PSYCHOANALYSIS AND THE BIRTH OF THE SELF

This book draws psychoanalysis out of unsubstantiated, hermeneutic speculation and into the science and philosophy of the Self. Mark Leffert offers a survey of where we as human beings come from, going back into prehistory, and our development as individuals. *Psychoanalysis and the Birth of the Self* is written to provide psychoanalysts with interdisciplinary information drawn from fields that they may have had little access to.

Leffert undertakes a novel integration of topics not frequently discussed together, resulting in a radical critique of the theorization of psychoanalysis. The book begins by setting the story with a short analysis of the history of psychoanalysis. A new science has been founded on the recognition of the impossibility of separating evolution from development; it is called Evo-Devo. Applied to the human condition, it integrates development with paleoanthropology and forms the basis for exploring such topics as the neurophilosophy of consciousness, the birth of the Self, and its neurodevelopment. It includes epigenetics in the conversation. Leffert then takes a radical turn, integrating the biological Evo-Devo of the Self with the study of its Existence that is, Existentialism and Phenomenology. The integration of these two threads, Evo-Devo and Existentialism, offers a powerful and unique tool for exploring the Self. The author offers an innovative way of understanding an individual that pulls together their biology, their development, and the way they choose to exist in the world. It steps outside of the traditional ways of clinically understanding an individual not by abandoning them but rather by powerfully supplementing them.

Psychoanalysis and the Birth of the Self offers a novel, interdisciplinary braiding of disparate strands of knowledge that will be of interest to psychoanalysts as well as those in the disciplines of neuroscience, existentialism and phenomenology, and anthropology.

Mark Leffert is a Training and Supervising Psychoanalyst with fifty years of clinical and teaching experience who has been exploring an interdisciplinary epistemology of psychoanalysis through several papers and, including the present work, five books. He maintains a practice in psychotherapy and psychoanalysis in Santa Barbara, California.

PSYCHOANALYSIS AND THE BIRTH OF THE SELF

A Radical Interdisciplinary Approach

Mark Leffert

First published 2018
by Routledge
2 Park Square, Milton Park, Abingdon, Oxon OX14 4RN

and by Routledge
711 Third Avenue, New York, NY 10017

Routledge is an imprint of the Taylor & Francis Group, an informa business

© 2018 Mark Leffert

The right of Mark Leffert to be identified as author of this work has been asserted by him in accordance with sections 77 and 78 of the Copyright, Designs and Patents Act 1988.

All rights reserved. No part of this book may be reprinted or reproduced or utilized in any form or by any electronic, mechanical, or other means, now known or hereafter invented, including photocopying and recording, or in any information storage or retrieval system, without permission in writing from the publishers.

Trademark notice: Product or corporate names may be trademarks or registered trademarks, and are used only for identification and explanation without intent to infringe.

British Library Cataloguing-in-Publication Data
A catalogue record for this book is available from the British Library

Library of Congress Cataloging-in-Publication Data
Names: Leffert, Mark, author.
Title: Psychoanalysis and the birth of the self : a radical interdisciplinary approach / Mark Leffert.
Description: Abingdon, Oxon ; New York, NY : Routledge, 2018. | Includes bibliographical references and index.
Identifiers: LCCN 2018001989 (print) | LCCN 2018005524 (ebook) | ISBN 9780429492273 (Master) | ISBN 9780429960406 (ePUB) | ISBN 9780429960413 (Web PDF) | ISBN 9780429960390 (Mobi/Kindle) | ISBN 9781138588455 (hardback) | ISBN 9781138588462 (pbk.)
Subjects: LCSH: Psychoanalysis. | Self. | Psychotherapy.
Classification: LCC BF175 (ebook) | LCC BF175 .L444 2018 (print) | DDC 150.19/5–dc23
LC record available at https://lccn.loc.gov/2018001989

ISBN: 978-1-138-58845-5 (hbk)
ISBN: 978-1-138-58846-2 (pbk)
ISBN: 978-0-429-49227-3 (ebk)

Typeset in Bembo
by Wearset Ltd, Boldon, Tyne and Wear

For my teachers,
Abe Lit, Rosalie Nemir, Mel Worth,
Ernst Lewy, Irwin Berkman, Hal Galef,
Jim Thickstun, Joe Abrahams, and Norm Marks

CONTENTS

Acknowledgments   ix

Introduction   1

1 Psychoanalysis's yesterdays, todays, and tomorrows: a brief history of being with patients   8

Introduction 8
Psychoanalysis as it was 11
Psychoanalysis as it is 16
A psychoanalysis for tomorrow 23

2 The neurophilosophy of consciousness   37

Introduction 37
Some diverse data points 38
Putting it all together: elements of a successful theory of consciousness 47
Taking stock 51
Consciousness and its Neurophenomenology 53
Consciousness is interpersonal 54
The phenomenology of emergence 56

3 Psychoanalytic theories of development and the new science of Evo-Devo   63

Introduction 63
How evolution and development became Evo-Devo 65

Epigenetics I 66
What we can learn about humans from rats 69
The Evo-Devo of play 74
Epigenetics II 79

4 The origins of the Self and its consciousness: the Evo-Devo of human being — 93

Introduction 93
So how did we get to be us? 94
The first year of life 98
Some notes on the history of the Self 100
The origins of consciousness 104
Speech and language 117
To sum up 122

5 Being and nothingness or to be or not to be — 131

Introduction 131
Camus and Hemingway 133
The Existentialist approach 141
The absurd and the emotions that accompany it 146

6 Common ground — 152

Introduction 152
Consciousness and the Evo-Devo of the Self 154
Consciousness and it discontents 158
Being in World 161

Index — *166*

ACKNOWLEDGMENTS

There are a number of people without whom this book would not have been possible. Kate Hawes, my editor, has helped me to make a literary home at Taylor & Francis and has supported my work since its beginnings a decade ago. Two friends, Marshall Sashkin and Jeff Seitelman, have offered their interest and support over decades. Kristopher Spring has served as my personal editor. He has copy-edited my books and has always been available to discuss the fine points of meaning I am trying to get my text to convey. Lastly, my wife, Nancy Leffert, has supported me throughout the complexities that life has thrown at us over 42 years of marriage.

INTRODUCTION

Since 2007 (Leffert, 2007, 2008, 2010, 2013, 2016, 2017), I have been developing an interdisciplinary understanding of Psychoanalysis (or Psychoanalytic Psychotherapy: In these Contemporary times, I can't draw a clear distinction between the two) and applying it to therapeutic action in the clinical situation. If the clinical practice of psychoanalysis and psychotherapy were likened to driving a car and Neuropsychoanalysis is about what goes on under the hood, then this book is about how the engine is made, how the parts came to be designed as and when they did, and, finally, the operating history it develops.

This latest stand-alone book might be described as a study of Being, an Ontology, for dynamic psychotherapists and psychoanalysts. Its title, *Psychoanalysis and the Birth of the Self: A Radical Interdisciplinary Approach*, should not be taken metaphorically: It means precisely what it says. It is about the human Bio-Psycho-Social Self, how it appeared evolutionarily over the last 3 million years and developmentally over the first few years of life, and the relevance of these twin interwoven discourses to Psychoanalysts and Psychotherapists. It recasts what we look at and participate in clinically with our patients into a phenomenological frame with an interdisciplinary twist. It stresses the importance of present-being and can be thought of as seeking answers to three questions. The first, respecting the present, is: Where are we (an exploration of Being-There)? The second is: Where do we come from (again, honoring the present, we ask *do* rather than *did*)? And, finally: Where are we going? Although the questions sound strange, they are actually the kinds of psychoanalytic questions we ask our patients all of the time.

The study of Consciousness is a thread that runs through the book, making an appearance in some form across all of the chapters. There is something paradoxical here. Evidence drawn from many sources, the behavioral, the interpersonal, and the neuroscientific, to name but a few, supports the conclusion that, *quantitatively*, what is conscious comprises but a small amount of the mental activity of the Self.

The great majority of this mental activity takes place outside of awareness in descriptively different, overlapping, and interreferential forms of unconsciousness. Yet it is Consciousness, this small piece of ourselves that seems to have appeared in our ancestors around 70,000 years ago and appears in each of us at around the age of 5 that makes us uniquely human. Borrowing from Oliver Sacks (1973/1999), I use the term *Awakening* for these diverse advents. Among living creatures, we alone possess this Consciousness; as we will discuss, it both enriches our lives and makes them mentally much more difficult and, at times, painful. I am using the term *Consciousness* here as a kind of shorthand for what is called (Tulving, 1985/2003) Self-reflective, Self-aware, or *Autonoetic* Consciousness. It resides in a Self who is aware of herself as a being-who-thinks and has a past and a future that she can mentally visit at will.

A problem in introducing this book (and some of the others as well) is that, in developing a unique thread of theory and practice, there is more to catch the reader up on without seeming repetitious to readers of my earlier work. I have tried to solve the problem by offering as a first chapter a discussion of the new and the old. It offers a kind of Existential history of psychoanalysis, aptly termed: a history of Being with Patients.

In offering a narrative of Being with Patients from the earliest past times and moving forward into the present and then the future, I ran the risk of falling prey to the pitfalls inherent in any narrative construction. Since we cannot cover everything, narratives easily fall victim to decisions of what to put in and what to leave out. This is unavoidable. What *is* avoidable is making them into narratives expressing the *politics* of inclusion or exclusion that then contain power-knowledge (Foucault, 1980). Such knowledge defines a vocabulary that either demands that certain ideas be talked about or makes talking about others impossible. It becomes a vehicle for the expression of power.[1] I have tried to be very careful about this throughout the book. The first of these narrative truths is that psychoanalysis is *always, always* about two people in a room with batches of other people, both the analyst's and the patient's, in adjoining rooms. To be generous, it took 50 years (Tower, 1956) for the unavoidability of multi-person psychologies to begin to be recognized *in print*, along with the realization, still decades later that the one-person psychology of a patient who feels and talks and an analyst who listens and analyzes was a meaningless abstraction. We are discovering that what patients (our customers) value most, even though they may first choose a therapist based on her theoretical orientation, is understanding and a caring attitude (Leffert, 2016; Tessman, 2003). If the first period was largely about metapsychology (Sandler, Holder, Dare, & Dreher, 1997), the contemporary period was based on exploring this two-person relationality (I include here the Intersubjective and Relational schools with references too numerous to cite). The two disciplines that psychoanalysis has encountered towards the end of the Contemporary period are neuroscience and psychopharmacology.

The fate of psychoanalysis going forward into the future is a complex matter. It must grapple with grave challenges or lapse into irrelevancy. We must face the fact that the term *psychoanalysis* is perceived by the public as anachronistic and that a therapy calling itself that has little appeal. We must also accept as fact that we cannot change this perception; we have to live with it if we are to save our discipline. To accomplish this, the curricula of psychoanalytic institutes must be modernized and broadened to make them more relevant to our modern world.

We can't discuss being Human without discussing being Conscious. Chapter 2 takes on this task from the perspective of Neurophilosophy. It begins perforce with a discussion of the anatomical hardware that makes up the brain and how it operates. Although the nature and origins of consciousness have been debated for a very long time, going back at least to Descartes and Locke, the realization that there are different kinds of consciousness is relatively recent. Tulving (1985/2003) described three forms of Consciousness—anoetic, noetic, and autonoetic—and their hierarchical relationships with each other are discussed here. Although anoetic and noetic consciousness exist in some for in all vertebrates, autonoetic consciousness is uniquely human. Following folk psychology, psychotherapists and psychoanalysts equate consciousness with autonoetic consciousness, which is fine as far as it goes, but also involves ignoring anoetic and noetic consciousness. Since these can contain important areas of potential psychic dysfunction, defensive or otherwise, much is lost here.

Although Consciousness remains "the hard problem" as it is described in the literature, it is one that is defined by a series of ontological parameters—complexity, physicalism, Consciousness as a workspace, the uniqueness of individual Consciousness—that are discussed. If we are going to look at the state of our knowledge of the hard problem and the tools we have, both Neuropsychological and Neurophilosophical, we can say that we are well along in the process and can expect answers not in centuries (Churchland, 2002), but in decades.

Another property of Consciousness is that it does not occur, as it is often studied, in an individual in isolation: The existence of Consciousness is uniquely and necessarily interpersonal. These interpersonal influences can often operate *un*consciously. A profound corollary to this observation is the expression of the interpersonal through the rise of social media.

Chapter 3 offers an interdisciplinary integration of psychoanalytic theories of development with the new science of Evo-Devo, a science that most psychoanalysts are unfamiliar with. Evo-Devo is based on the premise that any separation of the two fields, Evolution and Development, is artificial and that they must be treated as one area of study with interreferential referents. A corollary to any definition of Evo-Devo is that it applies to *all* living things including Human Beings, *H. sapiens sapiens*,[2] that is, *us*. All of these discussions once again lead us back to the Self.

We have, until recently, understood Development as arising out of an interaction of the evolved human genome with the environment. A corollary to this was the perceived absence of any molecular/genetic events that could influence the course of Development. The science of Epigenetics has led us to question these beliefs. It involves the way historical environmental experience modifies the expression of the genome, often in stable, heritable ways. In other words, the transgenerational transmission of phenotype or, to put it in an old way, the much-debunked concept of the inheritance of acquired characteristics (Lamarck, 1809/2012) does, in fact, take place.

The early mother-infant relationship is the locus par excellence for studying the effects of maternal behavior, particularly stroking and cuddling, on the developing phenotype of the infant. Adult massage (Field, 2006, 2014) has been shown to have similar beneficial effects. Daily massage was a usual part of Freud's early psychoanalytic technique that he abandoned for unclear reasons. Holding and touch figured in Winnicott's work with patients, and Boss described holding his patient "Dr. Kobling." In recent times (2000), an issue of *Psychoanalytic Inquiry* (Volume 20, Number 1) was devoted to the subject of touch in psychoanalysis and psychotherapy. It was constructed as responses to an earlier paper by Casement (1982) in which his severely depressed and needy patient pleaded with him to take her hands at the end of a session. My reading of his ultimate refusal to do so was that it severely traumatized his patient and irreparably damaged the treatment. Two of the contributors (Breckenridge, 2000; Fosshage, 2000) treated touch as a normal part of being with patients, including a handshake or clasp, a hand on the shoulder or an occasional hug (my own practice is similar to theirs). The remaining authors are in deep trouble with the whole issue and try to offer a balanced account but, nevertheless, see touch as dangerous and on a slippery slope leading to sexual boundary violations. Many analysts would be sympathetic to their positions, while others go about touching patients as Breckenridge and Fosshage describe, but just don't talk about it. It is understandable that old taboos die hard.

None of these authors comment on their *patients'* reactions to being touched as a part of their therapy. Horton and colleagues (Horton, Clance, Sterk-Elifson, & Emshoff, 1995), however, studied this question. They found that touch deployed solidly *within the boundaries* of the therapeutic situation was experienced as fostering the *therapeutic* bond and deepening the trust by patients of their therapists.

PLAY (Panksepp & Biven, 2012) is a normal part of mammalian development that we understand clinically, which has also been shown to have important Epigenetic effects on the development of the neocortex and on gene expression profiles. Of the 1200 genes that are active in the cerebral cortex, fully a third are epigenetically modified by play.

We will discuss a growing body of research that is demonstrating the intergenerational transfer of epigenetically acquired information. These studies are controlled to rule out simple behavioral transfers of information in which mothering psychologically affects the subsequent maternal behaviors of offspring without cellular transfers of genetic information. The two major studies of these effects in humans have to do with the inherited effects of hunger and satiation: the study of the Dutch "Hunger Winter" of 1944–1945 and that of cycles of famine and satiation in the Överkalix province of Sweden during the late 19th and early 20th centuries. A case illustration is offered to bring this work into the clinical sphere.

Chapter 4 must be described as a short monograph. It deals with the wider question of the origins of the Self, a discussion that leans towards the "Evo" end of the

Evo-Devo spectrum. I would call it a non-clinical monograph with clinical implications. It first explores the origins of *H. sapiens sapiens*, its *Paleoanthropology*, in southern Africa some millions of years ago. *H. sapiens*, our immediate ancestor, appeared around 200,000 ya. *H. sapiens* appeared as a result of an unusual genetic event: the doubling of a gene called SRGAP2 around 3.4 million ya, and a very rare event, its redoubling a million years later. This gene has a great deal to do with being human. We also evolved far larger brains, most recently characterized as being made up of 86 billion neurons that, uniquely, is able to engage in parallel, distributed process thought (Parallel Distributed Processing).

The first year of life is a fascinating area to study. It brings together developmental neurobiology with vast increases in brain volume and the number of neurons comprising it with our advanced knowledge of bio-psycho-social development and our observations of the mother–infant (or infant–mother) dyad. We will discuss how both Evolution and Development play out in the first year.

We will look at hominin evolution over the last half million years or so, the changes in brain power that accompanied it, and the new and more complex ways of being that were both entailed and made possible. This will take us to a historical inquiry into the origins of consciousness, in other words, its phylogeny. We also want to take an interdisciplinary look at its ontology, at all the different kinds of things that are going on in the first few years of life.

If we want to talk about the phylogenetic and ontological pathways that led to our becoming us, speech and language must be important parts of the discussion. It turns out that we know something about its Evo-Devo and can speculate about more.

Chapter 5 draws Existentialism and Phenomenology into the discussion of the Evo-Devo of human beings. It discusses the differences and confluence of the two terms, leading to a discussion of an unfamiliar therapeutic project: the analysis of the Absurd. Camus observed that if you want to do philosophy, you should write novels, and following his suggestion, if we want to understand Existentialism we must read the authors' fiction as well as their essays. The chapter begins with an encounter with two novels that make an unlikely pair: Camus' *The Stranger* and Hemingway's *The Sun Also Rises*. The chapter treats these novels as Existential Monographs that explore different psychological problems suffered in the context of Human Being: a struggle with the meaninglessness of life. The books describe very different problems with being-in-the-world. The two novels are discussed as philosophy rather than fiction, and a clinical case is discussed. From the psychoanalytic side of things, they are studies of post-traumatic stress disorder (PTSD).

Existentialism came to psychoanalysis in the late 1950s as a result of the perceived (accurately, I believe) failure of metapsychology to address clinical problems. In other words, rather than appearing out of nowhere, it followed the long-established path of the way new clinical ideas found their way into practice and, secondarily, into theory-building. PTSD is very much a disease of Being. Some patients suffering from PTSD deny it to everyone including themselves, and may present with a multiplicity of somatic symptoms that lack any particular symbolic meaning.

A patient is discussed who suffered from such a form of PTSD. The discussion leads us to the appearance of a new way of describing these conditions: Functional somatic disorder (FSD) (Gatchel, Peng, Peters, Fuchs, & Turk, 2007) that must be treated with a mentalization-based therapy that is existential in nature. These patients manifest pathological secondary attachment strategies—either attachment deactivation or hyperactivation strategies—that fail to establish functional emotional connections to caring others. I present this case illustration as an example of contemporary Existential psychotherapy.

The final chapter attempts the daunting task of braiding together the strands of Existentialism and Paleoanthropology. These strands teach us, from radically differing perspectives, how we came to be human and the burdens, particularly the knowledge of our own eventual death, that the human condition forces us to shoulder. The definitive bridge between the two ways of thinking about the Self is Consciousness, its origins and its behavior.

Consciousness offers us great control over the world (*Mitwelt* and *Umwelt*), but it comes with a price: the fact that we must know of our own inevitable deaths occurring at some point in our future, and the deaths of our loved ones. Religion is an old way of dealing with death; Existentialism is a new way.

A caveat: I write in a vernacular first-person voice that may, at first, seem grating. I do so anyway because I want to be clear that ideas are just ideas, we all have them, and thinking otherwise involves great pretension. A bit of the vernacular brings with it a necessary touch of humility that is often lacking in psychoanalytic writing.

Notes

1 This has always been a problem for psychoanalysis, its teaching, and its debates (Kirsner, 2000).
2 I am using the term *H. sapiens sapiens* to refer to us, the "intelligent" *H. sapiens*, that evolved in southern Africa from *H. sapiens* about 70,000 years ago (ya).

References

Breckenridge, K. (2000). Physical touch in psychoanalysis: A closet phenomenon? *Psychoanalytic Inquiry, 20,* 2–20.
Casement, P. J. (1982). Some pressures on the analyst for physical contact during the re-living of an early trauma. *International Review of Psychoanalysis, 9,* 279–286.
Churchland, P. M. (2002). *Brain-wise studies in neurophilosophy.* Cambridge: MIT Press.
Field, T. (2006). *Massage therapy research.* Edinburgh: Churchill Livingstone.
Field, T. (2014). *Touch* (2nd ed.). Cambridge: MIT Press.
Fosshage, J. L. (2000). The meanings of touch in psychoanalysis: A time for reassessment. *Psychoanalytic Inquiry, 20,* 21–43.
Foucault, M. (1980). *Power/knowledge: Selected interviews & other writings 1972–1977* (C. Gordon, L. Marshall, J. Mepham, & K. Soper, Trans.). New York: Pantheon Books.
Gatchel, R. J., Peng, Y. B., Peters, M. L., Fuchs, P. N., & Turk, D. C. (2007). The biopsychosocial approach to chronic pain: Scientific advances and future directions. *Psychological Bulletin, 133,* 581–624.

Horton, J. A., Clance, P. R., Sterk-Elifson, C., & Emshoff, J. (1995). Touch in psychotherapy: A survey of patients' experiences. *Psychotherapy, 32,* 443–457.

Kirsner, D. (2000). *Unfree associations.* London: Process Press.

Lamarck, J. B. (2012). *Zoological philosophy: An exposition with regard to the natural history of animals.* London: Forgotten Books. (Original work published in 1809.)

Leffert, M. (2007). Postmodernism and its impact on psychoanalysis. *Bulletin of the Menninger Clinic, 71,* 15–34.

Leffert, M. (2008). Complexity and postmodernism in contemporary theory of psychoanalytic change. *Journal of the American Academy of Psychoanalysis and Dynamic Psychiatry, 36,* 517–542.

Leffert, M. (2010). *Contemporary psychoanalytic foundations.* London: Routledge.

Leffert, M. (2013). *The therapeutic situation in the 21st century.* New York: Routledge.

Leffert, M. (2016). *Phenomenology, uncertainty, and care in the therapeutic encounter.* New York: Routledge.

Leffert, M. (2017). *Positive psychoanalysis: Aesthetics, desire, and subjective well-being.* New York: Routledge.

Panksepp, J., & Biven, L. (2012). *The archaeology of mind: Neuroevolutionary origins of human emotions.* New York: W. W. Norton & Co.

Sacks, O. (1999). *Awakenings.* New York: Vintage Books. (Original work published in 1973.)

Sandler, J., Holder, A., Dare, C., & Dreher, A. U. (1997). *Freud's models of the mind: An introduction.* Madison: International Universities Press.

Tessman, L. H. (2003). *The analyst's analyst within.* Hillsdale: The Analytic Press.

Tower, L. (1956). Countertransference. *Journal of the American Psychoanalytic Association, 4,* 224–255.

Tulving, E. (2003). Memory and consciousness. In B. J. Baars, W. P. Banks, & J. B. Newman (Eds.), *Essential sources in the scientific study of consciousness* (pp. 575–591). Cambridge: MIT Press. (Original work published in 1985.)

1

PSYCHOANALYSIS'S YESTERDAYS, TODAYS, AND TOMORROWS

A brief history of being with patients

Introduction

Over its long history, Psychoanalysis has changed, in some ways hardly at all and in others so as to make of it a thing beyond the recognition of the early analysts. This is both good and bad; there is yet much more to be done. In this admittedly presumptuous chapter, I'm going to look at where we started from, where we've gotten to over the past century, and where we might be going in the next quarter century or so. Many, but not all of the events I will be talking about are well-known to all of us, but I will be talking about them in novel and perhaps disturbing ways. (Sadly, we have become known for rejecting ideas we find disturbing, and I ask only that you suspend belief and tolerate, for the moment, the accompanying uncertainty.) I write about all of these in the plural, since a number of different psychoanalyses (and I do not mean just metapsychologically different) have always been practiced, are being practiced in the present, and there are two possible outcomes for our profession going forward into the future. Although we should retain hope, some of the possibilities are ominous, intensifying the trivialization of our profession in the eyes of the wider world, a process that began to appear over recent decades, had we but the wit to apprehend it.

It should be obvious that a comprehensive account of a history such as I am proposing would be incomplete in a multiple volume work. What I want to offer here is a *selective*, warts-and-all narrative of the history of being with patients. Narratives contain knowledge that is actually power-knowledge (Foucault, 1980). Not including something in a narrative, for example, all too easily becomes an exercise in the power of exclusion. A deservedly obscure illustration of this can be found in *Fruition of an Idea: Fifty Years of Psychoanalysis in New York* (Wangh, 1962), which offers a history of the activities of the New York Psychoanalytic Society and the New York Psychoanalytic Institute as if it was the whole of psychoanalysis in New

York *and that no other psychoanalytic ideas even existed.* I have tried as best I can to avoid this power trap in the choices I have made concerning what I would talk about (and, by exclusion, what I have chosen not to talk about), but such efforts can, at best, only be partially successful.

Trying to offer a definitive history of clinical practice at once faces a number of problems. Such a report is, *inevitably*, subjective. No one, not even a like-minded individual, would offer a similar, let alone identical, account. I offer this unashamedly for what it is: a claim to be knowledgeable about the subject and speak of it from a perspective honed over the past half-century, *without making any claims of any sort of unique or special standing.* Another source of the subjectivity is the relative dearth of hard data on these subjects. Surveys have been mostly limited to practice metrics and degree of analyst or therapist satisfaction. Participant self-selection tends to limit survey results to a description of the behavior and feelings of a subset of like-minded individuals. There *is* a small but significant literature (Hill, 2010; Leuzinger-Bohleber, Stuhrast, Rüger, & Beutel, 2003; Leuzinger-Bohleber & Target, 2001; Schechter, 2014; Tessman, 2003) about how patients feel about their analysts and the results of their analyses. We can also fall back on a series of subjective assessments gleaned from listening to how analysts talk in seminars and conferences, what they write, and what we hear from supervisees and patients about what *they* do and hear. A final source of inevitable subjectivity is the unknowable gaps between what clinicians think they do, say they do, what they actually do, and how aware they are of any of these (I've seen enough, Leffert, 2016, to confirm that this is a real issue).

The history of psychoanalysis is not a smoothly linear sequence of events, which makes the telling of it that much more difficult. As a card-carrying Postmodern,[1] I (Leffert, 2010) think of history in Derrida's terms (1978) as a group of individual threads, interreferentially braided into a sheaf of *différence*. Some threads, like the Relational thread, make their appearance and then continue while others, like the Existential thread, can come and go. Despite the efforts of many metapsychologists to the contrary, all of these threads must inevitably influence each other.

Most of us already know the salient facts of psychoanalytic history (although "younger" analysts may be forgiven for some uncertainty about some of the less recent yesterdays). Unfortunately, all too few of us think of what psychoanalysis will be like tomorrow, beyond asserting the comfortable platitudes that it is alive and well, etc., and has a bright future. I have been recasting our historical narratives (Leffert, 2010, 2013) for some time and will do so yet again in this chapter. I will use phenomenological[2] tools to do so here, following Husserl's (1937/1970, 1913/1983) admonition, which became a kind of phenomenological battle cry, to *Return to the Things Themselves.* (The *Things* here are two people in a room, talking to each other mostly about the life problems of one of them.) So, with these caveats firmly in place, let us proceed.

Allow me to turn, for a moment, to metaphor. It is in the form of a story I want to tell you. One can presume that, in the 19th century, there were many firms successfully engaged in the making of buggy whips. With the advent of the automobile in the 20th century, the need, and hence the demand, for buggy whips fell. As this happened, the less efficient of these firms and the ones producing an inferior product began to go out of business. Finally, perhaps by 1925 or so, only one firm remained. It admittedly created a superb buggy whip (or at least it thought that it did) for an ever-shrinking market. Maybe it still survives, maybe not, but what *is* clear is that the world is now interested in gas pedals.

So how does this metaphor translate to the fate of psychoanalysis, poised to move forward as it is, in the early 21st century? A friend recently told me of an analysis she had had with a largely silent analyst 30 years ago. The analyst did begin to speak, and rather vociferously I might add, when my friend told her of an exciting job opportunity in another city. The analyst was aghast and expressed outrage that my friend would *even consider* moving before "completing" her analysis. Fortunately, she was able to not just consider it but to *do* it and has sought, as needed, psychotherapy over the intervening years. Her tone in telling me this was somewhat accusatory, and she asked me to justify the analyst's behavior as if it were my own; I told her that I could not. What makes this an even more difficult situation to discuss is that I must admit that, if confronted with it when I was a practicing analyst in the later 1970s, I would have responded in much the same way as my friend's analyst (hopefully without the outrage). Her present-day perceptions of psychoanalysis highlight a *secular* problem facing us all; it is not a subject for finger pointing (I could not say the same if the treatment itself had occurred in the present).

I have noticed another disturbing trend in the choices made by our colleagues. Over the years, I have come upon perhaps a half-dozen instances in which analysts who have had a couple of analyses (or more) feel in need of further help and seek out not another analyst, but an experienced social worker whom they usually see weekly, or occasionally biweekly, with great satisfaction. When psychoanalysts, who are presumably the savviest of analytic consumers, vote with their feet, we are in *very* serious trouble as a profession. These two illustrations would seem to exemplify the problems we have going forward. But there is more.

As a profession, we have not made our peace with psychotropic medication, becoming comfortably fixated on its abuses rather than its therapeutic benefits. Although we have been tackling the very thorny problem of therapists and analysts who have sex with their patients for three decades, we have largely done so on a case-by-case basis and are only beginning to get beyond that to address the wider social and cultural issues plaguing psychoanalytic groups of which it is but one example. We no longer even have a definition of psychoanalysis or its frequency that satisfies the 30,000 members of our profession (of which the American Psychoanalytic Association [APsaA] only boasts 3000) who have had training in psychoanalysis. (Laplanche and Pontalis had already acknowledged this problem in 1973.)

A further series of problems exists around the metapsychologies, a term that I use to refer to the differing theoretical orientations by which members of our profession tend to identify themselves, taking some overarching concept, or the name of some founding psychoanalytic mother or father as self-signifiers. (Such theoretical ultra-orthodoxy tends to be less of a problem for psychoanalytic psychotherapists who have not trained/been indoctrinated at psychoanalytic institutes.) These theoretical differences have been pursued with increasing civility in recent years; sometimes, they are even able to coexist in the same institute. But this doesn't solve the problem. There is often little or no evidence for the theoretical positions taken by these groups, and repeated studies (Leuzinger-Bohleber et al., 2003; Leuzinger-Bohleber & Target, 2001; Tessman, 2003, to mention but a few) have demonstrated that the theoretical orientation of the analyst has nothing to do with clinical results or what is valued by the patient (in psychotherapy and psychoanalysis, the customer is usually right). What patients seem to value above all else in their therapists is understanding and a caring attitude. The problem we face today is that, while many analysts are aware of these findings, more or less all try to elide the issue and *avoid considering its clinical and educational implications.*

In dividing our history into what are, after all, identity categories, we ignore the fact that some issues persist over the course of more than one period. In these cases, I have had to make a somewhat arbitrary assignment, expecting the reader to understand the carryovers. Bearing this in mind, let's begin with the first of our inquiries: Psychoanalysis Past.

Psychoanalysis as it was

The history of the "facts" of yesterdays of psychoanalysts is well-known to contemporary psychoanalysts and psychotherapists and does not bear repeating here. An excellent summary of these "facts" of the theory is to be found in Sandler, Holder, Dare, and Dreher's (1997) *Freud's Models of the Mind: An Introduction*. We, however, are after bigger game.

A phenomenological inquiry into the birth of psychoanalysis

In pursuing this inquiry into *the things themselves* (Husserl, 1937/1970, 1913/1983) of psychoanalysis, I am going to go about it phenomenologically. What that means here is that we must always begin with an inquiry into what can be observed directly in the therapeutic situation, as opposed to what can be theorized or hypothesized about what's going on and its theoretical (as opposed to existential) meaning. Husserl relied on direct observation, and if something could not be observed directly then he placed it in brackets, or *epoché*, saying in effect let's go on through to the thing and then come back to explore the bracketed material. If these ideas are unfamiliar, they will not make total sense, but will become clear the first time they are employed.[3] The narratives I'm constructing in this way will look very different than the customary history of psychoanalysis all of us are used to.

In the late 19th century, Sigmund Freud was a hardworking young neurologist struggling to raise a family.[4] During this period he made his greatest discovery (*not* any of the metapsychologies that appear in the *Standard Edition*). What he discovered, if we look at the memoirs of patients who saw him, was that regularly and frequently scheduled appointments in which patient and [psychoanalyst][5] engaged in a *caring* discourse *focused on the patient's life, problems and unhappinesses* usually[6] resulted in the patient feeling better or at least being able to feel at home (*heimisch*) in her life. These salutary effects often persisted. What went along with this in that far-off time was [the affect-trauma frame of reference (Rapaport, 1958/1967; Sandler et al., 1997)]. If we *honestly* consider the contents of this particular *epoché*, given what we have come to know about psychic trauma and post-traumatic stress disorder today, we must conclude that they are meaningless.

Going forward into the teens of the new century and beyond, the theoretical situation became so complex that it is best to replace it with a new *epoché*, [metapsychology].[7,8] This is the first period of multiple schisms appearing within psychoanalysis; [metapsychology] would never be singular again. For those of us trained in Freudian institutes, this did not appear the case. As Christ cleansed the Temple by expelling the merchants and moneychangers, so Freud, first in his inner circle, and then among their spiritual descendants, labeled these heretics (Bergmann, 1993) apostates and erased them from institutional consciousness. For the Freudian psychoanalyst, [metapsychology] continued on in its singular way.

If Freud's proto-relational discovery heralded the birth of psychoanalysis, major late mid-century discoveries that continued this psychoanalytic thread derived from Kohut's research (Kohut, 1966, 1971, 1977; Kohut & Wolf, 1978) into the forms and transformations of normal and pathological narcissism and the treatment of the latter. Prior to Kohut, we were essentially dealing with Freud's original work (1914/1957) "On Narcissism: An Introduction" and its later derivatives. I single out Kohut's contributions because they advanced a phenomenological/developmental rather than a metapsychological approach to the treatment of pathological narcissism and disorders of the self that had proved refractory to treatment for three-quarters of a century. Sadly, in spite of these discoveries, inadequately treated narcissism still remains a problem within as well as outside of our profession.

There was another important mid-century thread: the infusion of European Phenomenology and Existentialism into American psychoanalysis. This involved the thing itself, not a return to some metapsychology. Briefly (Chapter 5 will be devoted to a discussion of these ideas), Existential analysts (e.g., May, 1983, 1953/2009) described patients as suffering from a crisis of Being. They manifested experiences of hollowness and emptiness, from which followed anxiety and/or depression. Treating such patients required being able to open ourselves to the full experience of such suffering human beings rather than treating them as patients subjected to the *regard médicale* (Foucault, 1973/1994). However, these developments did not at the time lead to a truly two-person psychology involving two human beings joined in discourse.

A separate thread, Interpersonal Psychoanalysis (Stern, D. B., Mann, Kantor, & Schlesinger, 1995/2014), appeared in the United States in the 1940s[9] among analysts who left (and/or were ejected from) the New York Psychoanalytic Institute and founded the William Alanson White Institute. It prefigured the later development of Relational and Intersubjective Psychoanalysis. What characterized the Interpersonal movement involved a phenomenological study of relations in and out of the Therapeutic Situation. It made use of the terms *object relations* and *transference/ countertransference*, which were innovative at the time but at best only partially describe the therapeutic phenomena. Today, we have multiple and more complex languages with which to discuss them. Contrary to its critics, Interpersonal Psychologists did not deny the existence of the intrapsychic, although they could not conceptualize the Post-Cartesian connection between the two that we explore today (Leffert, 2016, 2017). Whereas the Interpersonals were self-described eclectics, even their existence was hardly acknowledged by orthodox Freudian psychoanalysts.

A major event of the late 1990s was the publication by D. N. Stern and colleagues (1998) of their paper on non-interpretive mechanisms in psychotherapy. It soon became one of the most often cited papers in the psychoanalytic literature. They discussed the "something more" than interpretation that was required in any successful therapy. What was important was not the paper itself, which was not remarkable in its own right, but rather its widespread interest. It was an indicator of a phase shift in clinical psychoanalysis of the way therapists thought about their work: if published a decade earlier, it would have been ignored and, a decade later, it would have seemed passé.

The appearance of care in clinical psychoanalysis

But what happened to the thing itself: clinical psychoanalysis? Surprisingly or not, when we ask the question about how psychoanalysts really go about their work, the thing itself, the story becomes rather murky. Psychoanalysts and psychotherapists have always written about theory, that is, [metapsychology]. In recent decades, we have written about *clinical* theory, that is, therapeutic action. There is, unfortunately, almost no writing about what it has been like to be a patient over the course of our history, and the implicit assumption was probably made that any such accounts would only represent unreliable narratives of transference distortions.[10] In the early years of psychoanalysis, what we know of the clinical situation and the patient's experience pertains mostly to Freud and comes from the accounts, published or otherwise, of his patients' analyses with him.

In Freud's case notes that were appended to his account of his analysis of the "Rat Man" (1909/1955) in the *Standard Edition*, there is a reference to the Rat Man's appearing for a session hungry; he was fed (passive voice; Freud thus, removed himself from the transaction), herring no less. This observation perplexed generations of psychoanalysts (and reveals something of their work in the process): What *on earth* did Freud think he was doing, *gratifying* his patient like that?[11,12] Indeed, memoirs (e.g., Andreas-Salomé, 1964; Blanton, 1971; Kardiner, 1977) written by a number of Freud's patients of their experience of being with him, indicate that he was simply going about psychoanalytic business (that of caring discourse) as usual. Gay (1988) interviewed Jeanne Lampl-de Groot about her analytic experience with Freud (beginning in 1921) for his biography. She found him "charming," "polite," and "considerate" (p. 464). He asked her if he or any of his daughters could be of any help getting her settled in Vienna. He was humane and accessible. When she told him that she needed to purchase a piano, Freud told her that he was not musical because, he said, if she found out later it might lead to disappointment. When she told him about the recent death of a beloved sister, he replied by telling her of the death of his cherished daughter, Sophie. So what are we to make of this? It seems *possible*, given his writings, that Freud maintained a separation in his head between his patients as subjects of analysis and as human beings whom he cared for and about. Roazen (1975) had observed the presence of a distinction between Freud's personality, tact, and oral teaching, and the rigid written rules of psychoanalysis, noting that other analysts tended "to follow these written regulations rather than his actual practices" (p. 119). Later on, when he struggled with the pain from his cancer, he spent patient hours suffering in silence and, inadvertently, taught this silence to his patient-pupils as analytic technique.

I focus on Freud not for the usual reasons that analysts focus on Freud but because this seems to be where the early published accounts of *patient* experiences are; as for the rest, we are left mostly with inference. It is significant, I think, that beyond process narratives describing transference, symptoms, and affective states, little is said about patients' experiences of their analysts or of their analyses.[13] At some point, a well-informed guess would be; beginning circa 1930, analysts became largely silent, with their vocalizations limited to interpretations of resistance, genetic transference, or unconscious contents gleaned from a patient's associations. There was only one person in the room in those days, with the therapeutic discourse consisting of an annotated monologue. The analyst was not present except as the wielder of the medical gaze, the *regard médicale* (Foucault, 1973/1994), the subject observing the object as anonymously as possible. Some number of psychoanalysts continues to operate in this way even though some of them may, surprisingly, identify themselves as Relational analysts.[14]

The reasons for this "shift to silence" had, alas, nothing to do with evidence-based observations of clinical praxis. I would suggest a darker origin. The most prominent psychoanalysts in 1930s America (and hence, those having maximal control over psychoanalytic education through conducting training analyses and teaching seminars) fell into two groups. One was made up of American psychoanalysts who had traveled to Vienna and Berlin to be analyzed, usually for six months, by one of the masters (if at all possible by Freud himself), and the other constituted the European émigrés who had fled the Nazi plague. (Perhaps needless to say, there were ongoing battles for standing between the two groups.) What they had in common, for differing reasons, was their relative silence. The traveling Americans had been analyzed by a Freud who had become largely silent as he bore the chronic pain of his cancer of the jaw (his work with Kardiner, 1977, being an exception) and learned to do likewise, while the émigrés spoke little because of their uncertain, heavily accented English (Jacoby, 1983).

The medicalization of psychoanalysis in America: pitfalls and legacies

Out of the battles fought for the medical dominance of American Psychoanalysis, battles fought beginning in the 1920s and initially "won" by physicians, grew a social milieu within psychoanalysis (Jacoby, 1983) that stifled creativity and healthy radicalism.[15] During those times, the APsaA and its member institutes essentially controlled the psychoanalytic training market in the United States. By restricting training first to physicians and later to psychiatrists, it imposed a series of filters that determined who became psychoanalysts and how they thought about the world and their work. As Jacoby observed (and as I experienced in the 1960s), the market for places in medical school classes was highly competitive, and successful applicants displayed certain characteristics and underwent educational experiences that did not select for people who would become creative, humanistic psychologists. As undergraduates, future applicants favored the sciences over the humanities to gain a competitive advantage, and medical school curricula stressed rote memorization of the sciences, administered with a large dollop of sadism. (Humanism, with rare exceptions, did not formally arrive in medical school curricula before the 1990s.) The process turned out physicians who thought rigidly, abhorred change, and, as a profession, rejected, and even ridiculed new ideas.[16] Nowhere were these trends more obvious than in psychoanalysis, where century-old ideas are seen as fresh and every new idea has been fought against. Our continued celebration of Freud in clinical practice cannot be found elsewhere in medicine or psychology; if we were to create an analog, it would be something like practitioners of internal medicine referring on a daily basis to the ideas of William Osler.

My own experiences date to the late 1960s including analyses, supervision, clinical coursework, and the psychoanalytic literature, with myself in the roles of patient and analyst, supervisee and supervisor, candidate and teacher, and reader and author. Since my analysts, supervisors, and teachers were sometimes in their 60s, I was drawing my experiences from psychoanalytic education and training dating back to the 1920s. Much of this involved an insistence on neutrality, marketed under the rubric of not "gratifying" a patient and trying to be a "blank screen." I have described (Leffert, 2016, Chapter 6) the actions and discourses that fly in the face of these rules as the care of the patient and the relief of pain and suffering.

I have, however, encountered a number of examples of second-generation psychoanalysts whose work, at least by the 1970s, manifested this split between the written word and how they actually dealt with their patients. In her last session, a control patient I treated in the 1970s brought me a gift: a large brass paperweight in the shape of a key. (This was the only gift I received from her throughout her analysis.) It was immediately clear that she would be profoundly and irrevocably hurt if I refused it or equivocated; I thanked her, but asked her, why a key? She told me that she had thought long and hard about what to bring me and decided on the key when she saw it because she felt the analysis had provided a key to so much. My supervisor, Douglass Orr, a second-generation analyst analyzed by Lionel Blitzsten, thought my technique appropriate, but when I went to write up the case for certification (1981) suggested I leave this episode out, that it was between the patient and me as he put it (he knew, as I then did not, that I might well have been turned down if I included it). I spent a year in analysis (1969–1970) with Ernst Lewy, a second-generation Berlin psychoanalyst (then aged 82) analyzed by Boehm.

I recall that, while he said relatively little, he radiated a personal warmth and caring throughout the sessions, something I only understood decades later. At the time it just felt good, and warming, to be with him. A colleague described an analytic experience he had with Edith Jacobson in the 1970s. (She was analyzed in Berlin by Otto Fenichel in 1925.) I have always found her published works icily neutral. As I read *The Self and the Object World* (Jacobson, 1964), I found it to be about neither. Again, my colleague described his experience with her as warm and caring.

From its earliest days, psychoanalysis has been afflicted by vicious turf wars surrounding what amounts to issues of money (referrals) and power (Leffert, 2010, Chapter 7). Although these wars have become more civil, they still exist. (The recent creation of the American Board of Psychoanalysis by self-designated psychoanalytic "experts" as an attempt to perpetuate the political power of the now defunct Board on Professional Standards [BoPS] offers one example.)

Psychoanalysis as it is

The birth of a relational psychoanalysis

The major "discovery" (acceptance, acknowledgment, or realization are perhaps better terms) in the Contemporary Period is that the therapeutic situation involves two Human Beings, two Daseins.[17] Later it was observed that relations with others in the world (the *Mitwelt:* the Relational or the Interpersonal World) played an important role for both. I am not using any *epoché* here because the secondary discoveries (and they are discoveries) of the Relational and Intersubjective schools do also rest on phenomenological observations rather than recourse to theory.[18] I tend to focus on these similarities rather than the differences between these two schools. One cannot say that Relational psychotherapists do not think about intersubjectivity just as one cannot say that Intersubjective analysts do not think relationally.

To avoid confusion about just what constitutes a two-person psychology, it might be best to begin with what it is not. The terms *transference* and *countertransference* are one-person psychologies because they imply that there is only one Dasein in the room, only one Being who is actually There. Some time *c.*1990 some analysts began dealing with their feelings in a new way. This sometimes manifested itself in taking process notes in a different manner. Down the center of the page they wrote down the content of the sessions. Then, in the wide margins they had thus created, they wrote down their feelings about the patient and what he was saying and any associations they had about it. This switch from exclusive cognition to emotion was certainly laudable, but did not define a true two-person psychology (one person was talking and one person was taking notes).

A two-person psychology manifests a discursive process, taking place on a number of levels. Most immediately, Hoffman (1998) describes "an ongoing dialectic between the patient's perception of the analyst as *a person like himself or herself* and the patient's perception of the analyst as *a person with superior knowledge, wisdom, judgment, and power*" (pp. 83–84). The process hence, manifests a "ritualized asymmetry," he says, and is characterized by the analyst's "ironic authority" (Hoffman, 1996). What Hoffman and other Relational and Intersubjective analysts failed to realize is that the analyst's power, wielded inevitably, and at times unconsciously, can be extremely dangerous to patients, and part of the analyst's task is to guard the patient against the power differential inherent to the therapeutic situation (Leffert, 2013, Chapter 1).

Meanwhile, the development of our understanding of the discursive process rested on a series of shifts in the epistemology of meaning. (The discussion that follows is roughly based on Leffert, 2010.) The first involves a shift from "what does the patient lack/need/desire" to "what does the analyst know and how does s/he know it" (Goldner, 2002, p. 160). The second shift is "from the subject who theorizes to the relational context through which any form of knowing is created and meaning performed" (p. 160), from a one-person to a *true* two-person psychology or, in Benjamin's (1988) terms, from subject-object to subject-subject interaction. The third shift takes things beyond the coconstructed present of relational theory and intersubjectivity, moving from "the dialogic to the discursive, from the intersubjective cocreation of meaning to the discourses and cultural narratives that set the terms for what the dialogic partners can think and know" (p. 160). Most relational analysts have gotten as far as the second shift. The exceptions are those groups of analysts whose work is informed by the study of race, gender, and queer theory (Dimen, 1991; Flax, 1990; Goldner, 1991; Layton, 2000; Walton, 1997). What is being described is four entirely different ways in which the analytic partners may choose to interact. I have argued (Leffert, 2010) that these four levels must coexist in the therapeutic situation, with the partners being able to shift from one to another as it meets the epistemological needs of the moment. It is also necessary to spell out the fact that discourse is *not* exclusively a verbal process; it includes emotional as well as language elements and takes place both consciously and unconsciously.[19]

Regressive group process in psychoanalytic organizations

In recent decades, there has been a concerted and therapeutic (for the group) effort to violate the *cordon sanitaire* that analytic communities had deployed around those analysts who *have been caught* having sex with their patients. (We don't seem to speculate much about those who aren't caught.) This topic has been well covered (e.g., Celenza, 2006; Celenza & Gabbard, 2003; Gabbard, 1995; Gabbard & Peltz, 2001) in our literature. The catastrophic and at times primitive reactions of shock on the part of psychoanalytic communities when forced to confront the presence of such "rotten apples" in their midst has also been discussed. For example, it has been the subject of a series of articles in a recent issue of the *Journal of the American Psychoanalytic Association (JAPA)* (Dimen, 2016; Gabbard, 2016; Levin, 2016). These discussions have offered interesting psychoanalytic interpretations of individual (the perpetrator) and group (the psychoanalytic community) behaviors and psychology. They have also suggested institutional ways of dealing with the problem. But this is not what I want to talk to you about. What I'm interested in here are the origins of the dread and denial that accompany the subject or the experience of it by psychoanalysts.[20] What I *do* want to discuss is what exactly these shattered reactions tell us about the groups that make up what we call organized psychoanalysis and our individual reactions to it as group members, beyond the fact that such boundary violations (and there *are* others, financial exploitation and verbal abuse to name two important ones) are indeed bad and unfortunate things. Our reactions go beyond the act. Sex between two people, when one of them manifests, for whatever reasons, and for whatever duration, diminished capacity (in this case a patient in therapy), is wrong, and reprehensible. But analysts and psychotherapists have no problem in discussing subjects such as rape, date rape, or domestic violence with their patients or among themselves. When the daughter of a psychoanalyst was the victim of date rape at college, it became a topic of public psychoanalytic discourse. So how is this different?; how does an analyst having sex with a patient produce an existential crisis for a psychoanalytic community or for the profession itself (it does not seem to have *that* effect on psychiatry, psychology, social work, or internal medicine)? And finally, how does all of this impact our ability to be with our patients because, inevitably, it must?

I would offer the unpopular answer that the dread speaks to a lapse, the presence of pathological narcissism and a vulnerability to at times massive regressions that have existed almost from the very beginnings of psychoanalysis. We are dealing not with "rotten apples" and our response to them, but rather with a profound secular problem present in our profession. Only *one* of the triggers of its symptom, regression, denial, and depression, is finding out that a colleague has had sex with a patient. The symptoms themselves involve narcissistic injury and depression, psychic trauma, and massive conflicts over pathological idealizations (in structural language, damage to the superego and ego ideal) of psychoanalysis and psychoanalysts. The problem is made that much more intense by the fact that many of its perpetrators are respected, even idealized members of our profession: In recent years, they include several deans of institutes, the editor of a respected psychoanalytic journal, and a past chairman of the Board on Professional *Standards* of the APsaA. Some of them have actually been involved in working with colleagues who have had sex with their patients. The more prominent the individual, the greater the reaction, and the more likely that, after the initial explosion, a *cordon sanitaire* is reestablished and vigorously defended.[21] At times, however, a psychoanalytic community manages the problem "successfully" with denial and repression.[22]

So if analyst-patient sex and our reactions to it are only symptoms, what then is the actual problem, and what possible solutions might be applied to it "Tomorrow?" The answer speaks to the very Being of our profession. Its roots lie in the tripartite model of psychoanalytic education we prize so much, the power relations issues present in psychoanalytic organizations between power elites and dominated classes (Lukes, 2005), and the inevitable emersion of psychoanalysts in therapeutic situations.

That a student undergoes his own psychoanalysis coincident with his coursework and clinical work with patients *is* essential in the education of psychoanalysts or psychoanalytic psychotherapists, but it also is a two-edged sword. The use of the terms *candidate* or *clinical associate* and *training analysis* serve to further define those edges and alter their Being; that is, they change what they are.[23] Although the analysis offers the student essential knowledge about himself and highlights the presence of defenses that may interfere with his clinical work and his studies, it does so at the price of having a student experience these activities in a state of regression.[24] So what the analysis helps explicate, it may also impair. All too often, elements of this regression persist after graduation and plague the relations of the young analyst (as we know, these people can easily be in their 50s) with her senior colleagues. I recall my experience of my first day of classes in 1975; I felt the very air of the classrooms to be so heavy with transference as to be able to cut it with a knife. One way to mitigate this problem is to make the training analysis at the hands of a training analyst (a designation that has its own long-debated problems) into a personal analysis with an analyst of the student's own choosing, unaffiliated with, and uncredentialed by the institute where that student is being educated. Another way is to provide each class with a group process or T-group experience (Bradford, Gibb, & Benne, 1964). Some institutes are, laudably, beginning to offer such experiences, but they tend to be led by *faculty members*. To be optimally useful, leaders should be trained in *group process* and hired for that purpose from *outside the institute*. The easy criticism here is that such experiences contaminate an analysis. We can, however, see beyond this. Talking about experiences contaminating analyses is like saying that *life* contaminates analyses, and there is nothing to say that life or group process experiences cannot be analyzed.

Absent these remedies and in the presence of the kinds of psychopathology described above, the vulnerable student becomes a vulnerable graduate analyst. This trend is exacerbated as a result of an unsatisfactory or traumatizing personal analysis,[25] particularly if the training analyst is struggling with his or her own narcissistic problems. The result, phenomenologically, is a re-projection of certain interpersonal self-regulatory functions and idealized self-representations onto a psychoanalytic group, its leaders, and its canonized ancestor(s). When threatened by opposing ideas, the responses of groups mingle rage and disparagement.

The situation is further complicated by the analyst's or psychotherapist's clinical work. We inevitably spend our days immersed in our patients' transference, our importance to them, and the inevitable narcissistic gratifications that they provide. The situation brings with it the temptations of power. There are two problematic results from this emersion in the vulnerable analyst. One occurs if an analysis is going badly. The analyst may assume a position of arrogance, blaming the patient's pathology (Casement, 2002) rather than entertaining the possibility that he or she is mistaken or has failed to grasp something. The other involves the analyst's behavior in groups. When one's colleagues fail to respond to one's ideas with the same admiration[26] and intense interest as one's patients, susceptible analysts regress, and become enraged. This phenomenon, if not an understanding of its causes, is so common that it is ignored. One of the ways analysts deal with it is to form power groups of like-minded colleagues that then involve themselves in long-term skirmishing or open warfare.[27] We will discuss possible solutions to this rather terrible problem in the section on the Tomorrows.

Neuroscience and its acceptance by psychoanalysis

At the risk of restating the obvious, Freud always believed that Neuroscience would one day replace psychoanalysis. Over the last few decades, research into neuroscience has borne fruit to a degree that, if not replacing psychoanalysis as Freud imagined, it can certainly lay claim to a place at its table. Be that as it may, some analysts see, and write about it as separate but equal. Pulver, for example, posited in 2003 that Neuroscience, while highly relevant to psychoanalytic theory, is entirely irrelevant to clinical practice. Solms (2013) explores the uses of neuroscience in rewriting classical metapsychology. Other 21st century authors (e.g., Meissner, 2006; Pally, 2010; Vivona, 2009) disagree, as do I (Leffert, 2010, 2013), seeing a burgeoning role for neuroscience in both psychoanalytic theory *and* practice Alan Schore (2003a, 2003b, 2011; Schore, J. R. & Schore, 2007) prominently writes in *this* vein. In a laudatory effort to begin a discourse between Neuroscience and Psychoanalysis, Mark Solms and Jaak Panksepp founded the journal *Neuropsychoanalysis* in 1999. In the "Editors' Introduction" to the first issue the editors (Nersessian & Solms, 1999) state "the goal of this new journal is to create an ongoing dialogue with the aim of reconciling psychoanalytic and neuroscientific perspectives on the mind" (p. 3). The goal seems to be for the members of the two disciplines to educate each other about what they do and to integrate neuroscience with psychoanalytic *theory*, that is, [metapsychology]. *Neuropsychoanalysis* has been successful in pursuing this goal, but what it has not done is to much explore the potential impact of neuroscience on *clinical* psychoanalysis.

Psychoanalytic institutes that offer courses in neuroscience (some, I don't know how many, do) teach it as a discrete discipline rather than in the wider context of relationally based clinical work. We are certainly in the early days of demonstrating neuroscience's relevance to clinical work, but already a number of points stand out. Functional neuroimaging studies already (Protopopescu & Gerber, 2013) have been used to demonstrate changes in size of brain areas known to be involved in various forms of psychopathology, following psychodynamic psychotherapy. Acknowledging these effects need not detract from the richness of clinical models of psychoanalysis but rather supplements that richness, offering as they do independent evidence of change. One area of functional neuroanatomy that I want to discuss for illustrative purposes involves the discovery of the Mirror Neuron System (MNS) and its role in decision-making in clinical psychoanalysis.

The discovery of the MNS, first in the inferior frontal cortex of macaque monkeys (Gallese, Fadiga, Fogassi, & Rizzolatti, 1996) and later in human beings (Gallese, 2009; Gallese, Eagle, & Migone, 2007; Iacoboni, 2007, 2008; Iacoboni et al., 2005), is both recent, and exciting. Briefly, the MNS is activated in someone if he observes goal-oriented behavior in another. When an individual performs an action, there is an unconscious tendency (it can, however, be made conscious) in an observer to *mirror* the action. It is also activated when one observes an action and *thinks* about performing it. It is first of all about unconscious empathic perception. If we *watch* someone being tickled or *imagine* being tickled, we have some feeling of *being* tickled. The MNS is a shared processing system that embeds "the self and consciousness in the interreferential social sheaf of community" (Leffert, 2010, p. 181). Developmentally, the MNS provides the infant with an innate capacity for bidirectional intersubjective exchange. And this information, while assuredly fascinating, has *what* to do with clinical psychoanalysis? Using the couch or doing therapy or analysis via telephone (Leffert, 2003) shuts off this visual means of patient-analyst communication. From its beginning, psychoanalysts have viewed use of the couch as the hallmark of psychoanalysis. It safeguarded [free association]:[28] Patients either were capable of using the couch, in effect they "made the grade," or not, and that was that. (One still hears this today, even coming from analysts who signify themselves as Relational.) In recent decades, the indications for psychoanalysis have expanded, and the discovery of the MNS could serve to initiate an entirely different sort of discourse about the couch. It raises the clinical issue: Do we want to turn off this system of bidirectional unconscious intersubjective exchange or else leave it on? The flexible rule of thumb I have come to use is that if a patient has been raised in an atmosphere of emotional deprivation, then cutting them off from me by shutting down the MNS only serves to isolate and even retraumatize her and she should be left sitting up. If, on the other hand, the patient has been raised in an atmosphere of overexcitement and overstimulation, then they need the opportunity for reverie and reflection in an unexciting safe space that the couch provides. Patients in the first group can sometimes, after analytic work, benefit from (not graduate to) the couch and the reflective opportunities it provides. Many patients fall somewhere in between these limits. Regardless, I explain the differences to patients, encourage them to try it out, and leave the final, revocable decision to them.

An abbreviated tour of psychopharmacology and its acceptance by psychoanalysis

Prior to 1962, there was no psychoanalytic problem with psychopharmacology because there *were* no medications that were relevant to the treatment of patients in psychoanalysis or psychotherapy. In that year, the tricyclic antidepressants Elavil and Tofranil became available and were shown to have a beneficial effect on our depressed patients. Because of the varying effects and considerable side effects of these drugs (prescribing tricyclics was and remains a task for the expert pharmacologist), those of us in outpatient practice who wanted to could comfortably ignore psychotropic medications for another 25 years. With the appearance of Prozac, the first selective serotonin reuptake inhibitor (SSRI), in the late 1980s, and the atypical antipsychotics in the mid-1990s this became much more difficult. Prozac was particularly troubling. First, despite its side effects (headaches and some gastrointestinal upsets), it proved highly effective as an antidepressant. There was more. Beth[29] was a patient I had seen twice weekly[30] for several years as she advanced from lab tech to medical student to intern and then to medical resident. In spite of these advances, she remained somewhat depressed, and I thought to try her on Prozac to see if we could do better. We could and we did. But wait. Beth was painfully shy, and after 4 years of treatment, she had still been unable to go out on a date. After a month on Prozac, she came in one day, following a long weekend, and announced that she had met someone with whom she had begun a relationship. I still can feel the sense of discovery that accompanied this observation all those years ago. Other psychiatrists (e.g., Cramer, 2016) were noticing the same kind of thing at the same time: *Prozac seemed to have the ability to change character.* This led to a wave of patients coming to psychiatrists and their primary care physicians asking for Prozac to treat their depressions, but also, even if they were not depressed, asking for it to treat character problems. Prozac had become a social phenomenon. Most analysts dismissed this phenomenon, and many (e.g., Buechler, 2010) continued to believe that, for an analysis to work the patient needed to continue to suffer.[31]

Beginning in the late 1960s, Lithium Carbonate began to be studied as a treatment for manic-depressive illness. At that time, this condition was considered to be a fairly rare psychosis and hence, mostly beyond the purview of psychoanalysts. Around the millennium, it became clear that milder forms of bipolar disorder were much more common and that mood stabilizers such as Lithium, and the newer drugs Depakote, Lamictal, and Carbamazine, rendered many patients suffering from bipolar disorder or borderline personality disorder much more treatable via psychotherapy or psychoanalysis. Absent the psychopharmacology, these patients had required heroic therapeutic interventions carrying with them only a chance of success. Around 2010, it emerged that some depressed patients who were refractory to SSRIs could be successfully treated with mood stabilizers, suggesting a bipolar origin to these depressions (this also was a matter left in the hands of an experienced psychopharmacologist or analyst-psychopharmacologist).

Let me insist that of course these medications are not panaceas.[32] Prescribing them is a complex matter. There can be serious side effects (bipolar patients, for example, may suicide on an SSRI). A patient who is prescribed a psychotropic medication by a primary care physician (often in response to the patient's demands) and left to languish on it for years is not likely to have a good result. Different patients respond to different drugs, but this fact is not taken into account when studying their efficacy. Lastly, psychopharmacological agents prescribed alone, or with concomitant psychoanalytic treatment, are entirely different animals, yielding different results.

There ought to be, at this point in time (2018), some consensus that psychopharmacology is a useful and necessary adjunct to some therapeutic situations and that it can be employed without violating the psychoanalytic field/frame.[33] Unfortunately, this does not appear to be the case. The frequency with which psychoanalytic patients as a group are treated concurrently with psychotropic medication is unclear, although there are promising signs.

There is some limited research on the prescribing or referring for prescription habits of psychoanalysts and psychotherapists, but no formal position statements or policies on the subject by any psychoanalytic organizations. (The APsaA *has* taken a position about Freud when it recently declared his birthday a day of celebration and has also taken a position on water quality in Flint Michigan, while it has never formed a study group to look at psychopharmacology as it relates to the psychoanalytic frame. So perhaps we have a problem here.)

The latest information on prescribing habits that we do have is contained in the survey, *2011 Psychoanalytic Professional Activities Benchmark Study* (Survey Advantage Whorton Marketing Research, 2011), of the professional activities of psychoanalysts who are members of APsaA. There are a number of caveats concerning the survey that might lead one to take it with a grain of salt. Of the 2715 active members of APsaA (there are roughly 30,000 clinicians in the United States that identify themselves as psychoanalysts), 879 or 32% completed and returned the survey. So, although the survey can reliably tell us nothing about the professional behaviors of psychoanalysts in general, it does tell us a lot about a small (roughly 3%) subset of them. We are safe in concluding that the returnees must identify themselves strongly as psychoanalysts and members of APsaA. We may *imagine* that this group of analysts falls on the more conservative end of the analytic population (a subset of questions could have revealed this).

The survey tells us that 31% of the patients treated by the respondents in psychoanalysis and 28% treated in psychotherapy were prescribed antidepressants, antianxiety agents were prescribed in 11% of cases in both modalities, and mood stabilizers were prescribed in 6% of analytic cases and 7% of psychotherapy cases. These numbers both surprised and heartened me; they were higher than I expected and suggest that we are further along than I had thought. This level of antidepressant usage is consistent with competent psychopharmacological practice. There is, however, little justification for the prescription of antianxiety agents beyond on a very limited as needed basis and the 11% is not consistent with good evidence-based practice. The prescription of mood stabilizers can be essential for the treatment of some patients; their use is an encouraging measure of expertise in psychopharmacology among psychoanalysts (as prescribers or referrers). Unfortunately, something we *don't* know, that could have been readily obtained for the survey results, casts all this in doubt: that is what percentage of psychoanalysts prescribes what percentage of psychotropic medication? At the absurd end of things, the 31% of patients taking antidepressants could be being treated by a small number of analysts while the majority of analysts still never prescribe. So we don't know anything about the *penetrance* of drug prescribing in even this small sample of psychoanalysts. The study is, all in all, a good beginning, but a great deal more has to be done.

A psychoanalysis for tomorrow

The question is whether psychoanalysis will be able to successfully grapple with the grave challenges it must face going forward or whether it will lapse into irrelevancy. An ancillary question is how well a psychoanalytic education prepares its students for practice in the world of the 21st century. The statements our psychoanalytic organizations make on the subject seem inappropriately sanguine in the face of what analysts say about their practices. I want to address the question in a number of areas: psychoanalytic research, psychoanalytic education, psychoanalytic politics and group process, and psychoanalytic practice. But before doing so it is necessary to discuss the win or lose problem: how psychoanalysis is perceived by the world of which it is trying to be a part.

The social and cultural situation of psychoanalysis

For most of us, psychoanalysis is a discipline, a vocation, a calling, and a way of understanding the world. For some of us, unfortunately, it is also a way of life. In that social world, it is something different, and unhealthy.

Psychoanalysts need, in Phenomenological terms, to be able to demonstrate to the communities in which they work that they are particularly able to understand and succor (Leffert, 2016) the Being of Human Beings. And for this to work, they need to actually *be* able to uniquely understand and succor the Being of Human Beings. Unfortunately, with the exception of those of us in the trade and the inhabitants of the Upper East Side and West Side of Manhattan, the term comes with a negative and anachronistic meaning. For large numbers of people in our culture, the term *psychoanalysis* has negative connotations. It is seen as old fashioned, involving lying on a couch (which most people don't understand), coming many times a week, digging into childhood at the expense of dealing with "real" present day problems, and taking years to complete, if it is ever completed. It is priced beyond the range that most people can afford.[34]

I'm not at all sure that, realistically, we can save the term *psychoanalysis*, but we can I think save the discipline if we constantly update it and keep the therapeutic marketplace in mind. Many analysts and analytic therapists have already taken this into account. They describe themselves instead as *psychotherapists*. It is fashionable, these days, to use personal websites as a way of introducing ourselves to the public. Many analysts do so without mentioning psychoanalysis.

If the market for 3 to 5 times weekly psychoanalysis is small, the market for once weekly psychotherapy and twice weekly psychoanalysis remains robust among the better educated members of society. I have had many patients come to me after getting little or nothing from other forms of treatment and benefit from a psychoanalytic approach. Unless they are psychoanalytic therapists or sophisticated laypeople, I tend not to use the term *psychoanalysis*. We have no data concerning how common this approach is.

Psychoanalytic research

If psychoanalysis is going to keep its place at the table, we are going to have to be much more thoughtful and proactive concerning efficacy research and how its results need to drive aspects of psychoanalytic education and its desperate need of reform. As psychoanalytic therapists and psychoanalysts, we have been dangerously complacent about such research and its results. There are two reasons for this. The first is that there are now numerous studies (e.g., de Maat et al., 2013; Leichsenring, 2005; Luborsky, Singer, & Luborsky, 1975) that *do* demonstrate the efficacy of psychoanalysis and psychodynamic psychotherapy.[35] The second is that we recognize that, phenomenologically, each therapy or analysis is such a complex and unique event that there are limitations in its knowability and it is nearly impossible to tease out significant strands of commonality.

We face darker problems around the results of efficacy research. For some time, we have known that therapeutic efficacy is independent of the metapsychological persuasion of the therapist or analyst conducting it (Asay & Lambert, 1999; Hill, 2010; Leuzinger-Bohleber et al., 2003; Leuzinger-Bohleber & Target, 2001; Tessman, 2003). When patients are asked about what they consider to have been curative in their therapeutic experiences, they always relate it to feeling cared for and understood by a kind therapist. I have previously (Leffert, 2016) written about these issues and the much maligned and misunderstood role of the placebo in these outcomes. Unfortunately, we tend to try to elide this conclusion as well as the profound effects it should have on psychoanalytic education.

A few authors *have*, over the decades, looked at what inevitably follows from these studies. Dating back to 1961, Frank and Frank (1993) posited in *Persuasion and Healing* that there are at least four components necessary for an efficacious psychotherapy:

1   An emotionally charged, confiding relationship with a helping person [emphasis added] (p. 40).
2   A healing setting (p. 41).
3   A rational conceptual scheme, or myth that provides a plausible explanation for the patient's symptoms and prescribes a ritual or procedure for resolving them (p. 42).
4   A ritual or procedure that requires the active participation of both patient and therapist and that is believed by both to be the means of restoring the patient's health.

[Original emphasis] (p. 43)

The third and fourth components should certainly disturb the sleep of all metapsychologists, particularly those that base their therapeutic practice on their metapsychology. They suggest that any therapeutic system, however arcane, can yield positive results as long as these criteria are met. Even worse, a therapist could make up his own conceptual scheme and therapeutic ritual about anything, and as long as he believed in it and his patient believed in it, it would work.

A great deal of work (Hubble, Duncan, & Miller, 1999) has been done on identifying the common factors in effective therapy and, by extension, effective psychoanalysis. None of this work has revealed *any* therapeutic factors relating to any particular metapsychology or to metapsychology in general. Effective therapists need to have an organized conceptual system (number 3 above), but it is enough if what they have is an organized belief system.[36] Nevertheless, consumers or potential consumers of psychoanalytic treatment usually ask the theoretical orientation of any therapist they come in contact with and are often upset, as are the ones who ask me, if told that I don't have one. In spite of the large volume of empirical work done on common factors and how they work, the information goes largely unmetabolized and entirely untaught in our discipline.

Psychoanalytic education

In a number of important ways, contemporary psychoanalytic education fails to prepare the graduating analyst for practice in the 21st century, leaving her to pick up information she needs in a hit-or-miss fashion. Regardless of affiliation, psychoanalytic institutes employ Eitington's tripartite model consisting of a personal analysis, seminars that teach the student the theory and practice of psychoanalysis, and conducting supervised analyses; this usually, but not always, means seeing three patients at a frequency of 4 or 5 times a week with the patients using the couch. APsaA's institutes require this and have been required to require it by the BoPS.[37] Here's the problem. The 2011 Survey (Survey Advantage Whorton Marketing Research, 2011) found that respondents averaged three patients in analysis. My admittedly informal sense is that frequencies in the wider world of psychoanalysis are far lower; I know many analysts who have never had a new analytic case after graduating. Schechter (2014) made similar observations when she studied recent graduates from the Chicago Institute for Psychoanalysis.[38] Regardless of this, we can say that the majority of the graduates of psychoanalytic institutes spend most of their time doing other things, things that their institutes do not specifically prepare them for. I know of no institute that discusses this reality with its applicants, yet Carlson (2016) would judge failure to do so as unethical.

The solution to this problem, in addition to being honest about it, is to increase the relevance of institute curricula to the wider professional lives of their students. Clinically, this means a number of things. The first is to teach and supervise some *psychotherapy* cases, since this will directly educate the students about what they spend most of their time doing. A formal education in both disciplines offers the student much more than, as we do now, making them try to integrate their knowledge without seminars to do it in. An important dividend in such an education is that it addresses the problem of the difficulty students have in finding suitable patients for analysis.[39] Typically, many institute classes waste their clinical seminars because they have difficulty finding cases; an advanced candidate then usually presents material, but it is not the same. Classes could begin with the psychotherapy cases everyone has that raise analytic issues.

The use of psychotropic medications as a part, often a necessary part, of psychoanalytic treatment is still contested. The best way to address this issue is to incorporate psychopharmacology into clinical seminars as opposed to not teaching it (current practice) or teaching it as a freestanding course. This way, students and faculty can hash out and study the subject together rather than simply offering Olympian pronouncements concerning it.

The relevance of neuroscience to what we do is increasing literally on a daily basis. Students need to be educated in this discipline if they are going to be able to follow developments in the field in the decades after their graduation. Again, the answer is *not* freestanding neuroscience courses; it is teaching it as a part of clinical and theoretical seminars.

I would offer our students, group process experiences led by outside non-reporting faculty. This idea is, admittedly, highly controversial. The strident complaint would be that it would "interfere" with the personal analysis. I know of no evidence for this, although there are students for whom it would be unsuitable. It is at least as likely that these experiences would bring up material that would further a personal analysis and that it would improve the citizenship of institute faculties going forward.

I have left the most serious educational problem for last. If there is no evidence for the validity of any arcane metapsychological system then the amount of time spent teaching students these various disciplines is largely wasted. Unfortunately, instead of dealing with it, analytic teachers elide it by acknowledging plurality and going about their business. Kernberg (2016), an otherwise thoughtful critic of psychoanalytic education, fails to consider this issue at all, while Kernberg and Michels (2016) simply suggest that the various psychoanalytic theories be taught and that students have the opportunity to hear from their proponents. The various commentaries on the paper that are to be found in *JAPA*, Volume 64, similarly do not consider the validity of metapsychology and its teaching going forward into the future.[40]

The acknowledgment of metapsychological irrelevancy poses a daunting problem for psychoanalytic education in the 21st century. There will be enormous resistance both inside and outside of institute faculties to making the changes in curricula that this acknowledgment should entail. Gerber and Knopf (2015) offer a model of an empirically-based psychoanalytic curriculum that is unlike any proposals I have encountered. As they note: "The stubborn refusal of psychoanalytic institutes to evolve with mainstream psychology has spurred 30 years of speculation about the impending death of psychoanalysis" (p. 118). What they suggest is metapsychology light, beginning with Contemporary theory, and limiting Freud to a single term in the third year. The curriculum is research heavy (it's not entirely clear what they include here) and a fairly usual (not a bad thing here) group of clinical courses. I am respectful of their efforts, but would do it differently.

I *would* downsize metapsychology as they do and teach Freud later rather than earlier. I would posit, however that it is not useful or necessary to teach Freud's cases and papers on technique for anything but historical interest. I would not teach the metapsychologies to just learn them; I would teach them critically looking at their inherent epistemologies. Psychoanalysis is scientific but not a science; I would want to teach the subjects discussed above, particularly neuroscience, and philosophy. Lastly, I would maintain a strong developmental presence, teaching it empirically, and neuroscientifically rather than metapsychologically.

Psychoanalytic politics and group dynamics

However disturbing and however much we use denial or disavowal to cope with it, a significant part of the behavior of psychoanalysts in groups is dysfunctional. Many of us, whether or not we maintain nominal connections with one or more psychoanalytic organizations, have dealt with the problem by voting with our feet, limiting our connections with each other to the [scientific].[41] The rest of the ways that psychoanalysts deal with each other involve, whatever may be claimed to the contrary, the pursuit of power, a pursuit sometimes accompanied by an infantile sense of urgency. This is true whether the pursuit is political, as it is with the "certification" issue, or the pursuit of theoretical primacy as a means of controlling psychoanalytic organizations at whatever level.

I'm not at all clear that these issues can be addressed by national organizations, but there are local ways of addressing them, one that I first saw in San Diego 35 years ago. The institute decided to form a "Thinking Committee." Its membership was drawn from those people in the analytic community who were not much involved in its politics. Its charge was to consider any aspects of institute or society functioning that it wished to and to report on the results. Our major accomplishment was to schedule a weekend retreat that was well attended and got people to actually talk to each other. I left San Diego for Minneapolis soon after the retreat. As a result, although the committee continued to function for a number of years, I do not know *how* it functioned. This was a very advanced effort for the times and, for that reason, can be forgiven for failing to engage the two hard problems facing that community in 1980: the discovery that one of the senior faculty members was a sexual predator, and the bitter conflict between two senior and beloved training analysts. Such committees could be of great benefit to the functioning of local psychoanalytic communities. I think that in the future, the tomorrows, they could capably deal with the kinds of issues that were too hot to handle in 1980. Based on what we know today, I would add a specific charge to such committees: That they help their communities to enter into a discourse about regressive group process. Sadly, since leaving San Diego, I have been a member of several psychoanalytic communities and I never saw such an explicit approach to group process even thought about.

A psychoanalytic praxis for tomorrow

If you have been following the arguments I have been developing throughout the course of this chapter, what I will have to say here will seem almost redundant. In order to be effective practitioners of our art, psychoanalytic therapists and analysts must be grounded in Interdisciplinary Studies that go beyond the psychoanalytic theories taught in out institutes today. [Metapsychology] is by its very nature reductionist, regardless of a practitioner's flavor of choice. In isolation, it can at best serve as a cartoon, a rough sketch that will guide the creation of the work that is to follow. The major interdisciplinary areas that must be included and, in our constantly expanding world, be kept up to date are Neuroscience, Neuropsychology, and Philosophy.

More focused fields that must be embraced are Neurophilosophy, Consciousness Studies, Network Studies, Complexity, Psychopharmacology, Epistemology, and Ontology. They can all valuably inform clinical work.

I have been writing about what must go into maintaining an effective clinical stance (Leffert, 2010, 2013, 2016, 2017) for some time now. Beyond that, while I think an entity termed *not-analysis* exists, I do not think that a distinction between psychoanalysis and psychotherapy serves us particularly well. In past decades, this distinction was made, and what the analyst did or did not do, said or did not say, then followed from it. Patients were not well-served by the distinction and I don't think its influence on praxis is anywhere as great now as it was.

I don't think a psychoanalysis uninformed by psychopharmacology (regardless of its use with a particular patient) can exist in the future. It seems likely as well that, in the decades ahead, other biological treatments for conditions like Major Depressive and Bipolar Disorder will become available. The new big thing in general medicine is Stem Cell transplants, and they might well be involved. Such treatments could offer the prospect of definitive cures rather than just effective maintenance and would profoundly influence—influence *not* replace—what we do discursively with our patients. Should we fail to celebrate these developments, we will relegate our discipline to the status of Astrology; followed by some as a matter of belief, ridiculed by many. Psychoanalysis is largely not well thought of by the public today. It is mostly seen as arcane, obsolete, lengthy, costly, and its therapeutic goals unserviceable and irrelevant. I am *not* saying psychoanalysis is any of these things (although lengthy and costly *are* accurate) but that it is largely *perceived* as being these things. Unfortunately, in the market place, perception is what matters. Our organizations do try to grapple with public perceptions; we could be much more effective in doing so. (APsaA's declaring a day of celebration to commemorate Freud's birthday is just not helpful.) One thing our organizations could do in the future and haven't done is to develop ways of using therapy and analysis via telephone (Leffert, 2003) or Skype to offer excellent treatment in rural areas where it is not otherwise available. To be successful, this would need to have an organization behind it; it is beyond the scope of the individual.

The degree to which these ideas are followed will determine whether a revitalized psychoanalysis takes its justified place in the community or sinks back to occupy a little known or cared about niche in society. The rest of the book offers the knowledge base necessary to pursue these goals.

Notes

1 Postmodernism, I would posit, offers a sound "base from which to engage the ambiguities, uncertainties, simultaneities and pluralities of the therapeutic encounter" (Leffert, 2010, p. 2).
2 Phenomenology, a somewhat slippery, and elastic term, can be difficult to define. I prefer Reynolds' (2012) simple definition gleaned from Husserl's work: "Phenomenology is the sustained attempt to describe the structure of experience without *theoretical* [emphasis added] expectations" (p. 486).

3 We will deal with Husserl and Heidegger in Chapter 5.
4 A far different Freud than the Freud of the 1920s, who commanded a then unimaginable fee of $20 and later $25 per session (Gay, 1988), The equivalent of somewhere between $500 and $1000 in today's dollars.
5 If I consider the meaning of the contents of this epoché I must argue, controversially to be sure, that a psychoanalyst is simply a particular kind of discursive partner with her nature changing somewhat over the decades.
6 Dora (Freud, S., 1905 [1901]/1953) stands out as a horrible exception to both.
7 It is worth noting that this problem, although little noted, nor long-remembered, is not entirely foreign to psychoanalysis. It is contained in the ideas of *Psychology versus Metapsychology* (Gill & Holtzman, 1976) and that "Metapsychology Is Not Psychology" (Gill, 1976). Klein (1969/1976) also argued for two versions of psychoanalysis; a valid clinical one and a dubious theoretical one. At the same time, in an essentially unknown paper, Rubinstein (1967) caught the link between these concepts and Existentialism as he explores the possibility of a purely clinical theory of psychoanalysis.
8 A phenomenological view of ego psychology would describe it simply as a series of identity categories that some psychoanalysts use to classify the data they collect in the therapeutic situation, but lacking in ontological significance.
9 Some of the early Interpersonal authors, like Clara Thompson (1964), trace their roots back even further to Sándor Ferenczi (Thompson, 1944/1964, 1964); others do not.
10 In keeping with this, books dealing with the history of psychoanalysis and the unfolding of psychoanalytic theory have almost nothing to say on the subject; Peter Gay's (1988) biography of Freud/history of psychoanalysis constitutes a rare exception.
11 I remember participating in such debates as a candidate in the 1970s.
12 Positions ranged from viewing the case as defining Freud's technique as he practiced it (Lipton, 1977) to describing it as an example of technical and countertransference errors (Gottlieb, 1989).
13 There are important but sparse recent exceptions (Hill, 2010; Tessman, 2003) to this observation.
14 I have observed this in supervision.
15 I have written elsewhere (Leffert, 2010, Chapter 7) about this history from a power relations standpoint, but this account speaks particularly to its effects on the very being of American psychoanalysts.
16 There are hundreds of examples of this. Just one is the *turn of the century* discovery that gastric ulcers were infectious in origin, that the offending organism was *H. pylori*, and that the definitive treatment was a course of antibiotics.
17 Dasein is a rather obscure and strange sounding Heideggerian term, but it can serve us as a kind of shorthand for a group of concepts: the Being of Human Beings, the Being of the Self, and Being *there*, that is Being or *located* in the inner and outer World. Its converse is the loss of Self-experience.
18 The absence of the latter makes it difficult in a good way to precisely define what these schools entail.
19 See the concept of a Relational Unconscious (Gerson, 2004) as an only partially successful attempt to deal with this problem.
20 For example, Dimen (2011) describes her own experience as the object of her analyst's violation of her. In spite of the fact that, by her own account, she was severely traumatized by the event, that it had remained an issue for her all of her life, and that her analyst was currently deceased, she was unwilling, or unable to name him in the article. To some extent, the *cordon* remained intact.
21 The BoPS chair simply resigned his positions in the APsaA via fax, and the only action taken by the then president of the APsaA was to accept his resignations. When someone questioned on the Members List why more was not done, the then president responded with rage and the matter was *never* publicly mentioned again.
22 In a Midwestern psychoanalytic community, a prominent training analyst unsuccessfully propositions two patients who refuse and report him to the state's licensing board. The

board investigates, but does nothing since nothing physical took place. Then other analysts in the community step in to suppress knowledge of the incident.
23 However well-meant, they signify the student as childlike and immature and the student *accepts* that signification.
24 Whether this is a therapeutic regression as it is billed as being or an iatrogenic and pathological regression should be a subject of some debate (I have written about this in the past [Leffert, 2016] and have argued that it is the latter).
25 Tessman (2011) in her survey of graduate analysts found that 22% were highly unsatisfied with their analyses, 39% were moderately satisfied, and 39% were highly satisfied. The study did not address how the clinical behavior of psychoanalysts, for good, or ill, is influenced by their analysts or supervisors.
26 An obvious criticism at this point would be that our patients sometimes respond to us with anger, contempt, or rejection. One must remember, however, that even in these cases, the patient's rage and contempt indicate to the analyst just how important he is.
27 The Klein Wars in the Los Angeles Psychoanalytic Institute occurring in the 1970s (Kirsner, 2009; Leffert, 2010) and the Certification Wars in APsaA (Leffert, 2010) are examples of this.
28 I bracket this because we all know that, strictly speaking, associations are not "free."
29 The story of Beth, like all the patients I will talk about, is a composite narrative, drawn from my work with many patients that manifest the essential features I want to discuss. I use this format to protect patient confidentiality. Psychoanalytic authors often write about case material as if they are offering veridical accounts that have evidential value: neither is correct. In talking about my "patients" I do so only for purposes of illustration, *not proof*, and composites are, for this purpose, as valid as any form of patient narrative.
30 I am happy to admit that my positions concerning frequency of sessions and a distinction between psychoanalysis and psychoanalytic psychotherapy is controversial. Psychoanalysis has become hard to define, with little agreement concerning theory or practice. (I do not believe that frequency of sessions, which has emerged into this vacuum, is of any help here.) For my purposes, I find that there is a discrete group of patients who are in "not-analysis." The rest are a highly heterogeneous group for which the distinction is meaningless and relies on artificial identity categories that do not inform our epistemologies. Given all of this, it remains obvious to me that it is extremely difficult (but not impossible) to maintain a psychoanalytic situation in once weekly treatment.
31 I have discussed this idea at length in the past (Leffert, 2016, Chapters 6 and 7), including its rather dubious ethical and medico-legal underpinnings.
32 A panacea is a substance that counteracts illness, preferably all illnesses, and returns the subject to normality. It is named after Panacea, the goddess of universal remedy in Greek mythology. The search for a panacea is as old as humanity; in their time, opium, cocaine, and dopamine were all considered panaceas.
33 The idea of a psychoanalytic frame has been with us for a long time and retains at least some of its value. There has been a postmodern shift in recent years to the concept of interreferential fields of influence (Benjamin, 1988) between patient and analyst making up a psychoanalytic field. I have argued (Leffert, 2010) that it is not necessary to abandon the former in order to enjoy the latter and that a dialectical constructivist view comfortably retains both.
34 Psychoanalysis is mostly not covered by insurance. If we do a rough estimate based on a fee of $150 per session (low!) 4 times weekly we are talking about $25,000 per year, after taxes, give or take. In these times this prices most people out of the market. Out of a wish to work psychoanalytically with patients multiple times a week some analysts solve the problem by accepting a nominal fee.
35 There are, however, no studies that test the efficacy of 4 times weekly psychoanalysis head to head with twice weekly psychoanalysis or psychoanalytic psychotherapy. Such studies may well be ethically precluded.
36 Some systems do iatrogenic damage to the patient (many years ago I had a supervisor who told me he preferred to work with negative transference) and have little or no relationship to efficacy.

37 Although BoPS is, as of this writing, being phased out, it is not clear how, if at all, this will affect the now self-imposed training requirements of these institutes.
38 No survey takes psychoanalytic fees into account, and if we are talking about nominal analytic fees, we are making psychoanalysis a hobby rather than a profession.
39 There is a darker side to this. As candidates become more desperate for cases, they are prepared to analyze virtually anyone that will lie down for it. Well-meaning case selection committees and supervisors pass on these cases so as not to impede the student's progress. The result of the actions of all of these well-meaning people is that unanalyzable patients get into analysis, the student has a terrible clinical experience, and the patient is either not helped (the usual result) or sometimes is seriously harmed.
40 These authors do acknowledge the dysfunction of psychoanalytic communities, but offer no suggestions about how to understand it and no remedies to address it.
41 This term fails to accurately describe clinical or theoretical study and interchange, but colloquially most of us know what we mean by it.

References

Andreas-Salomé, L. (1964). *The Freud journal of Lou Andres-Salomé* (S. E. Leavy, Trans.). New York: Basic Books.

Asay, T. P., & Lambert, M. J. (1999). The empirical case for common factors in therapy: Quantitative findings. In M. A. Hubble, B. L. Duncan, & S. D. Miller (Eds.), *The heart & soul of change: What works in therapy* (pp. 33–55). Washington, DC: American Psychological Association.

Benjamin, J. (1988). *The bonds of love*. New York: Pantheon.

Bergmann, M. S. (1993). Reflections on the history of psychoanalysis. *Journal of the American Psychoanalytic Association, 41*, 929–955.

Blanton, S. (1971). *Diary of my analysis with Sigmund Freud*. New York: Hawthorne Press.

Bradford, L. P., Gibb, J. R., & Benne, K. D. (1964). *T-group theory and laboratory method: Innovation and re-education*. New York: John Wiley & Sons.

Buechler, S. (2010). No pain, no gain? Suffering and the analysis of defense. *Contemporary Psychoanalysis, 46*, 334–354.

Carlson, D. A. (2016). Review: Illusions of a future: Psychoanalysis and the biopolitics of desire. *Journal of the American Psychoanalytic Association, 64*, 245–249.

Casement, P. J. (2002). *Learning from our mistakes: Beyond dogma in psychoanalysis and psychotherapy*. East Sussex: Brunner-Routledge.

Celenza, A. (2006). Sexual boundary violations in the office: When is a couch just a couch? *Psychoanalytic Dialogues, 16*, 113–128.

Celenza, A., & Gabbard, G. O. (2003). Analysts who commit sexual boundary violations: A lost cause? *Journal of the American Psychoanalytic Association, 51*, 617–636.

Cramer, P. D. (2016). *Ordinarily well: The case for antidepressants*. New York: Farrar, Strauss and Giroux.

de Maat, S., de Jonghe, F., de Kraker, R. D., Leichsenring, F., Abbass, A., Luyten, P., ... Dekker, J. (2013). The current state of the empirical evidence for psychoanalysis: A meta-analytic approach. *Harvard Review of Psychiatry, 21*, 107–137.

Derrida, J. (1978). *Writing and différence* (A. Bass, Trans.). Chicago: University of Chicago Press.

Dimen, M. (1991). Deconstructing difference: Gender, splitting, and transitional space. *Psychoanalytic Dialogues, 1*, 335–352.

Dimen, M. (2011). Lapsus linguae, or a slip of the tongue? A sexual violation in an analytic treatment and its personal and theoretical aftermath. *Contemporary Psychoanalysis, 47*, 35–79.

Dimen, M. (2016). Rotten apples and ambivalence: Sexual boundary violations through a psychocultural lens. *Journal of the American Psychoanalytic Association, 64*, 361–373.

Flax, J. (1990). *Thinking fragments. Psychoanalysis, feminism, and postmodernism in the contemporary west*. Berkeley: University of California Press.

Foucault, M. (1980). *Power/knowledge: Selected interviews & other writings 1972–1977* (C. Gordon, L. Marshall, J. Mepham, & K. Soper, Trans.). New York: Pantheon Books.

Foucault, M. (1994). *The birth of the clinic: An archealogy of medical perception* (A. M. Sheridan Smith, Trans.). New York: Vintage Books. (Original work published in 1973.)

Frank, J. D., & Frank, J. B. (1993). *Persuasion & healing: A comparative study of psychotherapy* (3rd ed.). Baltimore: Johns Hopkins Press.

Freud, S. (1953). Fragment of an analysis of a case of hysteria. In J. Strachey (Ed.), *Standard edition* (Vol. VII, pp. 3–122). London: Hogarth Press. (Original work published in 1905 [1901].)

Freud, S. (1955). Notes upon a case of obsessional neurosis. In J. Strachey (Ed.), *Standard edition* (Vol. X, pp. 155–318). London: Hogarth Press. (Original work published in 1909.)

Freud, S. (1957). On narcissism: An introduction. In J. Strachey (Ed.), *Standard edition* (Vol. XIV, pp. 73–102). London: Hogarth Press. (Original work published in 1914.)

Gabbard, G. O. (1995). The early history of boundary violations. *Journal of the American Psychoanalytic Association, 43*, 1115–1136.

Gabbard, G. O. (2016). The group as complicit in boundary violations: Commentary on Dimen. *Journal of the American Psychoanalytic Association, 64*, 375–379.

Gabbard, G. O., & Peltz, M. L. (2001). Speaking the unspeakable: Institutional reactions to boundary violations by training analysts. *Journal of the American Psychoanalytic Association, 49*, 659–673.

Gallese, V. (2009). Mirror neurons, embodied simulation, and the neural basis of social identification. *Psychoanalytic Dialogues, 19*, 519–536.

Gallese, V., Eagle, M. N., & Migone, P. (2007). Intentional attunement: Mirror neurons and the neural underpinnings of interpersonal relations. *Journal of the American Psychoanalytic Association, 55*, 131–176.

Gallese, V., Fadiga, L., Fogassi, L., & Rizzolatti, G. (1996). Action recognition in the premotor cortex. *Brain, 119*, 593–609.

Gay, P. (1988). *Freud a life for our time*. New York: W. W. Norton & Co.

Gerber, A. J., & Knopf, L. E. (2015). An empirically-based psychoanalytic curriculum. *Psychoanalytic Inquiry, 35*, 115–123.

Gerson, S. (2004). The relational unconscious: A core element of intersubjectivity, thirdness, and clinical process. *Psychoanalytic Quarterly, 73*, 63–98.

Gill, M. M. (1976). Metapsychology is not psychology. In M. M. Gill & P. S. Holtzman (Eds.), *Psychology verses metapsychology: Essays in honor of George S. Klein* (pp. 71–105). New York: International Universities Press.

Gill, M. M., & Holtzman, P. S. (Eds.). (1976). *Psychology verses metapsychology: Essays in honor of George S. Klein*. New York: International Universities Press.

Goldner, V. (1991). Toward a critical relational theory of gender. *Psychoanalytic Dialogues, 1*, 249–272.

Goldner, V. (2002). Relational theory and the postmodern turn. In S. Fairfield, L. Layton, & C. Stack (Eds.), *Bringing the plague toward a postmodern psychoanalysis* (pp. 157–165). New York: Other Press.

Gottlieb, R. M. (1989). Technique and countertransference in Freud's analysis of the Rat Man. *Psychoanalytic Quarterly, 58*, 29–62.

Hill, C. A. S. (2010). *What do patients want? Psychoanalytic perspectives from the couch*. London: Karnac Books Ltd.

Hoffman, I. Z. (1996). The intimate and ironic authority of the psychoanalyst's presence. *Psychoanalytic Quarterly, 65*, 102–136.

Hoffman, I. Z. (1998). *Ritual and spontaneity in the psychoanalytic process*. Hillsdale: The Analytic Press.

Hubble, M. A., Duncan, B. L., & Miller, S. D. (Eds.). (1999). *The heart and soul of change: What works in therapy*. Washington, DC: American Psychological Association.

Husserl, E. (1970). *The crisis of European sciences and transcendental phenomenology* (D. Cairns, Trans.). Evanston: Northwestern University Press. (Original work published in 1937.)

Husserl, E. (1983). *Ideas pertaining to a pure phenomenology and to a phenomenological philosophy: Book one: General introduction to a pure phenomenology* (F. Kersten, Trans.). New York: Springer (Original work published in 1913.)

Iacoboni, M. (2007). Face to face: The neural basis of social mirroring and empathy. *Psychiatric Annals, 37*, 4, 236–241.

Iacoboni, M. (2008). *Mirroring people: The new science of how we connect with people*. New York: Farrar, Strauss and Giroux.

Iacoboni, M., Molnar-Szakacs, I., Gallese, V., Buccino, G., Mazziotta, J. C., & Rizzolatti, G. (2005). Grasping intentions of others with one's own mirror neuron system. *PloS Biology, 3*, e79.

Jacobson, E. (1964). *The self and the object world*. New York: International Universities Press.

Jacoby, R. (1983). *The repression of psychoanalysis Otto Fenichel and the political Freudians*. New York: Basic Books.

Kardiner, A. (1977). *My analysis with Freud*. New York: W. W. Norton & Co.

Kernberg, O. F. (2016). *Psychoanalytic education at the crossroads: Reformation, change and the future of psychoanalytic training*. New York: Routledge.

Kernberg, O. F., & Michels, R. (2016). Thoughts on the present and future of psychoanalytic education. *Journal of the American Psychoanalytic Association, 64*, 477–493.

Kirsner, D. (2009). *Unfree associations: Inside psychoanalytic institutes* (updated ed.). Lanham: Jason Aronson.

Klein, G. S. (1976). Freud's two theories of sexuality. In M. M. Gill & P. S. Holtzman (Eds.), *Psychology verses metapsychology: Psychoanalytic essays in honor of George S. Klein* (pp. 14–70). New York: International Universities Press (Original work published in 1969.)

Kohut, H. (1966). Forms and transformations of narcissism. *Journal of the American Psychoanalytic Association, 14*, 243–272.

Kohut, H. (1971). *The analysis of the self*. New York: International Universities Press.

Kohut, H. (1977). *The restoration of the self*. New York: International Universities Press.

Kohut, H., & Wolf, E. S. (1978). The disorders of the self and their treatment: An outline. *International Journal of Psychoanalysis, 59*, 413–425.

Laplanche, J., & Pontalis, J. B. (1973). *The language of psycho-analysis* (D. Nicholson-Smith, Trans.). New York: W. W. Norton & Co. (Original work published in 1967.)

Layton, L. (2000). The psychopolitics of bisexuality. *Studies in Gender and Sexuality, 1*, 41–60.

Leffert, M. (2003). Analysis and psychotherapy by telephone: Twenty years of clinical experience. *Journal of the American Psychoanalytic Association, 51*, 101–130.

Leffert, M. (2010). *Contemporary psychoanalytic foundations*. London: Routledge.

Leffert, M. (2013). *The therapeutic situation in the 21st century*. New York: Routledge.

Leffert, M. (2016). *Phenomenology, uncertainty, and care in the therapeutic encounter*. New York: Routledge.

Leffert, M. (2017). *Positive psychoanalysis: Aesthetics, desire, and subjective well-being*. New York: Routledge.

Leichsenring, F. (2005). Are psychodynamic and psychoanalytic therapies effective?: A review of empirical data. *International Journal of Psychoanalysis, 86*, 841–868.

Leuzinger-Bohleber, M., Stuhrast, U., Rüger, B., & Beutel, M. E. (2003). How to study the "quality of psychoanalytic treatments" and their long-term effects on patients' well-being: A representative, multi-perspecitve follow-up study. *International Journal of Psychoanalysis, 84*, 263–290.

Leuzinger-Bohleber, M., & Target, M. (Eds.). (2001). *Outcomes of psychoanalytic treatment perspectives for therapists and researchers*. London: Whurr Publishers.

Levin, C. (2016). Fear of breakdown in the psychoanalytic group: Commentary on Dimen. *Journal of the American Psychoanalytic Association, 64*, 381–388.

Lipton, S. D. (1977). Clinical observations on resistance to the transference. *The International Journal of Psychoanalysis, 58*, 463–472.

Luborsky, L., Singer, B., & Luborsky, I. (1975). Comparative studies of psychotherapies: Is it true that "everyone has won and all must have prizes?" *Archives of General Psychiatry, 32*, 995–1008.

Lukes, S. (2005). *Power a radical view* (2nd ed.). New York: Palgrave Macmillan.

May, R. (1983). *The discovery of being*. New York: W. W. Norton & Co.

May, R. (2009). *Man's search for himself*. New York: W. W. Norton & Co. (Original work published in 1953.)

Meissner, W. W. (2006). Prospects for psychoanalysis in the 21st century. *Psychoanalytic Psychology, 23*, 239–256.

Nersessian, E., & Solms, M. (1999). Editors' introduction. *Neuropsychoanalysis, 1*, 3–4.

Pally, R. (2010). *Frontline*—The Brain's shared circuits of interpersonal understanding: Implications for psychoanalysis and psychodynamic understanding. *Journal of the American Academy of Psychoanalysis and Dynamic Psychiatry, 38*, 381–411.

Protopopescu, X., & Gerber, A. J. (2013). Bridging the gap between neuroscientific and psychodynamic models in child and adolescent psychiatry. *Child and Adolescent Psychiatric Clinics of North America, 22*, 1–31.

Pulver, S. E. (2003). On the astonishing clinical irrelevance of neuroscience. *Journal of the American Psychoanalytic Association, 51*, 755–772.

Rapaport, D. (1967). A historical survey of psychoanalytic ego psychology. In M. M. Gill (Ed.), *The collected papers of David Rapaport* (pp. 745–757). New York: Basic Books. (Original work published in 1958.)

Reynolds, J. (2012). Existentialism. In S. Luft & S. Overgaard (Eds.), *The Routledge companion to phenoomenology*. New York: Routledge.

Roazen, P. (1975). *Freud and his followers*. New York: Alfred A. Knopf.

Rubinstein, B. B. (1967). On the possibility of a strictly clinical psychoanalytic theory: An essay in the philosophy of psychoanalysis. In M. M. Gill & P. S. Holzman (Eds.), *Psychology versus metapsychology: Psychoanalytic essays in memory of George S. Klein* (pp. 229–264). New York: International Universities Press.

Sandler, J., Holder, A., Dare, C., & Dreher, A. U. (1997). *Freud's models of the mind: An introduction*. Madison: International Universities Press.

Schechter, K. (2014). *Illusions of a future: Psychoanalysis and the biopolitics of desire*. Durham: Duke University Press.

Schore, A. N. (2003a). *Affect dysregulation and disorders of the self*. New York: W. W. Norton & Co.

Schore, A. N. (2003b). *Affect regulation and the repair of the self*. New York: W. W. Norton & Co.

Schore, A. N. (2011). The right brain implicit self lies at the core of psychoanalysis. *Psychoanalytic Dialogues, 21*, 75–100.

Schore, J. R., & Schore, A. N. (2007). Modern attachment theory: The central role of affect regulation in development and treatment. *Clinical Social Work Journal, 36*, 9–20.

Solms, M. (2013). The conscious id. *Neuropsychoanalysis, 15*, 5–19.

Stern, D. B., Mann, C. H., Kantor, S., & Schlesinger, G. (Eds.). (2014). *Pioneers of interpersonal psychoanalysis*. New York: Routledge. (Original work published in 1995.)

Stern, D. N., Sander, L. W., Nahum, J. P., Harrison, A. M., Lyons-Ruth, K., Morgan, A. C., ... Tronik, E. Z. (1998). Non-interpretive mechanisms in psychoanalytic therapy: The "something more" than interpretation. The process of change study group. *The International Journal of Psychoanalysis, 79*, 903–921.

Survey Advantage Whorton Marketing Research (2011). *2011 Psychoanalytic professional activities benchmark study*. New York: American Psychoanalytic Association.

Tessman, L. H. (2003). *The analyst's analyst within*. Hillsdale: The Analytic Press.

Thompson, C. M. (1964). Ferenczi's contribution to Psychoanalysis. In M. R. Green (Ed.), *Interpersonal psychoanalysis: The selected papers of Clara M. Thompson* (pp. 72–82). New York: Basic Books. (Original work published in 1944.)

Thompson, C. M. (1964). Ferenczi's relaxation method. In M. R. Green (Ed.), *Interpersonal psychoanalysis: The selected papers of Clara M. Thompson* (pp. 67–71). New York: Basic Books.

Vivona, J. M. (2009). Embodied language in neuroscience and psychoanalysis. *Journal of the American Psychoanalytic Association, 57*, 1327–1360.

Walton, J. (1997). Re-placing race in (white) psychoanalytic discourse: Founding narratives in feminism. In E. Abel, B. Christian, & H. Moglen (Eds.), *Female subjects in black and white: Race, psychoanalysis, feminism* (pp. 223–252). Berkeley: University of California Press.

Wangh, M. (Ed.). (1962). *Fruition of an idea: Fifty years of psychoanalysis in New York*. New York: International Universities Press.

2
THE NEUROPHILOSOPHY OF CONSCIOUSNESS

Introduction

Traditionally, Philosophy has concerned itself with, among other things, the nature of consciousness, the nature of mind, and the relationship of both to brain and body. These inquiries are as old as civilization: to the extent that one considers religion to also involve an exploration of these areas, they are even older. As neuroscience began to gain traction around the middle of the last century, researchers and philosophers began to add ever-larger dollops of it to try to better understand consciousness, and the field of Neurophilosophy was born. The field is expanding. There is a *Journal of Consciousness Studies* and a continuing flow of books on consciousness. I have discussed Consciousness and Neurophilosophy in the past (Leffert, 2010, Chapter 6) and my perspective on both has widened in the interim. There is more to the latter than a study of the former, and later chapters will deal with that more: the appearance of consciousness in the family tree of *H. sapiens sapiens* and the Neurophilosophy of Postmodernism, Existentialism, and Phenomenology. In effect, I am positing that Neurophilosophy and a discipline strange to most psychoanalysts, Paleoanthropology, are essential parts of any general ontology.[1]

This chapter will begin by laying out some of the data points that describe the Neurophilosophy of consciousness as required for a multidimensional discourse on the subject. I will then go over some of the conclusions I reached in 2010 about the nature of consciousness; I would call these conclusions neuropsychological rather than neurophilosophical. As far as they go, they are, mostly, holding up well after 8 years. Consciousness has been a central issue for Phenomenology since the days of Husserl (1937/1970, 1913/1983) and for psychoanalysis from its beginnings; we need to consider how a century of neuroscience research has impacted this position. In particular, I want to look at how studying consciousness, mind, and their relations to brain and body can further inform our work as psychoanalytic clinicians. For both philosophy and psychoanalysis, consciousness has been king for a long time, with a focus on understanding its origins and its relation to the Self.[2] If it is *not* king, as I am going to argue, if it is a necessary but not a sufficient part of Human Being, then just what is it? While accounting for only a relatively small part of what goes on mentally, it is also what makes us uniquely Human. It is a system of executive functions that initiates (agency and intentionality) and experiences (knows and reflects). Neuroscience tells us that experience is not in the sole purview of consciousness, an issue that we will need to take up; however much initiation beyond the reflexive certainly seems to be. Orthodox psychoanalysis attempts to adhere to the Topographic frame of reference. It defines a system Unconscious delineated by Repression as by far the more important site of therapeutic action, there is, as I have previously discussed (Leffert, 2010, 2016), *no evidence for the existence of either.*

This is the first of two chapters in which I am going to develop a much broader Neurophilosophy in contrast to those authors whose object is philosophy as it pertains to a neuroscience (the subject of only the present chapter) cast in terms of a Metaphysics of Consciousness.

Some diverse data points

Data point 1: vegetative states

I began my earlier (Leffert, 2010, Chapter 6) discussion of consciousness with a case illustration: "In 1997, a 26-year-old schoolteacher named Kate Bainbridge fell into a coma following an obscure illness that progressed to a vegetative state[3] (Groopman, 2007; Owen et al., 2006)" (p. 157) and was hospitalized at Addenbrooke Hospital at Cambridge University. By a lucky coincidence, Adrian Owen, a British neurologist, had recently moved there to study PET (Positive Emission Tomography) scanning, and the hospital's neuroimaging center was located down the hall from the Neurological Intensive Care Unit. Owen heard about Kate and decided to study her. PET scans reveal increased blood flow and metabolism, showing what parts of the brain are cognitively active (very exciting in 1997). Pictures of Kate's family caused her brain to light up in the same way as such pictures did for normally conscious people: different from the response to random photographs. To avoid the problem of whether the pictures succeeded in capturing her glance, Owen switched to voice recordings and got the same result.

The next question was whether the speech had been understood or only recognized. It seems that if you begin a sentence with an ambiguous noun, the Self assumes the most common meaning, and if the sentence bears out that usage, the same area of the brain lights up in some vegetative patients and in normal volunteers. If, however, it turns out that the sentence involves a less common meaning, a different area of the brain, the left inferior frontal cortex, lights up to correct the meaning. This too was seen in some vegetative patients and in all normal volunteers.

Owen and colleagues (2006), in an attempt to document the conscious awareness of these patients, wanted to see if they could follow commands to perform complex memory tasks. They asked Kate to first imagine playing a game of tennis (a motor task) and then to visually take a guided tour of her home (a memory task). Again, she performed as did the volunteers. In an accompanying editorial, Naccache (2006) attempted to answer the question: "Is She Conscious?" He was unsuccessful.[4]

Data point 2: the anatomy

As good logical positivists, we are drawn to the idea that any anatomical localization of consciousness broadens our knowledge. Unfortunately, anatomy is not destiny: It promises much, but delivers little.

> Beginning subcortically and plunging into the brain stem is a tangly, snarly collection of neurons called the reticular formation (RF), which seems to collect information "downstream" from the brain stem and the peripheral and autonomic nervous systems and connects bilaterally "upstream" with the nucleus reticularis of the thalamus (NRT) and the intralaminar nuclei (ILN) of the thalamus. From there, connections branch out all over the brain.
>
> *(Leffert, 2010, p. 168)*

Somewhere in this group of structures, I thought in 2010, we would find the origins of Consciousness.

Bilateral lesions of even a few cubic millimeters (the size of a couple of grains of rice) in these areas can produce irreversible coma. The anatomy would seem to imply Bogen's (1995/2003) property of consciousness "C": To wit, whatever else consciousness is, without C there can be no consciousness. But it doesn't, not really. We don't know *anything* about what actually goes on in this area: Location and ablation prove nothing. We also know that while this tiny area of the brain is essential to consciousness, relatively large chunks of the rest of the brain can be damaged or removed without affecting it at all.

Other authors (Crick & Koch, 2005; Koch, 2012) have taken a wider view of the neural apparatus of consciousness to include not only the thalamus but an adjacent area of the neocortex forming a *cortico-thalamic complex*. The complex includes the hippocampus, the amygdala, basal ganglia, and the claustrum. The claustrum is a thin layer of cells located beneath the inner surface of the neocortex. In 2005 Crick and Koch described its function as "enigmatic," noting that it is unusual, both receiving and sending out input to almost all areas of the cerebral cortex. More recently Koch and colleagues (Reardon, 2017) discovered three *very* long branched claustral neurons in the mouse that completely encircle the brain "that seem to connect to most or all of the outer parts of the brain that take in sensory information and drive behaviour." Reardon further reports that "Koch sees this as evidence that the claustrum could be coordinating inputs and outputs across the brain to create consciousness" (p. 15).

Consciousness is the product of two sorts of brain systems (Blumenthal, 2016): those determining the *content* of consciousness and those determining the *level* of consciousness. The former is determined by complex, hierarchically organized bilateral systems that interact intimately with memory (see Tulving, 1983), while the latter influences all of these functions through the regulation of alertness, awareness, and attention.

The consciousness system involves the complex interactions of disparate parts of the brain. It involves the collective activity spread bilaterally across the association areas of the cerebral cortex that determine the level of consciousness.[5] The brain self-organizes into shifting parallel distributed processing networks (McClelland & Rumelhart, 1986; Rumelhart & McClelland, 1986) of neurons. These networks vie for attention (Marinsek, Gazzaniga, & Miller, 2016). When the activity of one or another of them is boosted to a sufficient level of activation (an admittedly inexact concept), it enters consciousness and remains there until it is superseded by another Parallel Distributed Processing (PDP) network. Subcortical areas of the brain, including the upper brainstem, thalamus, hypothalamus, and basal forebrain, involve activation and arousal and function through multiple neurotransmitters. There is widespread disagreement concerning the relationship of attention to consciousness (Blumenthal, 2016) with some authors considering them dissociable while others consider them identical, and still others take differing positions in between. That said, Koch and Tsuchiya (2007) argue convincingly for the presence of two discrete systems capable of operating independently. Somehow, these systems come together by a process termed *binding* (Singer, 2001) that yields a unified experience of consciousness. As yet, these findings have only limited clinical relevance except that when these connections are damaged they lead to a fragmented experience of consciousness called *simultagnosia*. What is important for our immediate purposes is that the structure of these areas of the brain is, for the individual, uniquely affected by experience, and development so that, although consciousness has shared components of experience, the *experience* of consciousness is also different for each of us (Kunzendorf & Wallace, 1999), a point that is mostly ignored. We will return to it presently.

Data point 3: split brains

The central nervous system, like most of the rest of us, manifests bilateral symmetry. Although there are some complex connections deep in the midbrain and even the brain stem, the major ways in which the cerebral hemispheres are connected to each other and exchange information is through a fibrous structure, the corpus callosum, comprised of 200 million or so axons, the long processes of neurons that transmit action potentials (information) to distal neurons. It is responsible for the "hemispheric transfer of sensory, motor, perceptual, and semantic information" (Marinsek et al., 2016, p. 271). Beginning in the 1940s (Wolford, Miller, & Gazzaniga, 2004), neurosurgeons found that severe and intractable epilepsy could be successfully treated by performing a commissurotomy: cutting the corpus callosum and separating the hemispheres. (It interrupted the transmission of self-reinforcing seizure activity across the brain.) Bogen and Vogel (1962) perfected the procedure. Their patients who now had, in effect, "split brains" appeared to function quite normally; they became the subjects of intense neuropsychological interest (Galin, 1974; Wolford et al., 2004). Sperry and colleagues (Sperry, Gazzaniga, & Bogen, 1969) developed experimental protocols allowing them to "interview" each hemisphere in isolation, and they filmed the interviews. Except for Sperry (1969), these researchers believed they were studying the unconscious residing in the Right Cerebral Hemisphere, as did psychoanalysts (e.g., Hoppe, 1977). In fact, what they were studying were consciousnesses, albeit from a different perspective than Owen and his colleagues (2006).

In Sperry's first experiment (Sperry et al., 1969), a young woman is shown a series of geometric images in her left visual field (going to the right cerebral hemisphere [RB]) using a tachistoscope.[6] A nude pinup is mixed in with the images of geometric shapes; the woman blushes and giggles. When she's asked what she saw, she confabulates, and says she saw a flash of light. Her left cerebral hemisphere (LB) did not see it, and her RB is unable to use words; it can only react. In another film, the subject is asked to arrange a series of colored blocks to match a colored geometric design. The left hand (RB) easily completes the task (the RB is nonverbal but manages visio-spatial recognition). When the right hand is asked to perform the same task, it is slow, and makes errors. Suddenly, the *left* hand snakes out and successfully completes the assembly. Language skills are predominantly located in the LB, while the RB is only able to understand words as symbols. Causal inference is a LB capacity, while the RB is capable of lower-level sensory inference and higher-level parallel processing. The reason for these differences is that, over the course of lifelong development and experience, each hemisphere has developed different specializations that can be thought of either as residing in cognitive modules or as in less sharply demarcated interreferential areas of Brain.

What we have is not a conscious and an unconscious, but *two separate consciousnesses* that, in normal individuals, are in communication with each other through the corpus callosum. In another study, Risse and Gazzaniga (1978) demonstrated that the RB could "keep secrets" from the LB, that these were two *dissociable* memory systems, two dissociable consciousnesses. Right-handed individuals are usually LB dominant. The consciousness of the Self is thus divisible, yet split-brain individuals still experience a unity of Self *even when it isn't there*. This is a product of the synthetic functions of the LB that, in normal individuals, smoothes out narratives, gives consciousness a continuous feel that belies how it is made up of chunks, and fills in the blanks, not necessarily accurately.

This bicameral mind, somewhat unusually, violates a principle of folk psychology: What we *experience* as consciousness is Left Brain verbal, reflective consciousness. What is actually going on is that LB consciousness is *dominant*. We are prepared to treat the Right Brain as unconscious in spite of the fact that these experiments demonstrate it *is* conscious; it is only that the LB is unconscious *of* it.

42 The neurophilosophy of consciousness

Data point 4: development and laterality

The development of each of the cerebral hemispheres is very different. The RB[7] develops from birth with its rate of anatomic and physiological growth peaking at 10–12 months (Thatcher, 1991, 1994). The LB goes through its own growth spurt from 18 to 36 months. The RB is dominant during the earlier period as measured by cerebral blood flow being greater on the right (Chiron et al., 1997; Schore, 2003). After age 3 this is reversed, with blood flow becoming greater on the left. Chiron and colleagues posited that this shift paralleled the development of first visio-spatial recognition on the right and then language on the left.[8] Schore further posited that left-sided dominance is the result of the growth of the axons of left prefrontal neurons across the cerebral commissures to the right hemisphere and the beginning of communication between the two halves of the brain. It occurs at the same time that speech beyond the use of single words develops. We could ask the neuroscience question: Which came first? But this is where the postmodern component of meaning comes into play. We have these two processes going on at about the same time: There are these changes in the toddler's brain, and she starts to speak. Speech is driven by attachment and its cognitive expression in a push to communicate that, although it precedes age 3, does not exist in the absence of life experiences with the parents that call it forth. Speech is the outcome of the mother and child's quest for *dyadic meaning* (Tronick, 2009). If the process of normative language learning does not begin before age 3, it can only be because the brain is not developmentally ready to do so. What we have then must be an interreferential process in which the Self is driving speech and phase-ready anatomical structures are developing to enable it. What participates in the acquisition of speech is the development of left-sided dominance; the connection is not necessary to *maintain* it, as we see in our commissurotomy patients. The question we will want to ask later (in Chapter 4) is how the advent of language affects consciousness.

We know other things about how the hemispheres differ from each other. The LB thinks slowly (taking seconds or longer to reach a conclusion) and serially processes information; it burns a lot of calories doing so. The RB operates very fast (2 msec, give or take) using parallel processing; it is energy efficient, the Prius of consciousness. Why have such a system at all? Baars (1993/2003) asks that very question in a paper entitled: "How Does a Serial, Integrated and Very Limited Stream of Consciousness Emerge From a Nervous System That is Mostly Unconscious, Distributed, Parallel, and of Enormous Capacity?" The answer, it seems, comes independently from an analysis of computer design. If you are designing a computer to handle the largest and most complex of problems, you *require* a global workspace architecture that turns out to mimic the bimodal LB-RB architecture of the human brain. We also know that although the LB experiences its consciousness as *continuous* and serial, that is not the case. It is a broken chain, with discontinuities, often experiencing mini-epiphanies as ideas pop into it from the RB. It makes use of a synthetic self-function that creates the *experience* of continuity, and its absence, or interruption is at least disconcerting. There is evidence for this. Nisbett and

Wilson (1977), in a now classic study proved that preferences, biases, and choices are not accessible to LB consciousness. They first asked their subjects about their judgments or explanations of a series of events they were exposed to. They readily supplied the information. They were then asked how they had come up with them. They readily supplied this information as well. It took, however, relatively little inquiry to determine that these were ex post facto explanations and that these LBs *had no idea* how they had reached their conclusions. This was not an unconscious process; it was simply a parallel RB process that fed the decision to the left. In terms of the concepts we are about to discuss, such decision-making draws on affect-rich interactive algorithms. Decision-making under conditions involving uncertainty employs cognitive shortcuts called heuristics and biases (Tversky & Kahneman, 1974/1982) that I have previously discussed at some length (Leffert, 2016).[9] They function on the level of what is called *anoetic* memory (we will talk about this term shortly). It is possible to become self-knowing about these processes. One can learn to attend to how and when such ideas pop up, seemingly out of nowhere. In other words, *it is possible to change one's consciousness by reflecting on it*.

Data point 5: unconsciousnesses

No discussion of consciousness can be considered complete without dealing with its relationship to what isn't conscious. I have written (Leffert, 2010, Chapter 5, 2016, Chapter 4) at considerable length about the nature of unconsciousness. I have offered systematic critiques of the existence of a dynamic unconscious separated from consciousness by a process called repression that cannot be shown to exist (Willingham & Preuss, 1995). As Holmes (1990) put it, "despite over 60 years of research involving numerous approaches by many thoughtful and clever investigators, at the present time there is no controlled laboratory evidence supporting the concept of repression" (p. 96). That such critiques have proven unpopular goes without saying. Some majority of psychoanalysts and psychotherapists maintain *at least implicitly* that bringing unconscious things into consciousness through the undoing of repression is a significant, perhaps *the* significant, source of therapeutic action. What I have argued for instead is that, phenomenologically, there are many different, interreferential kinds of unconsciousness, and what I would argue for now is that there are also many different kinds of *consciousness*. What we are after therapeutically, I would posit, is not moving some contents from one category to another, but rather an expansion of our very Being that is entailed in a comprehensive search for meaning (Leffert, 2017, Chapter 2). *This* is a major focus of therapeutic action.

Tronick (2009) argues convincingly that what therapy is mostly about is dyadic meaning making that, involving multiple levels of mind/brain function, establishes a polymorphic and polysemic flow of meaning. In applying his work to things conscious and otherwise, Tronick moves from neuroscience into philosophy, implicitly becoming an ontologist of consciousness. He defines meaning as biopsychological (as I would define it as bio-psycho-social and locate it in the Self: Leffert,

2016, Chapter 1). Meaning is created or cocreated in a state of consciousness, where Tronick defines a state of consciousness as "a dynamically changing biopsychological state integrating biological and psychological meaning, purposiveness, and intentions made at every level and site of operation in the organism from physiology to awareness" (p. 94). The changes have to do with what are polymorphic states of Being, of consciousness, and unconsciousness that occur in the Bio-Psycho-Social Self. If we try to deal with them as identity categories, as have philosophy and psychoanalysis to date, they break down if one is serious about observing what goes on in the Self. If we rather treat the Self as a holistic system, it is ontologically permissible for all these things to come and go, flit in, and out of consciousness, manifest physical, neurochemical states of being, and constitute a sheaf of Being and *différence* (Derrida, 1978) progressing through time.

Data point 6: different kinds of memory, different kinds of consciousness

If these were not already enough different ways of describing consciousness, there are also different kinds of memory and different kinds of consciousness to go with them. This observation brings us to Neurophilosophy. Going back to 1983, Endel Tulving defined three memory systems: in ascending order the *Procedural*, the *Semantic*, and the *Episodic*. As he puts it (Tulving, 1985/2003), "procedural memory is concerned with how things are done—with the acquisition, retention, and utilization of perceptual, cognitive and motor skills" (p. 580). Vanderkerckhove and Panksepp (2009) argue that knowledge, knowing, is largely comprised of *raw affects*, the extents of which are underestimated by most authors. Procedural Memory, then, is not just the stuff of riding bicycles, an outcome of systematic motor learning, largely on a spinal level, but also involves affectively primitive ways of knowing Self and World. Semantic knowing leads to our store of accessible *cognitive* knowledge about, well, *everything*, Self and World. The knowledge is fact-based, not event-based. Semantic knowledge (e.g., the world is flat) is not necessarily *accurate* knowledge. Episodic knowing involves the memory of past events; that is, narrative, self-reflective memory containing event-based knowledge.[10] It too need not be correct, it is capable of errors (Schacter, 1996), and it can house fantasies or stories. Errors or fantasies can result from internalized systematic errors in judgment that can flow from psychopathology. Judy, a patient who sought me out when she found herself in dire financial straits, had discovered in childhood that fantasy was often more pleasant than reality. She learned to simply deny those realities she found unpleasant, entering into disastrous relationships in which she was exploited and squandering a fortune in the process. She was highly defensive about her distortions of procedural and semantic processing, and they could not be approached in the present. Instead, I helped her to explore the origins of the small psychotic core that "needed" to produce these errors. We were ultimately, affectively led to the death of a beloved father when she was 5.

Semantic and episodic memory also harbor projections into the future (Schacter, Addis, & Buckner, 2008) of simulations or fantasies. Episodic memory enables "mental time travel," the ability to remember sequences of events from the past and project possible events in the future. Tulving believed that the three forms of memory have a hierarchical relationship, with Semantic Memory being a subset of Procedural Memory and Episodic Memory being a subset of Semantic Memory (Semantic is built on Procedural and Episodic is built on Semantic). This represents a "class inclusion hierarchy" (Tulving, 1985/2003, p. 580) in which specialized sub-categories are *entailed*. Each of these involves a different kind of consciousness. They constitute a neurophilosophy of memory.

Procedural Memory is characterized by *anoetic* ("unknowing") consciousness (Tulving, 1985/2003). It is tied to a current situation: It perceptually registers, internally represents, and leads the individual to behaviorally respond. It includes no references to non-present internal or external elements. It is phylogenetically ancient (Feinberg & Mallatt, 2016), going back at least to reptiles.[11] Autonoetic states are automatic and independent of voluntary attention: They can, however, if made objects of attention, be brought into reflective awareness. Anoetic states are prereflective; they are involved with intense affective and sensory information. They are a prerequisite for the higher, phenomenological states of awareness. Perhaps surprisingly, anoetic consciousness is fundamentally involved in self-experience (Vanderkerckhove & Panksepp, 2009). It produces the feeling of "who we are": a fundamental state of self-experience that cannot be put into words. It forms the background of experience with higher forms of consciousness in the foreground. "There is always a foreground and a background to consciousness determined by the limited capacity of the brain at a given moment" (Vanderkerckhove & Panksepp, 2009, p. 1020).

Semantic Memory involves noetic ("knowing") consciousness. It "allows an organism to be aware of, and to cognitively operate on, objects and events, and relations among objects, in the absence of these objects and events" (Tulving, 1985/2003, p. 581). Vertebrates are capable of Semantic Memory. Episodic or narrative memory involves autonoetic (self-knowing) consciousness. These two consciousness systems represent different complimentary ways of knowing: Although an individual can operate on semantic memory alone, episodic memory yields more information, making possible more effective action. Tulving (2005) forcefully argues that autonoetic consciousness is uniquely present in *H. sapiens sapiens*, that is, us. Other authors argue that autonoetic consciousness is present in primates and also in some of the higher mammals and birds (Terrace & Metcalfe, 2005) such as the African Grey Parrot (Pepperberg, 2000, 2008). The answer, I think, is that both are right. It seems evolutionarily unlikely that autonoetic conscious would suddenly snap into being in a fully realized form and that these higher primates, including our hominin ancestors manifested self-awareness without the capacity for mental time travel into the past or the future. (We'll return to this point in Chapter 4.) In folk psychology, autonoetic consciousness is what we mean by consciousness, and its damage, or absence results in amnesia. (In the presence of amnesia, anoetic, and noetic consciousness can remain intact.) Purposeful, psychological errors in anoetic consciousness can serve defensive purposes and lead to dysfunction. The process is amenable to uncovering in psychotherapy and psychoanalysis if only the therapist will seek it out. Tulving (1983) describes autonoetic consciousness as manifesting six properties: It manifests a personal time sense of past, present, and future; it is a necessary part of remembering events; it appears later in development; it is capable of being selectively lost in brain damage; it varies among individuals and situations: it is capable of being measured. A final property is that it presents knowledge in its context.

No particular argument can be made for parsing out the different orders of consciousness between the hemispheres. The split-brain studies (Sperry, 1969; Sperry et al., 1969) do not demonstrate, as we might expect, that there is no autonoetic consciousness in the RB, but only that it is qualitatively different from what it looks like in the LB. Indeed, some studies (Keenan, Wheeler, Gallup, & Pascual-Leone, 2000) localize autonoetic consciousness in the Right Hemisphere, but others (Tulving, Kapur, Craik, Moscovitch, & Houle, 1994) demonstrate that, while it exists in both hemispheres, the two must work together to accomplish encoding and retrieval.

These formulations have important consequences for the neurophilosophy of consciousness. They describe a dynamic, interreferential flow of memory through these systems. Unfortunately, this is not so for many authors who prefer to think of things by sticking them into categories rather than the harder alternative of understanding them, as we are trying to do, in terms of general systems theory (GST) (Laszlo, 1972/1996). We like to (feel at home with) name things, believing that the very act of naming creates knowledge and endows the namer with power. (Sadly, the latter is often the case within social systems, e.g., McCarthyism.) Elements of systems can exist at the same organizational level or can be nested one within the other without involving the attempt at boundary making inherent in defining identity categories.

As Psychotherapists and Psychoanalysts, we tend to equate Consciousness with autonoetic consciousness and, in the process, leave out a great deal of what is going on in the Self. As we have discussed, problems in anoetic, and noetic consciousness can both arise from and cause psychological dysfunction; this broader understanding of the different sorts of consciousness enables us to better understand out patients' problems with effective function and suffering (as we saw with Judy).

Phenomenologically, the experience of these systems in operation is very different. We can consciously deploy Procedural Memory, but if we try to know it, like the famous centipede being struck motionless when asked how he manages to walk, we usually fail. Anoetic consciousness is Phenomenal: it is what it is. It is noetic and autonoetic consciousness that are Phenomenological; they put us in touch with the Things Themselves (Husserl, 1937/1970, 1913/1983). We can know the past either noetically or autonoetically; they are different kinds of knowing. Thus, I know that John F. Kennedy was assassinated by Lee Harvey Oswald on November 22, 1963. But I *also* know that I heard about John F. Kennedy being assassinated by Lee Harvey Oswald on the radio after attending a physics lecture (it was a terrible lecture) and feeling lost for hours afterward. The information that Kennedy was assassinated can be retrieved noetically without retrieving the autonoetic memory. Adaptively, why develop autonoetic consciousness at all if we already have procedural and semantic knowing? The answer is that autonoetic consciousness accesses much more complex contextual information about out world, the people that inhabit it, and how to best dwell with them in it. It enables us to engage this complexity and to function more effectively in its presence. It seems likely that autonoetic consciousness had to evolve to handle increasingly complex social situations. The procedural, the semantic, and the episodic are different, interreferential kinds of consciousness that interact to form multi-dimensional states of Being.

Putting it all together: elements of a successful theory of consciousness

If consciousness remains "the hard problem" as it has been described, it is one that is very much defined by a group of ontological parameters. Although there is a massive literature on the subject, including at least two journals devoted to it, authors often do not much take this into account in formulating a theory of consciousness. The result is that at some point theorizing trails off into opinionating. A related problem is that what they call Neurophilosophy is sometimes neither; in these cases, it is only a theory of consciousness based on applied neuroscience. As Dehaene and Naccache (2001) observe, the phenomenology of an adequate theory of consciousness must allow for three things: a considerable amount of what goes on in the Self can take place without consciousness; attention is a prerequisite of consciousness; and that "consciousness is required for some specific cognitive tasks including durable information maintenance, novel combinations of operations, or the spontaneous generation of intentional behavior" (p. 1).

Complexity

Complexity theory (Leffert, 2010, Chapters 3 and 6) is the friend of consciousness theorists, even though I have not found anyone writing about it (hopefully this will change). The Bio-Psycho-Social Self is a complex system. Complex systems have properties that are of great interest to us. Although *some* of their properties can be found in the sum of those of their component part, others cannot. A complex system (like the Self) can thus, be greater than the sum of its parts and demonstrate characteristics that are not found in any of its components: These are *emergent properties of a holistic system*. Consciousness is such a property. The behavior of complex systems is nonlinear and cannot be predicted. *Emergent* does not signify something spooky and non-physical but only that it represents a property that emerges out of a complex system as a whole that is not to be found by tallying up the properties of its components. Emergence (and hence, consciousness) is *not* metaphysical. Complexity (Leffert, 2008) has been well studied, and emergence refers to a kind of property that such systems have, not some speculative, or spiritual notion about their behavior.

Chaos theory, on the other hand, describes the occurrence of catastrophic changes or tipping points in complex systems: phenomena like hurricanes, lakes freezing, earthquakes, or school shootings that are only predictable as probabilities occurring over broad ranges of time. Attempting to describe dysfunction in a complex system when it is defined as a series of modules that can be studied by looking at defects in one or more of them, the equivalent of lesions in the brain (e.g., Laureys, Gosseries, & Tononi, 2016), cannot lead to a working theory of consciousness.

Physicalism

Much of the writing on Consciousness has been shaped by the work of a single philosopher, René Descartes, writing in the Early Modern Period (1500–1800). He argued (1641/1999) that Brain and Mind were ontologically different and incapable of being integrated. Some of the philosophy done since has been derivative of his work while another thread begun by Baruch Spinoza continues into the present with the work of Antonio Damasio (1994, 2003). As Damasio (2003) puts it, Spinoza (1676/2011) posited, in contrast to Descartes, "that both the mind and the body were parallel attributes (call them manifestations) of the very same substance" (p. 12). Descartes remains alive and well. Arguing against both Spinoza and Damasio (and accusing the latter of hubris), Gluck (2007) proclaims that "The attempt to base metaphysics on empirical findings is doomed to failure because it presupposes that which it sets out to prove" (p. xviii). He argues that neural monism is only a possible solution to the mind-body problem, but it cannot be proved with empirical evidence. Damasio, in keeping with the mass of contemporary work on the neuroscience of consciousness, argues for a neural basis of mind. While I certainly support this position (as do the neural lesion arguments that necessitate the connection), I am after bigger game. Damasio remains vulnerable to the critique that, since we are unable to measure consciousness as opposed to its neural correlates, it cannot be understood in physical terms. In other words, if we are unable to measure consciousness, only to track the electrical activity of the brain that accompanies it, then how can there be a physical thing called Consciousness? There is an answer to this question that escapes these authors. It is another question: How do you know you *can't* measure it? We only know that you can't measure it *now*.[12] We take for granted our ability to measure all kinds of things that we were unable to understand or measure in the past: body temperature, blood pressure, Higg's Bosons, the list is endless. Consciousness can thus be a physical property that we are unable to measure now, but we should be able to measure it in the future. Indeed, P. S. Churchland (1986) argues that Neuroscience is still in its infancy and we could be facing centuries of work in order to understand the brain and consciousness. As P. M. Churchland (2002) rather elegantly put it, "*Consciousness*, almost certainly, is not a semimagical [sic] glow emanating from the soul or permeating spooky stuff" (p. 2). Casting the argument in philosophical terms, it involves a clash between Neuropragmatism and Metaphysics: The former proposes physical answers to questions of consciousness that are discoverable if not yet discovered, while the latter insists that the questions cannot be answered at all. Put still another way, Physicalism is an argument for the existence of natural answers to the question of consciousness as opposed to supernatural answers.

In making this argument for Physicalism, a physical explanation for consciousness, we must also consider that such an explanation could apply to the mental or the psychic in, at the very least, other animals. Strawson (2006) indeed argues for the extreme view, positing that Physicalism entails panpsychism, that *anything* could have psychic properties; we will just have to see.

There is an important corollary to the concept of physicalism. Metaphysics has been considered a higher form of reason and inquiry (even though it traces its name to the hodge-podge of subjects that a 1st century translator of Aristotle placed *after* Aristotle's first book, the *Physica*). Now, Physicalism is about the physical. Those things, like consciousness, for which we do not *yet* have physical explanations, are in a kind of holding pattern. While we await these explanations, they remain the subject of a *lesser* form of discourse: Metaphysics.

Consciousness as workspace

If we are going to look at Consciousness from a Cognitive Science (emotion and affect as well as thought are definitely included here) perspective, then it can be said to define a Cognitive Workspace within the Self. Unlike so many other mental properties of the Self, *it* could be said to reside in the brain. Dehaene and Naccache (2001) posit that the mental and neuroanatomical architecture that is capable of fulfilling our requirements for a theory of consciousness is of a global neuronal workspace. This approach to understanding consciousness involves the use of cognitive modeling (how *do* our brains do it?) of how neurons connect particular areas of the brain with their functions documented with imaging studies. These studies (Dehaene & Naccache) point to the prefrontal cortex and anterior cingulate gyrus as the location of this workspace: not a surprise, really, based on what we already know about cognition from functional imaging studies. Crick and Koch (2005) building on Dehaene and Naccache's work posit that the claustrum provides the connecting links joining these areas of the brain. Where it is easy to assemble the cerebral architectures associated with objective, measureable, events (raising the left arm, for example), consciousness involves introspective, subjective data, which are inherently messy and sometimes in error. To posit such assemblies, we must move from scientific objectivism to Phenomenology. The latter allows us to continue to observe consciousness objectively even though our data are ontically subjective. Although we can employ cognitive psychology and neuroscience as tools for understanding consciousness, we still require a Neurophilosophy of Being to make the most of our observations.

This should not be construed as a shift away from the Physicalism we discussed above. We should not, as Dehaene and Naccache (2001) observe, treat phenomena like visual hallucinations as parapsychological evidence of spirits or ghosts, but rather as physical properties of a broken brain that we already understand to some extent.

The PDP model of consciousness posits that there are a number of, perhaps many, distributed processing networks of neurons competing for attention. When a problem or a question appears, input specialists (Baars, 1993/2003) such as perceptual systems compete for access to the global workspace. When they gain access, "broadcast" neurons shop the problem out to the Mind/Brain where they sometimes find parallel networks already in place capable of addressing. If such networks do not exist, a vast parallel assembly is set loose until an effective network is constructed. The intelligence of the system lies not in the workspace, but in these wider organizations of the Mind/Brain. When one is recognized, it occupies and takes over the workspace of consciousness and forms a self-sustaining loop until another more urgently needed network displaces it. Greenfield (Greenfield & Collins, 2005) posits that there is such a vast assemblage of neurons across the brain for each experience of consciousness. It assembles, synchronizes, and then disbands.[13] To study their hypothesis, Greenfield and her colleagues (Collins, Mann, Hill, Dommett, & Greenfield, 2007) treated slices of rat brain with either an analgesic or an anesthetic. Analgesics, they found, affected only the level of synaptic connectedness. Anesthetics, unlike analgesics, temporarily modify consciousness. They found that "irrespective of the effects of the two drug classes at a synaptic level, the dynamics of transient neuronal assemblies are modified selectively by anesthetics and not analgesics" (p. 1). The study suggests that consciousness does not arise from synaptic activity, but rather from the ability of the Brain/Self to form these vast networks. Consciousness, again, is a holistic property of the complex, self-organizing system that is the Self.

Individual consciousness as unique

In thinking about consciousness, we unthinkingly make a systematic error. Two errors, really. The first is that we treat consciousness, the property, and consciousness, the state of being, as if they were the same in all of us. (Odd since, within defined limits, there is nothing much that is the same in all of us, and we know this.) The second, a corollary actually, is that we equate consciousness in ourselves with reflective, autonoetic consciousness and take it as a given that this is the consciousness that everyone experiences. We do realize that consciousness *is* subjective, but we consider it so in terms of its contents, not in terms of its neuropsychological building blocks whose very natures are individually shaped by development and experience.

Perhaps oddly, both errors are easily correctable. After reading this paragraph (and the part of the chapter leading up to it), you will immediately be able to think about different kinds of consciousness existing within yourself, but it will take a bit of further study to fully appreciate them. You will also, this time without further study, never again think of other people as being identical with yourself in that way. This adds an entirely new dimension to thinking about patients and what's going on inside of them.

This is, in fact, a discussion of the Neurophenomenology of consciousness, the nature of its Being within the Self, in relationship to Other, and to World.[14] Most researchers (e.g., Kunzendorf & Wallace, 1999) working in the field of individual differences in consciousness do not treat the problem in this way. Rather than consider the very Being of consciousness, they look at these differences in terms of psychopathology or idiosyncrasy. While these differences certainly exist (phantom limbs, colorblindness, hysterical paralysis, depression, and the like), and are more easily studied, they are not what we're talking about.

It is not that we aren't interested in pathology and difference, because we are. For example, the amount of time spent in a self-reflective state varies enormously with the individual: from almost always to almost never. These individual differences have never been quantified or studied, yet they have clinical relevance. Many of our patients spend a great deal of time in a state of autonoetic consciousness. The time is spent thinking rather than doing. There can be many reasons for this: a defense against anxiety, obsessional disorders, a form of disassociation. Such thinking is often circular, occurring in fixed cognitive loops leading nowhere. Roger, a patient now in his 40s that I have discussed elsewhere (Leffert, 2013, 2016) at considerable length, spent much of his time in self-reflection. This could be productive, leading to further understanding of himself, or circular. Either way, it interfered with his ability to become engrossed in World and relationships. In offering him an interpretation along these lines, I aimed for a shift in this way of Being. One can also properly guide a patient into self-reflection when he does not manifest it; an equally difficult task.

There is also a risk here that we don't attend to. An analysis or therapy tends to emphasize reflection. Although very useful for patients who appear seeming to lack a capacity for self-reflection, patients who are too much in that state may inadvertently be encouraged to stay there, intensifying rather than lessening the procedural influences on them. The concern then, one of the goals of therapeutic action, is to help the patient *out* of this state of Being. The issue of (for lack of a better word) overdoing things clinically is not one that has been much considered; I have previously discussed (Leffert, 2016, 2017) it in connection with treating post-traumatic stress disorder. Some amount of immersion in the trauma is necessary and therapeutic, but beyond a point that must be determined individually, it only serves to more firmly cement it in place. What is necessary is to clinically determine when that point has been reached and then move the patient away from the trauma.[15]

Taking stock

In reading over this material one cannot avoid a feeling of dissatisfaction, a question: Is this all there is? In 2010 (Leffert, Chapter 6) I answered in the affirmative: that consciousness is simply an emergent property of the self. Can we say more today? Imagine for a moment that we have a working time machine. We stock it with a battery powered TV and DVD player and a few DVDs and go back in time to 1920 or so, the age of wireless, radio, and silent movies. We demonstrate our devices to a man on the street or to someone in the broadcasting business. They will be amazed, will marvel at it, will not understand how the machine works, but will know generally what it is and what it is doing. Next, we load everything back in the time machine and go back to 1750, the age of enlightenment. We perform the same demonstration (not in a church). This time they will be more amazed and anxious, but they will know that this is a man-made device, a *machine*, that shows pictures, and projects language and music. Back in the time machine! We now go back to 1650. We demonstrate our stuff, and *here* it is supernatural and most likely has to do with the devil. We (luckily) escape back to 2018. Now, the question is where are we, analogously, with consciousness? The answer would seem to be somewhere past 1920, but it's not clear just how far past it we are. We are still in the early days of neuroscience research (Churchland, P. M., 2002).

If we are to take stock of where we are as of this writing (2018), we have to say that we are nowhere near an understanding of consciousness, nor do we possess an adequate theory of consciousness on which to base such an understanding.

An argument can be made, however, that we are reaching a point of singularity in the neurosciences. A. K. Churchland and Abbott (2016) observe that we have reached a point in our ability to document and manipulate neurons and groups of neurons that will, over the coming years, yield vast amounts of new data. What we now need is an expansion in theoretical neuroscience to use this data to increase our understanding of the Brain/Mind/Self. They argue for a three-stage process that involves extracting activity from the raw data, summarizing that activity to make it more compact and understandable, and creating models on macro and micro levels to link "underlying mechanisms and overlying principles" (p. 348).

As Patricia M. Churchland (2002) posits, we can approach the problem either directly or indirectly. A direct approach involves a search for what is known as the neural correlates of consciousness. Patricia M. Churchland bases it on what she calls Crick's Assumption: "There must be brain differences in the following two conditions: (1) a stimulus is presented and the subject is aware of it, and (2) a stimulus is presented and the subject is *not* aware of it" (p. 136). Experimental approaches are then directed at documenting and localizing the functional neuroanatomical difference in the brain when the two states are compared. A. K. Churchland and Abbott (2016) are suggesting that there might now be considerable hope in the success of such an approach.

Patricia M. Churchland's (2002) indirect approach goes at the problem very differently. It identifies a variety of functions of the Self, "attention, short-term memory, autobiographical memory, self-representation, perception, imagery, thought, meaning, being awake, and self-referencing; all of which would seem to be connected to consciousness in some way" (pp. 156–157). The indirect approach proposes, in effect, that, once we understand the neurobiology of these diverse functions and states of Being and the relations between them, a theory of consciousness will pretty much fall into place. She posits that once we have such a robust theory of brain function, we will then possess the means to develop a successful theory of consciousness *indirectly*.

Problems remain. Although the direct and indirect approaches taken together offer an overall plan for pursuing a theory of consciousness, we don't have a sense that success is close or yet on the horizon. It's not clear, however, that this is even what we are looking for. The problem may be that what we are really pursuing is a *subjectively satisfying* theory of consciousness. Consciousness is so important to us that we are looking for something comprehensive that we don't even understand. This is a very different sort of problem, one that involves the Being of Human Beings, Dasein, and takes us partly beyond the realm of neuroscience into the realm of Phenomenology.

Consciousness and its Neurophenomenology

Neuroscientists are interested in investigating what goes on in the brain when we are conscious and what goes on as thoughts and perceptions move in and out of consciousness. Although certainly laudable pursuits, like many others, it is not at all clear how interesting ultimately they are to those of us who identify ourselves as students of the human condition. *We* ultimately want to explore what it means to be human, and, as therapists and analysts, to understand how the process goes awry and what to do about it when we see it happening.

We, and this is folk psychology now, equate consciousness with sentience. We see consciousness and reason (which requires consciousness) as what makes us uniquely human. The clockworks of the process, the neuroscience of it, do not now serve our purposes (beyond our need to know that there *are* clockworks). This need not conflict with our understanding that most of what goes on in the Self goes on outside of awareness or that some of it, conscious *and* unconscious stuff, is implicitly a part of our humanness. Neuroscience can contribute to our understanding of these problems, but it cannot, at least for now, solve them. A. K. Churchland and Abbott (2016) offer a very thoughtful account of how it can do so, but the problem remains philosophy's to solve. Taken together, then, what we are after is a Neurophilosophy of consciousness.

To argue that right now neuroscience (the study of the claustral neuronal axons that surround the mouse brain, for example) doesn't help us to answer the questions we care most about should not be allowed to lead us down the path of breaking the two apart. Husserl, who was perhaps the last of the Cartesians, made this mistake as an unnecessary price to pay for returning to the Things Themselves.[16] The separation of the subjective from the objective falls into the trap that Latour (Latour, 1991/1993, 2005; Leffert, 2010) described as the *modern critical stance*, in which the hybrids of the social and the scientific are broken apart in the service of theoretical hygiene but at the price of a fundamental loss of meaning. A way around this might be to pose questions for neuroscience (how consciousness moves in and out of World and of Self, for example) that, even though they cannot be solved today, are in range of what might be answered in the near future.

If we move on to the Phenomenology of consciousness, as it pertains to the Being of Human Beings, we immediately come upon a problem that is shocking in its ability to elude us. Looking at humans in general, we find *vast* differences in the nature and kinds of consciousness that they display, how they *experience* being conscious, and the states of consciousness that they spend time in. (How, for example, an average voter comes to choose a candidate in an election, bearing in mind Nisbett and Wilson's [1977] warning that they don't consciously know.) To perplex us still further, it is necessary to acknowledge that *neuroscience offers no explanation for these differences*. They include taking into account such parameters as the amounts of time spent in Tulving's (1985/2003) various states of consciousness, the nature of Being in each of them, and the presence of emotion (Panksepp & Biven, 2012) in consciousness. If we approach these differences simply as things in themselves (Husserl, 1937/1970), we can investigate them in individuals therapeutically and in ourselves.

At the risk of repeating myself, consciousness is a phenomenal property of the Self, the Bio-Psycho-Social Self, and not of Mind or Brain. Some phenomenologists (Melnick, 2011) argue that consciousness exists in and through the whole body. But they also argue, erroneously I believe, that it is not located in the Brain and that the Brain is simply a generating organ of consciousness. This return to a Cartesian separation of mind and body (embodied consciousness in 21st century language) is both unnecessary and counterproductive. To put it more simply: Why can't it be both?

A central element in the phenomenology of consciousness that pure neuroscience doesn't deal with is Time (Heidegger, 1927/2010). Consciousness is inhabited by time on two levels. One has to do with inherent timescales in Semantic Memory and Narrative Memory of the past, the projection of time into the future (episodic simulation of future events [Schacter et al., 2008]): our sense of when things are *going* to happen. The other is the sense of time elapsing in the moment of consciousness. These are all experienced subjectively, loosely connected to histories (written *and* Narrative and Semantic), calendars, and watches in the world (consciousness lacks the little time stamp unwinding in the corner of the screen of a video camera). Husserl would signify this multimodal presentation of [*time*] by enclosing the term in brackets (as he does with all terms that have complex and often controversial definitions) and referring to it as *phenomenological time*: the measure of an object's duration. The phenomenological time stamp that *does* exist is our awareness (or denial) of the finiteness of life, that is, of *death*. Phenomenologists unpopularly argue that it is the conscious certainty of death that gives life meaning that *throws* us (Heidegger's language) into life and into the moment. Its opposite is conscious denial of death, embodied in the unconscious fantasy of immortality, a *fallen* state that treats death as an idiosyncratic event.

Consciousness is interpersonal

Nearly everything we have said about consciousness so far, with the exception of some brief comments on Discourse, has been from the perspective of the individual, discussed in isolation. There are inherent limitations in such an approach, which entail all of the Post-Cartesian critiques leveled at the concept of a mind in isolation and resolved by Heidegger (1927/2010) in his concept of Dasein, the Being of Human Beings *there*, in the World, Being with Others. Indeed, we know that if you completely isolate a person by placing him in a sensory deprivation tank, he will lose coherent consciousness in a matter of hours. To be conscious, one must be in the world, the world of things, and the world of others. Reflection requires these connections to sustain itself even if a person is in a seemingly solitary state.

Autonoetic consciousness, in other words, is fundamentally relational. To be fully developed, it requires linguistic competence. Language then shapes consciousness (and, of course, consciousness shapes language). For example, Eskimo-Aleut languages have dozens of words for different kinds of ice, while Navaho and Hopi have dozens of words for different states of water. The consciousness of native speakers of these languages is shaped by these differentiations, and the importance of their subjects, in ways that ours are not. English grammar lacks the familiar and formal pronouns (*tu* vs. *vous*, *du* vs. *sie*) that are found in French and German. French and German speakers thus, experience a hard distinction between the two where Anglophones do not. Similarly, nouns have gender in them while they lack it in modern English.[17]

As neurophilosophers, we have to incorporate in our discussions cultural definitions of consciousness as they relate to discursive partners, to a society, or to a Social Network (Christakis & Fowler, 2009). I have posited that Being conscious is not the same in all of us and that its very nature is affected by the often unconscious connections determined at each of these levels of social intercourse. Thus, information can unconsciously be exchanged through a process of social contagion (Christakis & Fowler), sometimes active at increasing degrees of separation that shapes *how* its members are conscious and what they are conscious *of*. Intimate relationships, pair bonding, and, yes, the therapeutic relationship shape the consciousness of both parties, at least when they are present and engaged with each other. We know that the Mirror Neuron System (Iacoboni, 2008) furnishes the mechanism by which this mutual influence takes place but have no specific knowledge about how it gets into consciousness. We also know, even if we don't think about it much, that societies profoundly influence (Erikson, 1950/1963) how people are (their Being) and what and how they consciously think. Understanding all of these requires Phenomenological investigation supported by Neuroscience research.

This brings us to the most recent and perhaps the least understood event in the evolution of consciousness: the advent of Social Media in human ontology. The numbers of us who have experienced the dawn of this age and lived in the times before it is trending towards zero as more and more of us appear on the scene who have known nothing else. Although the process began with emailing, it was the introduction of the cell phone that changed our Existence forever. Cell phones provide instantaneous connection to World: the World of information and the World of others. Texting and Social Media sites keep us in constant connection with each other, and games are always there to fill up our alone time.

Social Media *are* being exhaustively studied, but it is not clear that the studies will offer the Phenomenological Investigations we need. Those of us who think about the role of cell phones in society mostly deplore them, citing how often people together are "on" their devices rather than talking to each other. Further consideration reveals how people who are on Social Media a lot experience similar kinds and levels of emotion but are mostly unreflective about what is going on. That is, less time is spent in a state of autonoetic consciousness. The question that is left in all of this is that if it is *so* deplorable, why do people crave it so, a craving that exists across cultures? One could argue, I suppose, that it's because it's an addiction, like tobacco, or food. Although one can't argue the null hypothesis here, it is simpler to say that people like being connected: A young woman wants to tell all her friends that she has tried a new candy bar, so she posts it on her Facebook "wall." People have, in effect, elected to become cyborgs but with no implantation necessary (can anyone doubt that such implants are far away?). The great majority of us simply do not want to be conscious of being alone if we don't have to. We really can't say what this will all look like in the decades ahead beyond saying that the bonds that hold social networks together will continue to be strengthened.

The phenomenology of emergence

To return to our starting point, consciousness, looked at ontologically, is an emergent property of the complex system known as the Self. A number of properties are unique to complex systems. We are interested in the class of properties that are emergent. They are holistic properties of systems (Laszlo, 1972/1996) that cannot be determined by adding together the properties of the components of the system and, although the behavior of holistic systems can be predicted in the broadest of terms by studying the system, their specifics, and timing are unknowable and unpredictable. By studying the properties of the Self, we have come to understand that, in general terms, the Self is conscious, and our studies of its functional neuroanatomy have led us to understand that most if not all classes of vertebrates (Feinberg & Mallatt, 2016) possess some forms of consciousness.

Let's look at a hurricane (earthquakes would serve as well, as would non-chaotic properties such as airline flight arrivals on a given day) as an example of an emergent property of a climate system. Meteorologists spent decades trying to predict the formation, strength, timing and course of tropical storms before an understanding of complexity theory (Gleick, 1987; Mitchell, 2009) led to an understanding that this was an impossible endeavor. They understood that air and water temperature joined with shifts in barometric pressure could combine to produce a tropical storm with its timing, strength, course, and duration, the emergent properties of hurricane systems, being unpredictable.

If we apply this line of reasoning to consciousness, what do we come up with? Well, the neuroscience tells us that there is a snarly collection of neurons in the brain stem called the reticular formation (RF) that collects information downstream from the brain stem and from the autonomic and peripheral nervous systems. (So the whole Self is already involved at this level.) Bilateral lesions the size of a couple of grains of rice in the thalamic end of the system result in irreversible coma. We also now think that the claustrum, a thin lining of cortical neurons located near the insula and manifesting bidirectional connectivity with nearly all areas of the neocortex plays a fundamental role in consciousness. This is all rather fascinating, and we want to study the functional neuroanatomy some more, but has it taught us much about consciousness? Aside from knowing that the whole Self is involved (again, this is the Bio-Psycho-Social Self continuous with World that I am talking about), the answer is "no." We've identified only a choke point in the wiring of the system, and who's to say that we won't, in a few decades at the outside, develop a little implant that gets around the problem? The neurological investigations can, by themselves, only take us so far; in order to get farther, we have to rely on Phenomenological Investigations of the thing itself called the Self as we have been doing in this chapter.

If we ask ourselves who is the preeminent Neurophenomenologist of the 20th and early 21st centuries is, we have to come up with only one answer: It is Oliver Sacks (1985/1998, 1973/1999, 1992/1999, 2008). What makes Sacks unique is that he both studied the functional neuroanatomy of his patients and talked with them as Human Beings (that is as fellow Daseins) and their Being-in-the-World as they lived with their uniqueness. He practiced as a neuroscientist and a neuropsychologist but he was, implicitly, a Phenomenologist. Although there is no evidence that he was familiar with the Existentialist-Phenomenological literature, he always dealt with his patients from a Post-Cartesian perspective. Sacks was particularly interested in his patients' consciousness as it was impacted by cerebral malfunctions as Ramachandran (Ramachandran & Blakeslee, 1998) was interested in the distortions of consciousness manifested in phantom limb pain.

As psychoanalysts and psychotherapists, we have the option of approaching our patients in similar ways. We can, for instance, observe the various kinds of memory present in our patients and ourselves. As psychoanalytic clinicians we have mostly worked with narrative memory and autonoetic consciousness, trying to reshape strings of memories and fill in the blanks. We can also study our patients' Procedural Memory System (and our own) and determine whether they are functional or dysfunctional. Heuristics and Biases (Leffert, 2016; Tversky & Kahneman, 1974/1982) constitute a subset of these memories.

An area where we have been largely unsuccessful in approaching the Neurophenomenology of Dasein is in the common ground of the psychoanalytic and the psychopharmacologic. The great majority of prescriptions for psychotropic drugs are written in the absence of any psychotherapeutic interventions in the same way that more than half of psychoanalysis and psychotherapy (Survey Advantage Whorton Marketing Research, 2011) take place in the absence of these interventions. A Neurophenomenological approach to this issue involves the therapist's having an understanding of the neurobiology of mental illness, how it interacts with its psychology, and the role of psychotropic medications in its treatment (not management). Our job as Neurophenomenologists is to engage in a Discourse with our patients involving *all* of these areas.

We have not much considered how consciousness might have evolved and how it develops in each of us. These two threads have recently been braided into a new

58 The neurophilosophy of consciousness

sheaf of différance (Derrida, 1978) called Evo-Devo. Epigenetics has also been heating up in recent years, and both require a reassessment of how we understand development. Let's turn to it now.

Notes

1 Broadly speaking, I am concerned with ontology and epistemology: the study of Being and the nature of knowledge.
2 I define *Self* as a bio-psycho-social entity (Leffert, 2016, Chapter 1), in Heidegger's terms Dasein, the Being of Human Beings in the World.
3 In a vegetative state, a patient appears awake, but does not communicate, or initiate; a comatose patient appears to be asleep and is both motionless and unresponsive.
4 Kate subsequently awoke (Owen, 2017), but continued to manifest major cognitive deficits.
5 These include the medial and lateral parietal and frontal associative areas of the cerebral cortex that will be of interest when we discuss what enters in to consciousness. They are also, perhaps through the claustral neurons, the most important inputs to the subcortical arousal systems.
6 A device that flashes images for specific amounts of time, usually fractions of a second that can be used to stimulate different parts of the visual fields.
7 I am engaging in a kind of shorthand here: all this should be taken to refer to right-handed individuals. The situation with left-handedness is not so sharply defined.
8 Children obviously start to acquire *vocabulary* (word symbols) at a year give or take, but they do not develop *language*, which is meaning expressed in syntax, until later.
9 There are several types of heuristics. An example is the Availability Heuristic, which assesses the likelihood of an event coming to pass. It makes this assessment based on the ease with which past instances of the event can be brought to mind. Recent experiences tend to be more available. Heuristics are a kind of anoetic shortcut that facilitates decision-making. They only sometimes yield accurate results.
10 Semantic and episodic memory can be combined to enhance event-based knowledge. In the 19th century and less so today, people would intra-psychically construct *memory palaces*, imagined structures serving as filing systems that used episodic memory to enhance semantic memory.
11 A flood of recent work (e.g., Feinberg & Mallatt, 2016; Terrace & Metcalfe, 2005) is showing that consciousness, once thought of as uniquely human, is, *in some form*, present in at least all vertebrates. Some degree of fortunate demystification is inherent in this statement: Perhaps, consciousness is simply a property of brains that possess a sufficient level of complexity (Leffert, 2008).
12 We have already come a very long way from the telescope and the steam engine of Descartes' day to functional magnetic resonance imaging and the computer.
13 This offers a picture of therapeutic discourse in terms of these vast shifting assemblages of neurons in patient and therapist that interreferentially influence each other as the discourse proceeds. The image is clinically useful, I think, because it carries with it a sense of how little of the process is actually under conscious *control*.
14 In Heidegger's terms, it is the consciousness of Dasein.
15 I am well aware that this flies in the face of everything we have been taught and believe about free association. Alas, free association is *not* free. It is simply a tool we have, one among many, that can be over- or underused. The parable of having a hammer and therefore treating everything as a nail also comes to mind.
16 Contemporary students of Husserl and of Phenomenology (e.g., Petitot, Varela, Pachoud, & Roy, 1999) have recognized this problem and responded with a process they call Naturalizing Phenomenology, which is the use of an explanatory framework in which the things themselves are fully integrated with properties found in the natural sciences.

17 As an Anglophone with minimal competence in both French and German I *understand* these distinctions, but I'm completely unable to *feel* them, unable to make this gender distinction.

References

Baars, B. J. (2003). How does a serial, integrated, and very limited stream of consciousness emerge from a nervous system that is mostly unconscious, distributed, parallel and of enormous capacity? In B. J. Baars, W. P. Banks, & J. B. Newman (Eds.), *Essential sources in the scientific study of consciousness* (pp. 1123–1129). Cambridge: MIT Press (Original work published in 1993.)
Blumenthal, H. (2016). Neuroanatomical basis of consciousness. In S. Laureys, O. Gosseries, & G. Tononi (Eds.), *The neurology of consciousness* (2nd ed., pp. 3–30). San Diego: Academic Press.
Bogen, J. E. (2003). On the neurophysiology of consciousness: An overview. In B. J. Baars, W. P. Banks, & J. B. Newman (Eds.), *Essential sources in the scientific study of consciousness* (pp. 891–900). Cambridge: MIT Press. (Original work published in 1995.)
Bogen, J. E., & Vogel, P. J. (1962). Cerebral commisurotomy in man: Preliminary case report. *Bulletin of the Los Angeles Neurological Society, 27*, 169–172.
Chiron, C., Jambaque, I., Nabbout, R., Lounes, R., Syrota, A., & Dulac, O. (1997). The right brain hemisphere is dominant in human infants. *Brain, 120*, 1057–1065.
Christakis, N. A., & Fowler, J. H. (2009). *Connected: The surprising power of our social networks and how they shape our lives*. New York: Little, Brown and Company.
Churchland, A. K., & Abbott, L. F. (2016). Conceptual and technical advances define a key moment for theoretical neuroscience. *Nature Neuroscience, 19*, 3, 348–349.
Churchland, P. M. (2002). *Brain-wise studies in neurophilosophy*. Cambridge: MIT Press.
Churchland, P. S. (1986). *Neurophilosophy: Toward a unified science of the mind brain*. Cambridge: MIT Press.
Collins, T. F. T., Mann, E. O., Hill, M. R. H., Dommett, E. J., & Greenfield, S. A. (2007). Dynamics of neuronal assemblies are modulated by anaesthetics but not analgesics. *European Journal of Anaesthesiology, 24*, 1–6.
Crick, F. C., & Koch, C. (2005). What is the function of the claustrum? *Philosophical Transactions of the Royal Society Biological Sciences, 360*, 1271–1279.
Damasio, A. (1994). *Descarte's error: Emotion, reason, and the human brain*. New York: Grosset/Putnam.
Damasio, A. (2003). *Looking for Spinoza*. Orlando: Harcourt, Inc.
Dehaene, S., & Naccache, L. (2001). Towards a cognitive neuroscience of consciousness: Basic evidence and a workspace framework. *Cognition, 79*, 1–37.
Derrida, J. (1978). *Writing and différence* (A. Bass, Trans.). Chicago: University of Chicago Press.
Descartes, R. (1999). *Meditations and other metaphysical writings* (D. M. Clarke, Trans.). New York: Penguin Books. (Original work published in 1641.)
Erikson, E. (1963). *Childhood and society* (2nd ed.). New York: W. W. Norton & Co (Original work published in 1950.)
Feinberg, T. E., & Mallatt, J. M. (2016). *The ancient origins of consciousness: How the brain created experience*. Cambridge: MIT Press.
Galin, D. (1974). Implications for psychiatry of left and right cerebral specialization: A neurophysiological context for unconscious processes. *Archives of General Psychiatry, 31*, 572–583.
Gleick, J. (1987). *Chaos making a new science*. New York: Viking.

Gluck, A. L. (2007). *Damasio's error and Descartes' truth: An inquiry into epistemology, metaphysics, and consciousness*. Scranton: University of Scranton Press.

Greenfield, S. A., & Collins, T. F. T. (2005). A neuroscientific approach to consciousness. *Progress in Brain Research, 150*, 11–23.

Groopman, J. (2007, October 15). Silent minds: What scanning techniques are revealing about vegetative patients. *The New Yorker, 83*, 38–43.

Heidegger, M. (2010). *Being and time* (J. Stambaugh & D. J. Schmidt, Trans.). Albany: State University of New York. (Original work published in 1927.)

Holmes, D. S. (1990). The evidence for repression: An examination of sixty years of research. In J. L. Singer (Ed.), *Repression and dissociation: Implications for personality theory, psychopathology and health* (pp. 85–102). Chicago: University of Chicago Press.

Hoppe, K. D. (1977). Split brains and psychoanalysis. *Psychoanalytic Quarterly, 46*, 220–244.

Husserl, E. (1970). *The crisis of European sciences and transcendental phenomenology* (D. Cairns, Trans.). Evanston: Northwestern University Press. (Original work published in 1937.)

Husserl, E. (1983). *Ideas pertaining to a pure phenomenology and to a phenomenological philosophy: Book one: General introduction to a pure phenomenology* (F. Kersten, Trans.). New York: Springer (Original work published in 1913.)

Iacoboni, M. (2008). *Mirroring people: The new science of how we connect with people*. New York: Farrar, Strauss and Giroux.

Keenan, J. P., Wheeler, M. A., Gallup Jr., G. G., & Pascual-Leone, A. (2000). Self-recognition and the right prefrontal cortex. *Trends in Cognitive Sciences, 4*, 338–344.

Koch, C. (2012). *Consciousness: Confessions of a romantic reductionist*. Boston: MIT Press.

Koch, C., & Tsuchiya, N. (2007). Attention and consciousness: Two distinct brain processes. *Trends in Cognitive Sciences, 11*, 16–22.

Kunzendorf, R. G., & Wallace, B. (Eds.). (1999). *Individual differences in conscious experience*. Amsterdam: John Benjamins Publishing Company.

Laszlo, E. (1996). *The systems view of the world: A holistic vision for our time*. Cresskill: Hampton Press, Inc. (Original work published in 1972.)

Latour, B. (1993). *We have never been modern* (C. Porter, Trans.). Cambridge: Harvard University Press. (Original work published in 1991.)

Latour, B. (2005). *Reassembling the social: An intorduction to Actor-Network-Theory*. Oxford: Oxford University Press.

Laureys, S., Gosseries, O., & Tononi, G. (Eds.). (2016). *The neurology of consciousness* (2nd ed.). San Diego: Academic Press.

Leffert, M. (2008). Complexity and postmodernism in contemporary theory of psychoanalytic change. *Journal of the American Academy of Psychoanalysis and Dynamic Psychiatry, 36*, 517–542.

Leffert, M. (2010). *Contemporary psychoanalytic foundations*. London: Routledge.

Leffert, M. (2013). *The therapeutic situation in the 21st century*. New York: Routledge.

Leffert, M. (2016). *Phenomenology, uncertainty, and care in the therapeutic encounter*. New York: Routledge.

Leffert, M. (2017). *Positive psychoanalysis: Aesthetics, desire, and subjective well-being*. New York: Routledge.

Marinsek, N. L., Gazzaniga, M. S., & Miller, M. B. (2016). Split-brain, split mind. In S. Laureys, O. Gosseries, & G. Tononi (Eds.), *The neurology of consciousnes* (2nd ed., pp. 271–279). San Diego: Academic Press.

McClelland, J. L., & Rumelhart, D. E. (1986). *Parallel distributed processing* (Vol. 2). Cambridge: MIT Press.

Melnick, A. (2011). *Phenomenology and the physical reality of consciousness*. Amsterdam: John Benjamins Publishing Company.

Mitchell, M. (2009). *Complexity: A guided tour.* Oxford: Oxford University Press.
Naccache, L. (2006). Is she conscious? *Science, 313*(5792), 1395–1396.
Nisbett, R. E., & Wilson, T. (1977). Telling more than we can know: Verbal reports on mental processes. *Psychological Review, 84,* 231–259.
Owen, A. M. (2017). *Into the grey zone: A neuroscientist explores the border between life and death.* New York: Scribner.
Owen, A. M., Coleman, M. R., Boly, M., Davis, M. H., Laureys, S., & Pickard, J. D. (2006). Detecting awareness in the vegetative state. *Science, 313,* 5792, 1402.
Panksepp, J., & Biven, L. (2012). *The archaeology of mind: Neuroevolutionary origins of human emotions.* New York: W. W. Norton & Co.
Pepperberg, I. M. (2000). *The Alex studies.* Cambridge: Harvard University Press.
Pepperberg, I. M. (2008). *Alex & me.* New York: HarperCollins.
Petitot, J., Varela, F. J., Pachoud, B., & Roy, J.-M. (Eds.). (1999). *Naruralizing phenomenology: Essays on contemporary phenomenology and cognitive science.* Stanford: Stanford University Press.
Ramachandran, V. S., & Blakeslee, S. (1998). *Phantoms in the brain: Probing the mysteries of the mind.* New York: Harper Perennial.
Reardon, S. (2017). Giant neuron encircles entire brain of a mouse. *Nature, 543,* 14–15.
Risse, G. L., & Gazzaniga, M. S. (1978). Well-kept secrets of the right hemisphere: A carotid amytal study of restricted memory transfer. *Neurology, 28,* 487–495.
Rumelhart, D. E., & McClelland, J. L. (1986). *Parallel distributed processing* (Vol. 1). Cambridge: MIT Press.
Sacks, O. (1998). *The man who mistook his wife for a hat and other clinical tales.* New York: Touchstone. (Original work published in 1985.)
Sacks, O. (1999). *Awakenings.* New York: Vintage Books. (Original work published in 1973.)
Sacks, O. (1999). *Migraine.* New York: Vintage Books. (Original work published in 1992.)
Sacks, O. (2008). *Musicophilia: Tales of music and the brain* (rev. and expanded ed.). New York: Vintage Books.
Schacter, D. L. (1996). *Searching for memory.* New York: Basic Books.
Schacter, D. L., Addis, D. R., & Buckner, R. L. (2008). Episodic simulation of future events concepts, data, and applications. *Annals of the New York Academy of Science, 1124,* 39–60.
Schore, A. N. (2003). *Affect regulation and the repair of the self.* New York: W. W. Norton & Co.
Singer, W. (2001). Consciousness and the binding problem. *Annals of the New York Academy of Science, 929,* 123–146.
Sperry, R. W. (1969). A modified concept of consciousness. *Psychological Review, 76,* 532–536.
Sperry, R. W., Gazzaniga, M. S., & Bogen, J. E. (1969). The neocortical commissures: Syndromes of hemisphere disconnection. In P. J. Vinken & G. W. Bruyn (Eds.), *Handbook of clinical neurology* (Vol. 4). Amsterdam: North Holland Publishing Company.
Spinoza, B. (2011). *Ethics: Treatise on the emedation of the intellect and selected letters* (S. Shirley, Trans.). Indianapolis: Hackett Publishing Company. (Original work published in 1676.)
Strawson, G. (2006). Realistic monism: Why physicalism entails panpsychism. *Journal of Consciousness Studies, 13,* 10–11, 3–31.
Survey Advantage Whorton Marketing Research (2011). *2011 Psychoanalytic professional activities benchmark study.* New York: American Psychoanalytic Association.
Terrace, H. S., & Metcalfe, J. (Eds.). (2005). *The missing link in cognition: Origins of self-reflective consciousness.* Oxford: Oxford University Press.
Thatcher, R. W. (1991). Maturation of the human frontal lobes: Physiological evidence for staging. *Developmental Neuropsychology, 7,* 397–419.

Thatcher, R. W. (1994). Cyclical cortical reorganization: Origins of human cognitive development. In G. Dawson & K. W. Fischer (Eds.), *Human behavior and the developing brain* (pp. 232–266). New York: Guilford Press.

Tronick, E. Z. (2009). Multilevel meaning making and dyadic expansion of consciousness theory: The emotional and the polymorphic polysemic flow of meaning. In D. Fosha, D. J. Siegal, & M. Solomon (Eds.), *The healing power of emotion: Affective neuroscience, development, and clinical practice* (pp. 86–111). New York: W. W. Norton & Co.

Tulving, E. (1983). *Elements of episodic memory.* Oxford: Clarendon Press.

Tulving, E. (2003). Memory and consciousness. In B. J. Baars, W. P. Banks, & J. B. Newman (Eds.), *Essential sources in the scientific study of consciousness* (pp. 575–591). Cambridge: MIT Press. (Original work published in 1985.)

Tulving, E. (2005). Episodic memory and autonoesis: Uniquely human? In H. S. Terrace & J. Metcalfe (Eds.), *The missing link in cognition: Origins of self-reflective consciousness* (pp. 3–56). Oxford: Oxford University Press.

Tulving, E., Kapur, S., Craik, F. I. M., Moscovitch, M., & Houle, S. (1994). Hemispheric encoding/retrieval asymmetry in episodic memory: Positron emission tomography findings. *Proceedings of the National Academy of Science, 91,* 2016–2020.

Tversky, A., & Kahneman, D. (1982). Judgment under uncertainty: Heuristics and biases. In D. Kahneman, P. Slovic, & A. Tversky (Eds.), *Judgment under uncertainty: Heuristics and biases* (pp. 3–20). Cambridge: Cambridge University Press. (Original work published in 1974.)

Vanderkerckhove, M., & Panksepp, J. (2009). The flow of anoetic to noetic and autonoetic consciousness: A vision of unknowing (anoetic) and knowing (noetic) consciousness in the remembrance of things past and imagined future. *Consciousness and Cognition, 18,* 1018–1028.

Willingham, D. B., & Preuss, L. (1995). The death of implicit memory. *Psyche, 2*(15).

Wolford, G., Miller, M. B., & Gazzaniga, M. S. (2004). Split decisions. In M. S. Gazzaniga (Ed.), *The cognitive neurosciences III* (pp. 1189–1209). Cambridge: MIT Press.

3
PSYCHOANALYTIC THEORIES OF DEVELOPMENT AND THE NEW SCIENCE OF EVO-DEVO

Introduction

Psychoanalysis has, from its infancy, offered Development pride of place in its attempts to understand and find meaning in the human condition. It has done so first by mining the narrative memory of adult patients, then through nursery school, and infant observations and interpretations of the behavior of children in therapy and analysis. These techniques have yielded a great deal of information, but they also have well-known and inherent epistemological flaws that I have discussed in the past (Leffert, 2010, 2013). These flaws are not particularly germane to our discussions here. In the final decades of the 20th century, we clinicians, albeit a bit reluctantly, began to integrate the data and theory-building amassed by developmental psychologists over the past century into our thinking and our clinical work. If we were to identify a single area of developmental psychology that has most influenced us, it is certainly Attachment Theory.

A little later and, with even more ambivalence, we watched as Developmental Neuroscience began to peep over the horizon (Schore, 1994). While many analysts have been captivated by its emergence on the scene, many others, wrapping themselves in the mantle of hermeneutics have declared it irrelevant to clinical psychoanalysis.[1]

Psychoanalysis exploded into the intellectual world of the early 20th century. The twin biological disciplines of Evolution and Development were very much present at its birth (Hofer, 2014) and in the minds of early psychoanalytic thinkers. At that time, the two were quite close together, but, with the advent of molecular biology later in the century, they went their separate ways and lost as well their relevance to psychoanalytic theory-building. They never became relevant to clinical practice. More recently, a flood of discoveries has led to a reintegration of the two disciplines, and a new field of inquiry has taken shape in biology. It involves the recognition that any separation of Evolution and Development is artificial and that they belong in a single field, now called Evo-Devo. Included in it are Embryology and Epigenetics. Hofer argues that these developments have brought psychoanalysis and biology much closer together. Evo-Devo is so new and so apparently unrelated to psychoanalytic treatment that very few analysts and therapists (Hofer being an exception) have even heard of it, much less decided to reject its relevance or significance. One of the aims of this chapter is to correct that deficiency.

I particularly want to examine the question of how Existential Phenomenology can inform our understanding of childhood and Evo-Devo. Existential and Phenomenological authors have largely failed to consider children, childhood, or development, focusing instead on the dilemmas of Being that confronts us as adults.

One area of inquiry where Phenomenology, Psychoanalysis, Development, and Evo-Devo can come together is parenting. Developmental Psychologists and Evo-Devo researchers have separately studied parenting and mother-child bonding. Parenting has remained implicit in Existential Phenomenology, and psychoanalysts, while highly amenable to the findings of Developmental Psychology, have been mostly interested in it from the perspective of the individual psychologies of parents and children.

As clinicians, we tend to bring considerable implicit bias to Evo-Devo. We first think of the disciplines as separate, with evolution thought of as taking place over millions of years on average and, at the very least, over spans of tens of thousands of years. (Evolution would hence be of little or no interest in the therapeutic situation.) We also tend to think of *H. sapiens sapiens*, as evolutionarily and developmentally unique, with only few of our ways of Being extending *down* the evolutionary tree to the higher primates. Going further *down*, the development and bond formations of lesser mammals were seen to be the result of instincts, inborn patterns of behavior, reflexes, hormonal regulation, and noetic memories. Yet we already know that this is not the case. Panksepp's (Panksepp & Biven, 2012) *cross-mammalian* studies of primary affective states and the role of their secondary and tertiary development demonstrate that the complex emotional states present in humans are present in all mammals and perhaps all vertebrates. We've seen that the initial work on the Mirror Neuron System (Gallese, Fadiga, Fogassi, & Rizzolatti, 1996), now understood as essential to the development and maintenance of social bonds, was done using Macaque monkeys. However, as Hofer (2014) observes, "we vastly underestimated the extent to which basic developmental processes have been conserved by evolution over vast reaches of time" (p. 9).[2] He and Sullivan (Landers & Sullivan, 2012; Sullivan & Moriceau, 2005) have studied the appearance of attachment bonds, social relationships, and the long-term effects of early mother-infant experience in rodents. We will consider their work shortly.

There is one risk that we will have to be careful about. In these discussions, material seems to naturally fall into two distinct categories: the mental and the biological (the biology of Epigenetics). Unless we want to return to Cartesian-based thought (with all the problems inherent in it), we must constantly remember that what we are dealing with are two aspects of the same thing, a sheaf of *différance*, a psychobiological hybrid (Latour, 1991/1993; Latour & Woolgar, 1986). The thing that we are talking about here, the *thing* that subsumes everything, can only be the Self, the Bio-Psycho-Social Self (Leffert, 2016, Chapter 1).

How evolution and development became Evo-Devo

Until quite recently, the biology of Development was seen as the innate expression of an evolved genome with "no molecular/genetic mechanism for interactions with the environment to affect the course of [that genetic] development" (Hofer, 2014, p. 13). Hofer posited that this stance understandably led to biology being of even less interest to psychoanalysts. However, this began to change in the late 20th century. As Carroll (2005) tells it, the amount of genetic material present in human beings is not much different from that of mammals and birds generally, and much of it is held in common (only 5% difference between us and the great apes). It turns out that 1.5% of our DNA codes *all* the proteins we produce, while another 3% is regulatory, turning their synthesis on and off during Development and throughout the life cycle. These regulatory genes are widely shared across animal Phyla, with humans having 99% of them in common with fruit flies and yeast cells. Evolution thus turns out to be not so much a product of heritable mutation as it is a result of changes in the sequence and timing of the activation of these regulatory genes; that is, as a result *of*, and resulting *in* Development. These genes function as switches, and they are organized into circuits and circuits into networks (Hofer) that allow a wide variety of structures to be assembled from relatively few component proteins. It is this group of observations that led to the recognition of a field of evolutionary development: Evo-Devo.

We can also say when Development first appeared over the course of time. Prior to the advent of the Cambrian Period (540–485 million years ago [mya]), life was unicellular. It reproduced via cell division or budding and was modified as a result of spontaneous mutation and natural selection. These single-celled organisms could also alter their means of function (mostly via changes in protein synthesis) in response to environmental changes. Life progressed through pure Evolution. Beginning around 540 mya and lasting around 20–25 million years, a period occurred in which there was a rapid appearance of diverse multicellular life forms (aptly termed the Cambrian Explosion). By its close, the ancestors of all living Phyla (Gould, 1989) had appeared. Now there were two problems: First, these organisms started out life as single cells; second, they ended up with a large batch of specialized cells that all fit nicely together. There must have been a process that produced different kinds of cells and moved them around the growing organism. That process can only be Development: It has been with us ever since, accompanying Evolution. "From an Evo-Devo perspective, Development and its capacity to generate variation is seen as a major participant and *even a cause of Evolution* [emphasis added]" (Hofer, 2014, p. 15). From this perspective, Development becomes a very different animal, and its differences bear on our work as psychoanalysts. Development is not, as it was originally thought to be, a process designed to produce *uniform adults*.

Development (Devo) operates to produce transgenerational variation in organisms (humans, too) in response to individuals' interaction with their environment that ultimately results in evolution (Evo).

The flexibility of the system allows for rapid adaptation in the face of changes in the environment.[3] Carroll (2005), for example, credits climate change in Africa with the doubling in size of the Homonin brain over a comparatively short 1 million years, beginning 2 mya.[4] As we will see, smaller changes, such as the appearance of speech, occurred much more rapidly. We have not yet talked about how another major process affects all of this: that process is Epigenesis.

Epigenetics I

For once, Epigenesis is a term with which some clinicians are familiar. Two second-generation psychoanalysts, Erik Erikson (1950/1963) and Heinz Hartmann (1939/1958), deployed it to describe how development takes place during and (in Erikson's case) after childhood. Erikson described it in terms of *mode-epigenesis*, whereby what were originally psychosexual functions (toilet training) were shaped by the environment into stable adaptational configurations present in adulthood. Hartman talked about *secondary autonomy*, by which neurotic symptoms in early life can be shaped into stable patterns of behavior through a similar process of adaptation.

We now come back to the central question pertaining to the nature of Evo-Devo: How can structurally and functionally diverse cells end up precisely located all over the body with each of them having *exactly the same DNA*? The answer lies mostly[5] in the "chromatin." As Hofer (2014) puts it, "the exquisitely orchestrated regulation of gene activity by messenger molecules was found to result from minute local changes, or remodeling of chromatin" (p. 14). Chromatin is the stuff of chromosomes; it is a complex of macromolecules, the long strands of DNA, four proteins called histones, and ribonucleic acid (RNA).

The histone proteins were once thought of as inert packaging, cellular bubble wrap, which fold the DNA into a more compact, stable structure. This seemed to make sense since, without the histones to compact the structure of the chromosomes, the DNA strands residing in the cell's nucleus would constitute double chains up to 2 meters in length (Carey, 2012)! We have already said that more genetic material is involved in regulating protein synthesis in a cell than is involved in actually synthesizing these proteins. To simplify a highly complex process that regulation is accomplished by switching on and off different protein synthesizing sequences of the DNA. This is done in two ways. In one of them, enzymes may act to hang methyl groups at particular points in the DNA sequence.[6] Methylation of a DNA sequence shuts off a gene sequence (Carey, 2012; Jaenisch & Bird, 2003) involved in the synthesis of a protein (methylation at a sight with more than one methyl group also occurs; the more methylation the stronger the Stop! order). The other switch has to do with the histone proteins and is much more complex (Bannister & Kouzarides, 2001; Jenuwein & Allis, 2001). For a gene to become active, the bond between the histone proteins and the DNA helix must first be able to loosen locally to allow synthesis of messenger-RNA (mRNA) (transcription), which will be transported from the cell nucleus to the cell cytoplasm where protein synthesis then takes place. Unlike epigenetic DNA methylation, different groups (acetyl, methyl, or phosphate groups, with acetylation being the most prominent) can be added to histones in different ways. In fact, roughly 50 different kinds of histone modifications (Carey) have been discovered. Again, unlike DNA methylation, some modifications switch transcription on, while others turn it off. Many different enzymes within a cell's nucleus act to turn these switches on or off. Strictly speaking, on and off are misnomers: The effect is quantitative rather than qualitative, with the end result depending on the total number of modifications at some point, and a matter of degrees rather than absolutes. The specific methylations of DNA and histone modifications on chromatin are referred to in the trade as "marks," as in marked up. They do determine what happens when and where, which genes are activated, and which are silenced (starts to sound sort of Ecclesiastical). Since these processes occur *after* DNA synthesis, after the gene, they were christened *Epi*genetics.

Switching on and off occurs for two reasons: when a cell's activity must be changed due to some needed change in function, or when a cell undergoes cell division. While histone acetylation and de-acetylation occur recurrently, methylation is generally more permanent, shutting down the processes involved in cell division. With one exception, cell division occurs regularly throughout the body. The exception is the neuron; the nerve cells of both the central and peripheral nervous systems. Once neural development is complete, no further neurons are produced:[7] Our nerve cells live as long as we do, unless they are killed by toxins or disease processes.[8] One would expect to see a lot of methylation in these cells as a way of shutting down processes related to cell division for a really long time. One would also expect the longevity of these cells because of the need to not interfere with the neurons' information storage and transmission properties that are preserved in cell memory.[9,10]

Researchers studying Epigenesis often rely on small mammals, mice and rats (e.g., Whitelaw et al., 2010; Whitelaw & Whitelaw, 2006), or simpler organisms like the fruit fly *Drosophila*. They do this because they are able to rapidly breed multiple generations to produce strains whose members are genetically identical to each other and can be epigenetically manipulated in ways that would be impossible with human subjects. When human researchers study humans, they do so in particular ways. They look at populations that experienced severe environmental stress and about whom detailed records were kept. In Epigenetics II, we will talk about the study of two such populations, those who lived through the Dutch Hunger Winter of 1944–1945 (e.g., Painter et al., 2008) and those experiencing cycles of famine and plenty in northern Sweden (e.g., Kaati, Bygren, Pembrey, & Sjöstrom, 2007) during the late 19th and early 20th centuries. They also study monozygotic twins: Fraga and associates (Fraga et al., 2005) studied Epigenetic marks in 40 pairs of monozygotic twins. They found that the marks were highly similar in young twins, but older twins showed increasingly divergent marks. They posited that this divergence reflected the effects of divergent life experiences that led to epigenetic adaptation; changing cellular function to cope with different lifestyles.

Transgenerational Epigenesis includes *all* of the processes that have evolved to bring about the *transmission of phenotype* (Youngson & Whitelaw, 2008),[11] which are then added to *genetic* inheritance. To take Epigenesis back to Phenomenology, to *naturalize* it, is to connect it to the physical properties of mind, self, and world.[12] The existence and being of human beings in the world (Dasein) is an expression of phenotype. Epigenetics offers up a bridge between genotype and phenotype (Goldberg, Allis, & Bernstein, 2007) in which the DNA sequence remains unchanged. Phenomenologically speaking, Epigenesis is about the history of Dasein, a history of Being There (in the world). Cellular differentiation is a product of Epigenesis. "More specifically, epigenetics may be defined as the study of any potentially stable and, ideally, *heritable* [emphasis added] changes in gene expression or cellular phenotype" (p. 635). Many questions remain concerning how Epigenetic inheritance takes place, how histone modifications are maintained through replication, how newly formed histones "learn" from parental chromatin. These processes must in turn figure prominently in the process of Development.

While no doubt fascinating in its own right, what, if anything, does Epigenetics have to do with our work as psychoanalytic clinicians? The answer is a further set of questions: Can it tell us how parents produce children with particular ways of Being? How these children develop into adults? What kind of adults they develop into? How are they alike or different from their parents? And how are *their* children alike or different from them? Finally, how is this different from the old wine of the nature/nurture argument presented in the new bottle of Epigenetics? We are beginning to get tantalizing answers to these and other questions. Animal studies point to the existence of *two* operative systems of inheritance (Jablonka & Lamb, 2014): an Epigenetic system and a Behavioral system that operate in tandem. There is no reason to believe that humans would operate any differently and perhaps can provide an answer to the questions that have plagued us for some time: What kinds of things can be changed through therapy and analysis and what can't? And, if this wasn't already complicated enough, just how does neuroplasticity fit into it all?

In thinking about Epigenetics and Evo-Devo and their relevance and usefulness to psychoanalytic theory-building and clinical practice, we must remember one point: We are in early days. In the last chapter, I discussed Physicalism as it pertained to an understanding of Consciousness. My hypothesis there was that, although we lack the physical tools to measure Consciousness and understand it in 2018, it does not mean that such tools don't exist and won't be discovered in the future. Churchland (2002) believed that it would take many years, even centuries, to understand the physical properties of Consciousness. I do not believe the same can be said of the Evo-Devo and the Epigenetics of the Self. These disciplines are literally exploding before our eyes, with animal research expanding exponentially. I believe we will have some answers within a decade; I hope to be writing about them.

What we can learn about humans from rats

There once existed a now ancient joke among behavioral researchers to the effect that a human being is not a five-foot-tall laboratory rat. A modification of the human as rat hypothesis was advanced in the mid-20th century by the psychoanalyst and developmental psychologist John Bowlby (1958). As he famously observed at the time, "The longer I contemplated the diverse clinical evidence [of child development] the more dissatisfied I became with the view current in psychoanalytical and psychological literature and the more I found myself turning to the ethologists for help" (p. 351). The results of this developmental turn and the flood of animal research that followed it was an understanding that, to put it simply, the transgenerational study of the mother-child bond in rats had much to tell us about human mothers and their offspring. For our purposes, then, a rat might be considered a five-inch-tall human.

In the late 20th century, Hofer (1990) found that behavioral and physiological systems in the 2-week-old rat were maintained by different elements of the maternal relationship and were vulnerable to maternal separation. He identified components of mother-pup interaction, such as the mother's licking, warmth, odors, suckling milk, and the timing, and regulation of these interactions, that he termed "hidden maternal regulators." They have their obvious analogs in the human mother-child relationship. (By age 24 hours, an infant is able to recognize his mothers' odor [Trevarthen, 2009].) Hofer posited that his "findings appeared to be good evidence for a psychobiological symbiosis in which maternal behavior and nursing physiology interact with widespread infant physiological and behavioral systems in a shared homeostatic system" (2014, p. 7).

Supporting this psychobiological symbiosis, animal studies (e.g., Hillerer, Jacobs, Fischer, & Aigner, 2014) have demonstrated changes in the maternal brain during pregnancy and that these changes are long-lived. Until now, there have been no studies of changes in the human maternal brain during pregnancy. Hoekzema and colleagues (Hoekzema et al., 2017) studied the brains of pregnant, nulliparous woman with serial MRIs and found pronounced and characteristic reductions in gray matter (GM) and elaborations of white matter (axons of neurons) in areas involving social cognition. Reductions were diagnostic of pregnancy, occurred in women as opposed to prospective fathers, and were highly consistent. They proved to be valid predictive measures of post-partum attachment suggesting an adaptive process. Changes in GM volume could reflect various processes, such as "changes in the number of synapses, the number of glial cells, the number of neurons, dendritic structure, vasculature, blood volume and circulation and the reductions in GM volume observed in [their] study cannot be pinpointed to a specific molecular mechanism" (p. 7). They were analogous to changes in GM volume occurring during another period of great hormonal influence: the GM pruning (Abitz et al., 2007; Sisk & Foster, 2004) that occurs during adolescence. These changes also appear to be permanent: They are so in rats, and they were after a 2-year follow-up in this study of human mothers.

Beginning with Piaget (for example, Jea, Piaget, & Gruber, 1982), the study of infant development and its psychopathology in the 20th century proceeded along parallel but distinct tracks. Harlow (1958) studied the effects of maternal separation on infant monkeys and found irreversible effects even if structures of wire and terry cloth were provided as replacements. Spitz (1965) was, at the same time, studying the effects of moderate and severe maternal deprivation on hospitalized infants, leading to the concepts of anaclitic depression and hospitalism respectively: conditions of questionable reversibility.[13]

Meanwhile, Hofer (1990, 2014) had found that the hidden maternal regulators controlled and shaped levels of hormones, blood pressure, and sleep in rat pups. In the absence of the mother, *vigorous tactile stimulation of the pups* was found to also regulate growth hormone levels. But in the 1980s something happened: *Crossover occurred between animal and human studies*. Field and colleagues (Field, 2014; Field, Diego, & Hernandez-Reif, 2010; Field, et al., 1986) began to study the behavior of preterm infants in the Neonatal Intensive Care Unit. They found that periods of stroking and limb movement (15 minutes, 3 times a day) produced markedly increased growth and weight gain. Full-term infants of depressed mothers (Field, et al., 1996), when treated with massage over a 6-week period, also showed increased weight gain, and showed greater improvement in emotionality, sociability, and soothability. Field has pursued and elaborated these findings for 30 years, founding the Touch Research Institute, a part of the University of Miami health system. She has expanded her work (Field, 2006) from touching preterm infants to massage therapy in adults.

Researchers (Lucas, 2008; Urry et al., 2004) studying Subjective Well-Being (SWB) and happiness have found that SWB correlates with an asymmetry of prefrontal cortical activity in which there is increased activity on the left. Field (2006), noting frontal EEG asymmetry (Davidson, 1998) with a preponderance of right-sided activity in depression and a preponderance of left-sided activity in processing positive emotions and happiness, found that a shift from right to left preponderance occurred in depressed individuals treated with massage.

There is both an inescapable irony and a question that brings us back to Freud's early and long-abandoned clinical technique (Breuer & Freud, (1893–1895)/1955) in which he would massage his patients on a daily basis. Hofer (2014) and Field's (2006) work raise the question of whether there is a place for massage as an adjunct to psychoanalytic therapy. The goal would be to deepen, increase the efficacy, and/or shorten treatment. I think the cultural role of the 21st century psychoanalytic therapist differs from that of the 19th century physician to a degree that would preclude both modalities being provided by the same person.[14]

In gathering material for this section of the chapter, I found that, despite the institutional memory, and the prohibitions against touching a patient that it hands down to us, there *is* a diverse literature on touch, massage, and psychoanalytic therapy. The literature pertaining to massage refers to treatment outside of intensive psychodynamic or psychoanalytic treatment. Field and colleagues (2009), for example, found benefit in combining massage therapy with "group interpersonal psychotherapy" in the treatment of prenatally depressed women.

Touch is a different matter. Boss (1963), in his phenomenologically-based psychotherapy of the severely regressed patient he calls "Dr. Cobling," discusses holding her in his lap at her request and nursing her with a bottle of "sweet milk" that she brought with her to her sessions for that purpose. He viewed this as a necessary, *self-imposed* regression on the patient's part in which he provided her with reparative maternal experience that she had lacked. The analysis appeared to be highly successful; boundaries were undoubtedly *crossed but not violated*. Winnicott (1972) describes taking a patient's hands to emotionally hold her in his "metaphorical lap." Little (1985), however, in describing his work with her during states of "psychotic anxiety," says that he did in fact physically hold her and that he had done so with other patients.

This brings us to *Psychoanalytic Inquiry*, Volume 20, Number 1 (Breckenridge, 2000; Casement, 2000; Fosshage, 2000; Holder, 2000; McLaughlin, 2000; Pizer, 2000; Ruderman, 2000; Schlessinger & Appelbaum, 2000; Shane, Shane, & Gales, 2000), an issue devoted to touch in psychoanalysis and psychotherapy. The issue is organized around responses to a paper by Casement (1982). In it, he describes his work with a patient who, on a Friday, desperately begs him to take her hands. He tells her he will think about it over the weekend and then refuses her on Monday. In my reading of the paper, the patient was severely traumatized by his rejection, and the analysis irreparably damaged by it. While aware that things have not gone as well as they perhaps should, Casement (2000) appears oblivious to the extent to which he had traumatized his patient.

Two of the contributors (Breckenridge, 2000; Fosshage, 2000) treat touch as a normal part of their being with patients, including a handshake, or clasp, a hand on the shoulder, or an occasional hug. Shane and colleagues (2000) do not really offer a contribution that is on point. The remaining authors (Casement, 2000; Holder, 2000; McLaughlin, 2000; Pizer, 2000; Ruderman, 2000; Schlessinger & Appelbaum, 2000) convey unmistakably that touch is a subject with which they are struggling. Their prose is dense and they say little or nothing about their own experiences with touch. I think they try to offer a balanced account but come down on the side of the dangers inherent in boundary violations. Many analysts would, I believe, be sympathetic to their positions. Many of us continue to struggle with old taboos and the long-delayed appearance of the topic of therapist-patient sexual boundary violations in our literature has probably increased those concerns.

Unfortunately, none of these commentators (as is often the case) systematically considers the customer's (that is, their patient's) experience and response to being touched by their therapists. Horton and colleagues (Horton, Clance, Sterk-Elifson, & Emshoff, 1995), however, consider that very question. They found that touch deployed solidly *within the boundaries* of the therapeutic situation was experienced as fostering a therapeutic bond and deepening trust by patients of their therapists. To maximize the chance of getting negative evaluations, patients were not only recruited through their therapists, but through a variety of social settings including sexual abuse support groups and 12-step programs. Ultimately, there were 231 respondents: Only 10 of them reported negative experiences with touch, and 6 of those attributed their negative experience to their therapist's discomfort with the process.

To move on to my own experiences with touch, I have, in a non-systematic way, in violation of old taboos and prohibitions (*not* those prohibiting boundary *violations*), suggested to a number of patients that they seek massage on a weekly basis. They have generally been suffering from depressive and/or attachment issues, and those who have followed my recommendations have responded positively to massage. It would be relatively easy to study the effects of such an intervention in a *systematic* way in some kind of clinic setting if the will existed to do it. What I *do* have broader experience with is the handshake, an occasional pat on the shoulder, and, rarely, a hug. Many psychoanalytic therapists refuse to shake their patients' hands (as I did in the 1970s and 1980s), seeing it as a boundary violation and/or a gratification of the patient.[15] I always offer a handshake when I meet a patient for the first time. I find that some patients, mostly but not entirely men, continue to want handshakes: sometimes at the beginning of a session, sometimes at the end, and occasionally both. I initially found myself thinking about wanting to convey warmth through touch. More recently, I realized that this was entirely consistent with Hofer (2014) and Field's (2006) work. At this point, I can only say that patients who have sought out handshakes make it a regular part of their sessions; with others, they put their hand out on an occasional basis or I may offer a handshake after a difficult hour.[16] I can also say that none of these contacts led to subsequent boundary crossings, boundary violations, or patient requests for them.

Although I do have experience with patients who brought or developed an eroticized transference[17] in their therapy or analysis, I, *of course*, did not offer any physical contact to them, and they did not seek it out. Without any particular effort, their erotic feelings remained solidly within the physical[18] boundaries of Therapeutic Discourse. I don't know whether my experience is simply the result of a sampling error (possibly the case), my gender (doubtful), or some countertransference issue others have and I don't (also doubtful). On the other hand, Toronto (2001) offers a paper in which she acknowledges that touch would seem to be a part of the therapeutic situation in a two-person psychology but goes on to discuss it in terms of erotic maternal transference and offers three clinical vignettes in which she struggled mightily with her own reactions to her patients wanting to be touched and viewed touch as erotically inappropriate.

Moving on to levels of increasing controversy in the therapist-patient bond, I have posited (Leffert, 2013, Chapter 3) a place (and even a necessity) for the analyst's mature love for his or her patients in the therapeutic situation. Perhaps the term *Chesed*, drawn from Jewish theology and ethics, and meaning loving-kindness, also gets at this. Recent decades have seen a blossoming of literature on therapists' erotic love for their patients, the boundary violations that ensue (e.g., Celenza, 2006; Celenza & Gabbard, 2003; Gabbard, 1995), and its possible therapeutic action (Davies, 1994, 1996). As it turns out, there *is* a small literature (Friedman, 2005; Nacht, 1962a, 1962b; Natterson, 2003; Novick & Novick, 2000; Segal, 1962) concerning therapists' loving feelings for their patients that reside well within the boundaries of the therapeutic situation. It remains "a remarkably difficult subject to think about … talk about" (Leffert, 2013, p. 80) and write about. I want to posit that analysts do have "therapeutic" (for lack of a better term) loving feelings for their patients, but how prevalent such feelings are and how explicitly conscious of them therapists are, I do not know. Although therapists do, of course, have sexual feelings for their patients, *this is an entirely different matter*. There is evidence (Tessman, 2003) that analysands of affectless or "neutral" analysts do not speak well of their therapeutic experiences.

Such loving feelings cannot be uninflected by the two-person psychology of the therapeutic situation; this means that patients must have *some* role in evoking them, but not that the patient must return them *in kind*. Nor need it mean that the feelings represent some manifestation of transference/countertransference. To make things still more complex and obscure (as if we needed that), there would seem to be no reason that patients couldn't also have these kinds of loving feelings for *us*.

Novick and Novick (2000) deal with this dilemma by positing two sorts of love that the therapist is capable of: a mature adult kind of love and an infantile sado-masochistic variety, while Lear (1990/1998) and Loewald (1988) see the very act of the analyst's doing analysis as a manifestation of love.

There are other unanswered questions. Does this capacity to love our patients exist in some of us, or in most, or all of us? Is it present in us from the start, or does it develop over years of practicing therapy or analysis? If so, is it a manifestation of neuroplasticity in the therapist's brain? And, finally, would discussing love as part of one's education as a therapist alter any of these parameters?

There is ample evidence that our neuroplastic brains change over time (Doidge, 2007, 2015) as a result of particular disciplines or experiences. A now classic study of London taxi drivers (Maguire, Woollett, & Spiers, 2006) who must perform complex spatial navigation as they take fares around the city demonstrates that their hippocampal GM increases proportionately to their years of experience. Closer to what we might speculate as taking place in therapists who spend hours each day in a particular state of mind (being a participant-observer), subjects with extensive experience in meditation demonstrate neuroplasticity (Davidson et al., 2003; Lazar et al., 2005): increased cortical thickening and a decrease in age-related cortical thinning. There is no proof that these cortical changes account for the beneficial results of long-term meditation and beneficial increases in affect-regulation but there is no reason to assume they are unrelated. Indeed, both years of meditation practice and a reduction in respiratory rate (a physiological measure of cumulative meditation experience) correlate with increasing cortical thickness in the occipito-temporal visual cortex and the right anterior insula. Since these cortical changes take place in areas of the right cerebral hemisphere and relate to changes in body awareness and awareness of self, something very similar could occur in therapists and analysts with long-term experience in therapeutic practice. (Again, if one were but to study it systematically.)

If mature loving feelings for patients are not derived from infantile sexuality, how might we understand them? I would posit that they arise out of nurturant and attachment behaviors and normative social bonding. In our clinical theory, they would fit not in the transference/countertransference, but rather in the therapeutic alliance and the real relationship (Greenson, 1967). As Bowlby (1979[1977]/1984) put it, "What for convenience I am terming attachment theory is a way of conceptualizing the propensity of human beings to make strong affectional bonds to particular others" (p. 127).

The Evo-Devo of play

An area that we have not considered is the epigenetic and developmental role of play. Again, animal studies of play in normal development can cross over to human studies that may also have a place in therapy. As developmental psychologists, we have understood play as an essential part of normal psychological development, and as psychotherapists we have understood its role in the psychoanalytic treatment of children, in elucidating conflict-based problems, and problems of psychosexual development that the child cannot or will not formulate in words. Play therapy constitutes an important modality of therapeutic action. We have, however, not much understood the role of play in normative or pathological *neuro*-development and have not considered its possible role in *adult* life and *adult* psychotherapy and psychoanalysis.

In discussing play as behavior and neuroscience in animals and humans, and in juveniles, and adults, I am going to interweave a number of threads. One is drawn from the work of Panksepp and Biven (2012) that I have already referred to a number of times over the course of this book. They define PLAY as one of seven basic emotional states that have been described and verified in cross-mammalian studies. They describe these states as existing on primary, secondary, and tertiary levels depending on levels of cognitive processing.[19] Another is drawn from Pellis and Pellis' (2009) work on the neuroscience of play and its effects on brain development in murid rodents (particularly rats). (As of this writing, the neuroscience of play in humans has been much less studied.) Still another is drawn from studies of Desire and Positive Psychology (Leffert, 2017). It is the least well-developed as of this writing.

But first, what exactly *is* play? Although hard to define, it is not a primitive. Panksepp and Biven (2012) cite Burghardt's (2005) five factorial definition of play, which I would modify slightly: (1) The adaptive functions of play are not apparent when it first appears, developmentally; (2) play is an activity engaged in for its own sake because it is pleasurable or fun; (3) play is an exaggerated or incomplete form of adult activities that are not play; (4) it is repetitive and engaged in with multiple variations; and (5) in order to play, individuals must be comfortable, well-fed and healthy (stress reduces play). This definition is descriptive; it does not address the social significance of play or its neurodevelopmental consequences.

Play in rats is easy to study. Rat pups engage in play fighting and play mounting (Pellis & Pellis, 2009). The body maneuvers of attack and defense are complex but standardized and quantifiable. The degree of positive emotion, joy if you will, can be measured in rats by the frequency of 50 kHz vocalizations (the rats *sound* happy). It is highest during rough-and-tumble PLAY (Burgdorf, Kroes, Beinfeld, Panksepp, & Modskal, 2010) but also can be elicited by tickling (Burgdorf & Panksepp, 2001).[20] Play in juvenile rats has been shown to be necessary for normal brain development: "Cognitive, emotional, and social skills that are dependent on cortical mechanisms are influenced by play fighting experience in the juvenile period" (p. 93). Play leads to cortical thickening and increased arborization of dendrites of cortical neurons, particularly in the orbitofrontal cortex. The amygdala, which we know to have essential functions in affect-regulation, is crucial to "playful reciprocity." Play fighting among juvenile rats is the ultimate experience of social reciprocity. Juvenile rats who are prevented from engaging in play fighting, either through raising them in isolation (a complex independent variable), or raising them with their mothers but without litter mates (less complex), do not develop into socially successful adults.[21] The implications for human development have been little-studied but are of obvious importance. The prefrontal cortex, whose development is enhanced by play, helps to dampen the activity of the amygdala, allowing it to better regulate Primary-Process emotions and serve to prevent emotional overreactions. This suggests a neurodevelopmental mechanism whereby juvenile play fighting serves to produce socially healthy adults.

Rough-and-tumble PLAY is a normal part of developmental experience (Panksepp & Biven, 2012) actively sought out by all juvenile mammals. As these authors put it: "Physical playfulness is a birthright of every young mammal and perhaps of many other animals as well" (p. 352). Young human mammals enjoy play above all things, derive great joy manifested as euphoria from it, and will work, or perform unpleasant tasks in order to be allowed to engage in it. Like the other Primary-Process emotional states, the PLAY system is concentrated in subcortical brain regions, whereas the mechanics of play are Secondary-Process emotions. Tertiary-Process play involves complex states such as humor, reading, and viewing play. PLAY is closely allied with, but distinct from, SEEKING and *its* higher order experience of DESIRE (Leffert, 2017). Juvenile play enables the development of both non-social (hunting, working) and social (cooperation, courting, and parenting) skills.

Rough-and-tumble PLAY *has* been behaviorally and quantifiably studied in children (e.g., Boulton, 1996; Scott & Panksepp, 2003), although the studies seem not so far to have extended to hormonal and neurodevelopmental correlates. Panksepp and Biven (2012) argue forcibly for the developmental importance of supervised free play and the developmental dangers of psychostimulants, which have been shown to suppress play. Current social values have led parents to discourage rough-and-tumble PLAY, the consequences of which have not been studied. (Panksepp and Biven believe that in extreme cases, such deprivation can lead to named psychiatric conditions such as attention deficit hyperactivity disorder.)

PLAY arousal, mind development, and epigenesis are interreferentially linked. Rough-and-tumble PLAY (Panksepp & Biven, 2012) takes children to the edge of emotional knowledge. If promptly worked through with caring adults, it facilitates social development, whereas, if unsupervised, play can lead not to cortical development but to trauma compromising the amygdala. The increasing social awareness of bullying over the past decade or two, while certainly an acknowledgment of the problem, fails to consider its causes and prophylaxis.

Other forms of play do exist (Slade & Wolf, 1994). It can consist of symbolic, constructive, narrative, and relational activities. Psychoanalytic therapists working with children are generally concerned with the meaning of particular forms of play that their child patients spontaneously engage in or can be induced to engage in. We have more of a *process* interest here. Does the child have the *capacity* to engage in play and an *interest* in doing so? How have adults responded to a child's play? Beyond the interpretation of play (verbally to the child or for our own understanding), our role must be to teach children to play if they are unable to do so themselves.

As discussed above, PLAYfulness exerts a powerful effect on the neocortex that both follows from and leads to changes in gene expression profiles. Of the 1200 genes that are active in the frontal cortex (Panksepp & Biven, 2012), *a third* are epigenetically modified by play. Consistent with this, play increased levels of mRNA in the frontal and posterior cortex (Burgdorf & Panksepp, 2001).[22] Epigenesis leads to the creation of new prosocial pathways: the long-term modification of gene expression occurring as a result of experience.

PLAY influences human ontology and phylogeny[23] (Pellegrini, Dupuis, & Smith, 2007). These authors follow Burghardt's (2005) Surplus Resource Theory (SRT) of PLAY, to wit, that juvenile play can only occur in situations in which parents can or will provide adequate resources of safety and sustenance. They note, citing Groos (1898, 1901), that the concept that juvenile play is "critical" to later development is much older than we might think. Play allows juveniles to develop strategies for creative problem-solving that are low-risk and low-cost, ways of environmental sampling leading to more effective adult problem-solving. Play theorists tend to dismiss games over free play because they involve rules: I believe they are mistaken in doing so. Games teach both living *with* rules and the ability to develop creative solutions *within* them: As adults, we spend more time dealing with such situations than we do needing to think "out of the box." If we try to think about the way these experiences shape adult epistemologies, we could think in terms of the specifics of the Heuristics and Biases (Leffert, 2016; Tversky & Kahneman, 1974/1982) we develop. Heuristics and Biases are the particular emotional and cognitive shortcuts we create to find our way in an uncertain World where particular knowledges sometimes can't be found and sometimes don't even exist.

The long period of juvenile immaturity is an essential part of being human that conveys an evolutionary advantage (Lancaster & Lancaster, 1987; Pellegrini et al., 2007). It makes room for the developmental plasticity necessary to produce large-brained adults optimally adapted to function in their particular social and physical environments. Whether this also bestows selective reproductive advantages on an individual is obviously a debatable point: It does so in some societies but not others. Although we now deploy formal education to convey the knowledge base and problem-solving strategies necessary for survival in the modern world (how effective such education actually is, is a subject of debate) this is a relatively recent phenomena. *At best* prior to the 20th century, vocational, and social learning took place, for the overwhelming majority of individuals, not in schools but in the world, under the aegis of the surplus resources provided by the parents.[24] Play in the presence of surplus resources is, then, one manifestation of Erikson's (1950/1963) theory of epigenesis and the interdigitation of the generations.

What should have emerged here is the idea that PLAY is an essential piece of normal development, SRT, that it can be impaired by social circumstance and/or developmental psychopathology, and that the consequences of impairment for adult functioning are considerable. It would seem to make sense, then, to attempt to elicit a PLAY history from not only child, but also adult patients over the course of our work with them. We then face the questions of whether instilling PLAY into patients' lives (assuming they are first helped to develop the surplus resources allowing them to engage in it) is a good thing and, particularly, whether there is a place for play in the adult therapeutic encounter. If so, how might it alter standard therapeutic technique?

In my previous book (Leffert, 2017) on positive psychoanalysis, I mandated a place for the reawakening (or awakening) of play in our adult patients' lives. I considered suggesting that a patient convert a talent, such as sketching or making photographs, into a play activity (an avocation). Exercise, our own personal endorphin generator, can be prescribed and offers a path back to play (it also possesses psychopharmacological properties as an antidepressant and an antianxiety agent). Interacting with pets can be equally powerful.

So, should we play with our patients, or is it heretical to even think of it? One could, for example, play games with a patient or sing with them. Should one? I don't know. I'm less concerned with whether or not such practices are "analytic" than I am about whether there is a place for them in the Therapeutic Situation. I'm much more certain about and engage in elements of play with my patients that can be incorporated into the therapeutic discourse. The use of certain kinds of humor or joke-telling comes readily to mind. Obviously, there is a place for it with some patients and not others, and with some patients at some points in a therapy and not others. Surplus resources must be available to a patient to make use of humor (if a patient is exhausted by life's circumstances or depression, there is clearly no room for it). The humor must be devoid of hostility. It should not be inserted as a distraction into the discourse but should rather be illustrative. It can draw attention to the *absurdity* of a situation or event that would otherwise cause pain. Sharing spontaneous jokes imparts a powerful mutuality to the therapeutic situation, bringing it into pleasurable, even joyful territory.

Therapeutic discourse can *sometimes* be a form of play. There is an analytic literature (Cohen, 1996; Ehrenberg, 1990; Meares, 1992; Sachs, 1996; Winnicott, 1968) on the role of play in psychotherapy and psychoanalysis, with only some blurring about whether the patient is an adult or a child. Meares indeed suggests that a paradigm shift has occurred and that transference should be viewed as a form of play. Winnicott viewed psychotherapy as taking place in the overlapping space of the patient and therapist's areas of play. If a patient is incapable of this, then Winnicott saw the first goal of the therapeutic process being to get his patient to play. Play, he felt, was essential to that process. Ehrenberg also identifies playfulness and mutual pleasure in the process as necessary curative factors in psychoanalytic therapy. Sachs describes himself as making "a conscious effort to reduce analysis to play" (p. 39).

These are useful efforts, but I am going to take a somewhat different stance, one informed by epigenetics, and developmental neuroscience. I believe that play *is* an essential part of the therapeutic process. I would see a therapy as alternating periods of play and periods of non-play, usually both in the same session. What they involve are differing kinds of discourse. Both depend on a therapeutic space being safely removed from the overlapping worlds that patient and therapist inhabit. In non-play, the therapist retains the role that Bachelard (1958/1994) describes as the anchorite, the keeper-of-the-vigil in a cabin in the dark forest, in the office when the patient is not there, a lit candle in the window. This role is at once that of transference figure, but also that of teacher and religious leader. The non-play discourse involves figuring things out, experiencing, and understanding. It is a discourse that attends to problems in Being (Leffert, 2016, and Chapter 1 of this volume). The play discourse involves trying things out, ideas and feelings, making use of the therapist as a participant. The familiar goal of such therapeutic play is to serve as a field in which to work through previously discovered or elaborated material, often material that was outside of awareness. The additional goal (the two are often combined) is to help the patient develop and refine his capacity to play as an aspect of life and to foster its functional neuroanatomical goals derived from neuroplasticity.

Carol, an incest victim, returned to therapy after a hiatus of several of years. The narrative that emerged in *that* treatment (twice weekly psychoanalytic therapy) was of frequent physical and sexual abuse at the hands of a grandfather. Like many abuse victims I have treated, she tended to chronic illness, and had undergone numerous questionable surgeries for real medical conditions; these appeared to have a masochistic component. The abuse was apparently an open family secret, with Carol being offered up as a kind of sacrificial victim to the frightening, violent grandfather. I had diagnosed her with post-traumatic stress disorder. Carol had never spoken explicitly about the abuse to anyone before me; she had felt unable to do so. When she did, as a result of our work, attempt to talk to her parents and siblings about her experiences, she was first met with angry denial and then complaints that she was "making a big deal about something that had happened a long time ago." (This response is not uncommon.) Eventually, the mother refused to continue paying for the treatment, and I continued to see her at a reduced fee. As we discovered her family's exploitation of her, feelings of pain and anger directed at them appeared in the therapy. Carol experienced considerable relief as a result of the work we did, and the treatment tapered off. What disturbed me at the time was that she had never been able to fully Be in the World. She also had always held me in a high regard that precluded, perhaps defensively, negative feelings.

Significantly, it was this point that Carol took up when she came back to see me. Her parents, both now dead, had died in terror of their deaths, and she took some pleasure in this. She had studied to become a marriage and family counselor in the interim and announced to me (accurately) that she had never dealt with transference feelings in her therapy. What I want to tell you about is what ensued fairly rapidly as we began talking again. Carol told me that I had said something about her adult children in the previous therapy that had made her very angry with me. I had observed that, based on what she was telling me about their treatment of her, that they seemed to have joined the family conspiracy. In the present therapy she screamed for a minute or two (it felt far longer), that she *hated* me for having said this. It was hard to listen to her, and the thought flitted across my mind to say something to moderate the outburst, but fortunately I did not. Carol suddenly interrupted herself to tell me how good she felt to be able to give voice to these raw emotions and how good it felt to know that I didn't take them personally. I understood that she was playing with the feelings (play is often intense and not fun), identifying me as a willing partner in her doing so. This play has been repeated a number of times over the course of these sessions; she identifies it as taxing, but also pleasurable.

Having engaged this material on Evo-Devo, let's return to Epigenetics and see how it further informs our understanding of it.

Epigenetics II

As psychotherapists and developmental psychologists, we have, in the past, been accustomed, both theoretically and clinically, to thinking that intergenerational effects lay first within the purview of the mother-child relationship as it plays out in the attachment process and the development of maternal representations or internal working models, then within the elements of psychosexual development and their derivatives. It has been somewhat risqué to posit that such representations could begin to form in utero in response to sounds coming from the mother's voice and body. Schore (1994) added the neurodevelopmental component that the infant's and later the adult's capacity to regulate her autonomic nervous system is "burnt in" by that early relationship, largely mediated by pupillary reflexes in the mother-infant gaze. The question of how these processes could be understood in terms of unfolding biological developmental processes, particularly in those taking place in the developing immature[25] brain and nervous system, has not been much considered.

We have, up to now, discussed how epigenetic changes on a cellular level shape an individual's development and adult existence in order to function adaptively in a particular physical and social set of environmental circumstances. As therapists, we also know that some combinations of the social and the physical can lead to pathological adaptations that result in individuals who function at less than optimal levels, and that this is simply another way of describing what we are trying to address when we set out to heal (Leffert, 2016) our patients. Although it is comparatively easy to grasp the way these cellular changes take place, it is harder to understand how they could become heritable. In order to do so, epigenetic processes that affect somatic cells would also have to transform or mark (epigenetically) *germ* cells. Strange as such a process might at first sound, it has become the subject of the expanding study of *transgenerational epigenetics*.

There is increasing evidence that the effects of environmental influences on development can be mediated by epigenetic mechanisms. Data is piling up that epigenetic changes are heritable, and Lamarck's (1809/2012) old and discredited theory of the *inheritance of acquired characteristics* and *use/disuse* that he called *soft inheritance* is perhaps relevant in some instances after all.

Hofer (2014) seeks to close

> the causal ring between a particular set of maternal behaviors directed by a mother towards her offspring early in their development and the expression of adaptive behaviors with their supporting physiological responses in her adult offspring, even extending to the next generation.
>
> *(p. 14)*

Champagne (2008, 2010, 2013) observes that while we have previously viewed the transmission of traits across generations to occur as a result of inherited genomic information (parental DNA), there is now evidence for epigenetic mediation of this transmission. Intrauterine interactions between rat mothers and their offspring can profoundly influence development and affect the physiological and psychological health of adult offspring.

> Likewise, the care received by an infant early in life can produce changes in the development of neural systems regulating response to novelty and social behavior: The maternal environment experienced by a developing organism can play a critical role in shaping adult patterns of behavior.
>
> *(Champagne, 2008, p. 386)*

In some exciting preliminary research, Inaba and colleagues (Baker, 2017; Inaba, Buszczak, & Yamashita, 2015) demonstrated the presence of "nanotubes" in stem cells in the Drosophila that transiently connect different cells and allow for the exchange of genetic information. This could suggest how epigenetic information could be transmitted from cells of the phenotypic body to its germ cells.

Hofer (2014) describes a series of experiments performed with rats in his lab (Skolnick, Ackerman, Hofer, & Weiner, 1980) that demonstrate the effects of early experience on subsequent generations. He had posited a central developmental role for what he called "hidden maternal regulators": the mother's licking, warmth, odor, suckling, milk, and grooming of her pups. Early weaning of pups, he thought, would be an experimental way of shutting down those regulators. He found that early weaning was associated with the formation of gastric ulcers in the pups. They (Skolnick et al., 1980) posited that adult maternal behavior would be disrupted in those individuals who, as pups, were subjected to early weaning. Indeed, they found that *their* pups were subject to an increased incidence of stress ulcers even if *they* were normally weaned. This, of course, left as a possibility that deficits in maternal behavior were simply passed on behaviorally from mother to daughter (just like we analysts have always *assumed*). So they added another wrinkle to the experiment. It seems that normal pups of normally weaned mothers can be cross-fostered to another mother with no ill effects. So they cross-fostered the pups of early-weaned mothers to normally weaned mothers. They found that *these pups showed the same vulnerability to stress ulcers as their littermates raised by the early-weaned mothers did*. This change could not, then, be attributed to the behavior of the early-weaned mothers; it had to be caused by epigenetic changes occurring in utero or by an even earlier effect on the mother's germ cells. The effects could be traced across three generations to the grand pups of the original mothers.

Saavedra-Rodriguez and Feig (2013) found even stronger evidence for transgenerational epigenesis. They studied "female and male mice who were subjected to chronic social stress involving social instability and disruption of social hierarchy from postnatal day 27 to 76" (p. 44) (adolescence and early adulthood). They found that social instability was transmitted predominantly to females across three generations (to the great-grand pups). However, only the sons could transmit all of the signs and symptoms of social distress to *their* daughters and granddaughters. In keeping with these findings and others, Champagne (2010) concludes that there is evidence across species for the transmission of maternal behaviors across generations to offsprings and grand-offsprings.

How do we know if these results can make the trip from rats to humans? There is both behavioral and neurohormonal evidence justifying the transition (Hofer, 2014). Early responses of rat pups to maternal separation resemble the "protest response" seen in human infants, and long-latency responses to separation resemble the "despair phase" of Bowlby's attachment models. Investigation of the neural pathways involved in the rat pups' response to isolation found a high degree of similarity with the neurotransmitters involved in human anxiety. Psychopharmacological agents used to reduce anxiety in humans decreased stress vocalizations in isolated rat pups, where agents that increase human anxiety increased those vocalizations.

The results of these studies should be of profound importance to us as developmental psychologists in that we have always considered Transgenerational processes in mother-child interaction to be exclusively within the purview of conscious and unconscious mental processes. This is *not* a replacement for the psychology of development; the genetics and the epigenetics of gene expression are *additive* to it. However, in order to prove this Transgenerational Epigenetic hypothesis, there is one thing that we *must* demonstrate: environmental Epigenetic modification of germ line cells in succeeding generations of humans.

In their research into Subjective Well-Being (SWB), Lucas and Diener (Leffert, 2017; Lucas, 2008; Lucas & Diener, 2008/2009) argue that the most important determinant of a person's SWB is the personality he or she is born with. They

(Lucas & Diener) argue that personality is mostly a matter of biology and temperament. They found, however, that only 50% of the variance in SWB (Lucas, 2008) could be explained by top-down effects of biology and temperament; hence 50% of the variance had to appear as bottom-up effects of social experience. This SWB research (Leffert, 2017) gives us added reasons (if they should be necessary) to study the Epigenetics of personality.

It has been known for decades that if a mother has been malnourished during pregnancy, her child will be subject to ill health, not just post-birth but for decades thereafter. After going through all this evidence supporting the existence of Transgenerational Epigenetics in rats, you might still ask: Is there any *direct* evidence that the same process is active in us? It turns out that, due to devastating social circumstances and the comprehensive demographic records maintained by the Netherlands and Sweden, there is. The first is the infamous and intensively studied Dutch Hunger Winter (Stein, Susser, Saenger, & Marolla, 1975) of 1944–1945 when, in the last year of the war, the Nazis blocked any importation of food or fuel to the Netherlands, killing 22,000 people and causing extreme suffering to the entire population. The second took place in Överkalix, an isolated region of northern Sweden (Kaati, Bygren, & Edvinsson, 2002; Kaati et al., 2007) that was subjected, during the late 19th and early 20th centuries, to years of famine, and food shortages alternating unpredictably with years of plenty. Carey (2012) offers excellent descriptions of both.

Let's start with the Dutch Hunger Winter and its Epigenetics. Looking at women who were pregnant during that winter of 1944–1945, one could separate them into groups based on where their pregnancies fell over the course of the winter. Researchers (Carey, 2012; Heijmans et al., 2008; Painter et al., 2008; Stein et al., 1975) were particularly interested in two groups: women who had become pregnant in the summer of 1944 (let's call them P_1 to try to keep track of them) and were exposed to the famine during the last trimester of their pregnancies, and women who had become pregnant around mid-winter (P_2) and were exposed to the famine only during their first trimester. The F_1 babies (born to P_1 mothers) who suffered malnutrition during their *third trimester* were likely to be born small. Interestingly, the F_2 babies, who suffered from malnutrition during their *first trimester*, were born of normal weight; they had been able to catch up somehow when the mothers were well-fed towards the end of their pregnancies.

Now things get really interesting. The babies who were born small stayed small throughout their lives, while the F_2 adults (born to the P_2 mothers), although they were of normal birth-weight, were subject to a higher level of obesity throughout their lives. They were also subject (Carey, 2012) to higher levels of chronic illness and schizophrenia: "Something that had happened during their development in the womb affected them for decades afterwards" (p. 92). We know that Epigenetic marking by DNA methylation or histone protein modification in utero can account for such processes. We still have the question: Can acquired characteristics be inherited in this way?

The Dutch Hunger Winter provides some answers to these questions, thanks to the comprehensive record keeping of the Dutch. They maintained health records over the decades of the parents who had been alive during the winter, their children, and their grandchildren. It turns out that when the F_1 and F_2 daughters grew up, became pregnant, and delivered grandchildren, some even more interesting findings presented themselves. The first pregnancy of the low birth-weight daughters of the P_1 mothers resulted in the birth of normal weight babies (granddaughters of the original mothers) that were healthier than average throughout their lives. However, *the normal birth-weight daughters of the P_2 mothers gave birth to heavier than average babies.* This would seem like sound evidence for the existence of Transgenerational Epigenetics, but it does not completely rule in heritable DNA modification and rule out non-DNA uterine effects or factors carried in the egg proteins of the mother. However, there is a study that does precisely that: It is the Överkalix study of fathers and sons in northern Sweden that bypasses the possibility of uterine or egg protein effects.

It seems that during the late 19th and early 20th centuries, the Överkalix area was subject to years of lush harvests interspersed with years of famine. Isolation, poor transportation, and social unrest resulted in the famines not being relieved by shipments of foodstuffs from the rest of the country. Boys in middle childhood experience a slow-growth phase (SGP) that precedes the adolescent growth spurt. Researchers (Kaati et al., 2002; Kaati et al., 2007) studied food intake during the SGP in three cohorts of boys, born in 1890, 1905, 1920, and followed them until their deaths or until 1995. Parents' and grandparents' access to food was determined from general historical records, specifically those of harvests, and food prices. They found a number of things. If there was a scarcity of food during a father's SGP, his sons were less likely to die of cardiovascular disease, hypertension, or stroke. (This finding was similar to the Dutch results, in which the P_1 daughters of the F_1 mothers who were subject to famine were born small and remained small throughout their lives.) If, on the other hand, a paternal grandfather was exposed to a surfeit of food during his slow-growth period (and overate accordingly), his grandsons suffered an increased likelihood of dying of diabetes mellitus.

Kaati and colleagues (2002) posit that the Överkalix study revealed "a nutrition-linked mechanism through the male line seems to have influenced the risk for cardiovascular and diabetes mellitus mortality" (p. 682). These results would appear to rule out intrauterine or cytoplasmic effects and suggest that they were mediated by transgenerational epigenetics. If one is willing to return to the animal studies, Emma Whitelaw's (Whitelaw et al., 2010; Whitelaw & Whitelaw, 2006) work with coat color in the agouti mouse provides further evidence of transgenerational epigenetics, this time through documented DNA methylation.

I find this epigenetic stuff fascinating and would expect many of you to do so as well. You may, however, want to ask the question: Does epigenetics, however interesting, have any clinical relevance? I think that it does. Bear with me for a moment. The transgenerational effects of the Dutch Hunger Winter and the feasts and famines of Överkalix were caused by extreme environmental events. There is no reason to doubt that such effects can occur subtly, in response to smaller environmental and relational[26] factors that would be expressed equally subtly in the children and grandchildren of the people who experienced the events.[27]

Before we get to the bottom line, there is one more complication we have to deal with. In our usual way of thinking about the origins of psychopathology and cure, we view environmental and relational effects as operating through neuroplasticity (Doidge, 2007) and our efforts at cure as making contact with these effects through emotion-rich discourse. These must be expressed through synaptic facilitation and inhibition (Kandel & Tauc, 1965).[28] Subsequently, Kandel (2001) offered a more highly evolved version of this theory documented by work both with the sea slug *Aplysia* and the mammalian hippocampus. He described two phases of learning and memory: short-term and long-term memory, the former involving a single or a few stimuli and the latter involving exposure to repeated stimuli. On a cellular level, the difference between the two is profound: Short-term memory involves the actions of different chemicals, particularly neurotransmitters, within the existing cell architecture, while long-term memory involves changes in neuronal architecture through new protein synthesis. As we know, this requires signaling to and activation (or inactivation of inhibitory effects) of the neurons' DNA and can only result from new or temporary epigenetic marking. If you're still with me, neuronal architecture is also influenced by epigenetic marking that is inherited from both maternal and paternal lines.

As we've seen, this epigenetic marking can lead to dysfunction (it can also lead to positive function; perhaps, finally, an explanation of resilience) in succeeding generations. If we aim to get at these effects of life experience (both early or later) by getting back into those events in whatever ways that seem good to us, how do we deal with the inherited epigenetic effects with which they are involved?[29] To remind us to look at this process in a different way, these effects do make up the 50% of SBW and temperament (Leffert, 2017; Lucas, 2008; Lucas & Diener, 2008/2009) that are inherited.

As an optimistic clinician, I choose to believe that these transgenerational effects are treatable and that the complicated material we have just discussed provides a more effective way of understanding them. Another way of saying this in neurobiological language is that transgenerational epigenesis can be altered by neuroplasticity (Doidge, 2007). Thinking about transgenerational epigenesis also suggests a way out of some therapeutic impasses in which event-based work goes only so far and then fails. Therapeutic action on these effects will not be based at all on causative events but will play out entirely in the therapeutic relationship. Events *will* figure in this part of the therapeutic work, but as illustrations of the issues coming up in the relationship, not as history.

Let me offer a brief case illustration. Jennifer, a university professor in her 40s, sought therapy, and eventually analysis due to an intractable relationship with a verbally abusive, controlling husband. It emerged that she suffered from a masochistic character that developed in the childhood cauldron of a sadistically abusive older brother, a sweet hear no evil-see no evil-speak no evil father, and a mother who viewed her as competition and lost no opportunity to put Jennifer down and deny how her brother was abusing her. Now, here's what's interesting. The analysis successfully dissolved her masochistic character. She no longer allowed anyone to mistreat her and challenged such treatment, both in her intimate relationships and in her relationships and contacts in the wider world. However, she was unable to end any of the dysfunctional relationships. An old criterion for viewing a successful analysis that I believe still has some merit, involving the successful separation and moving on from the infantile objects, had not been met. Jennifer knew all these things about her parents and her brother (all long dead) and about her husband, but she tended to forget and dismiss them and was unable to separate from these people. (Forgetting did not involve her allowing them to treat her abusively: the character repair remained in place.) The analysis (and me) continued to bang unsuccessfully against this problem (Jennifer and I were banging on it together) until I recently came up with the idea that the nature of one's object relations was important enough evolutionarily to be a candidate for epigenetic transmission. According to this line of reasoning, Jennifer had inherited a tendency for very sticky object relations and while we could easily imagine situations where such a tendency would be highly adaptive and heritable, this was not one of them. At this point, I thought (as I would have outside of this line of reasoning) to take the dilemma directly to the patient: I asked Jennifer how I could help her. She responded that I should just be there, listen, and support her. Based on this clinical moment and my hypothesizing, I changed my clinical stance with her to simply allowing her to be in an interpretation-free relationship with me. It is too soon to know if this stance will prove effective in this kind of therapeutic situation, but preliminary results are positive.

In the next chapter, we will take up the subject of the Self and its origins in a less clinical and more speculative way. I hope it will prove interesting.

Notes

1 I have mounted a detailed critique of hermeneutics in the past (Leffert, 2010, 2013; 2016, especially Chapter 1) and cannot, within the constraints of space, reprise it here.
2 We have even found that the lowly octopus demonstrates evidence (Godfrey-Smith, 2016), of consciousness, social bonding, and a sense of humor. We are certainly not in Kansas anymore.
3 We will see how this has been shown to be true of humans as well, later in this chapter.
4 Like many of the landmarks found in Paleoneurology this claim has been questioned. Contrary to Carroll (2005), Falk (2011) describes the current view that hominin brain size began to enlarge from the $500\,cm^3$ range about 3 mya and did so steadily over the course of hominin evolution.
5 It is still very early in the game, but there does appear to be a role for mitochondrial DNA (Curley & Mashoodh, 2010) in the Epigenetic Process.
6 This can only occur on the nucleotide base cytosine, the "C" in the genetic code, but only if it's a C that is adjacent to a base G, short for guanine.
7 There is an exception to this (there is always an exception). It is the hippocampus, which functions in memory storage and organization: It adds or loses neurons throughout our lives in the face of experience.
8 Recent studies (Bourzac, 2016) have shown that stem cell transplants in areas of the brain damaged by stroke can produce new neurons that return functionality.
9 Indeed, in early to mid-adolescence roughly 20–30% of brain cells appear to be found redundant and disappear (Abitz et al., 2007; Gogtay et al., 2004) through a process aptly termed *pruning*. We will return to this observation later in the chapter.

86 Theories of development and Evo-Devo

10 Stable increases in the number of synapses, synaptic facilitation of inhibition, and changes in a neuron's dendrites and axons produce information storage.
11 Strictly speaking, then, Epigenesis includes a biological and a behavioral component. Usage among researchers and clinicians, however, takes the term *Epigenetics* to refer to the biological component and *Development* to refer to a psychobiological process, exclusive of any genetic components. Although it is inaccurate, it seems best for our purposes to come down on the side of usage.
12 Roy, Petitot, Pachoud, and Varella (1999) have brought together a series of essays whose goal is naturalizing Phenomenology. Their particular aim is to integrate cognitive psychology with Husserlian Phenomenology (1937/1970, 1913/1983), a "return to the things themselves." There is no reason not to apply the term to Heidegger's Phenomenology (1927/2010, 1998/2015) as well, and to include under it all of the processes that pertain to the functioning and adaptation of the Bio-Psycho-Social Self.
13 *Possibly* as a result of Spitz's work (they could just as easily have intuitively known [folk knowledge] to do this), in 1968 as a medical student on the infant ward of Bellevue Hospital, I observed how infants were routinely held, cuddled, and fed several times a day by nursing attendants.
14 In the 19th century, the treatment and its boundaries were so firmly medicalized that examining or manipulating a patient's body was seen as a normative aspect of the physician's social job description as it is not seen as being a part of the 21st century psychoanalytic clinician's.
15 As I wrote, perhaps heretically (Leffert, 2017), I see gratifying a patient as potentially therapeutic, so long as it is non-sexual and determined by therapeutic considerations of tact, timing, and extent.
16 Since moving to Santa Barbara from a Midwestern city, I continued to work with some patients there via telephone (Leffert, 2003). I would make a trip back there first twice a year and then annually, seeing them 2 or 3 times over a 3-day period. I *always* shook hands with them, making it a two-handed handshake when I first saw them and at the end of the last session. One or two patients, in the grip of anger and pain over my move, had no interest in handshakes, and I knew not to offer one. The other patients, however, always reached out eagerly for my hands.
17 Whether such feelings are a species of transference or are simply feelings is perhaps a more open question than we have tended to treat it as being.
18 I stress *physical* here because, as I hope I have been making the case for it, non-sexual non-violating touch is very much a part of the extended view of Therapeutic Discourse I described in Chapter 1.
19 Briefly, Primary-Process primordial affects (Panksepp & Biven, 2012) involve anoetic, unconscious, subcortical brain hardware at a midbrain level. Secondary-Process emotions are noetically conscious, developed through conditioning and cognitive priming, and form behavioral and emotional habits, whereas Tertiary-Process emotions are neocortically based, reflective, and autonoetic; they are complex higher order functions that are essential to being human.
20 Humans find tickling pleasant up to a level of intensity after which it becomes highly dysphoric.
21 Clinical experience suggests that some humans have similar problems.
22 Recall that synthesis of mRNA leads to protein synthesis.
23 For our purposes here, ontology refers to the sum of development from egg fertilization to adulthood and phylogeny to selective evolutionary advantage.
24 Parents purchasing an apprenticeship for a son in past centuries would be an example of this, as paying college or vocational tuition would today. Child and adolescent psychotherapy is also a manifestation of surplus resource allocation.
25 I use the term *immature* to signify preadult, a range from in utero to adulthood.
26 I make this distinction for purposes of clarity; relationships are, strictly speaking, part of the environment: Heidegger (1927/2010) handles the distinction by identifying two separate realms of Being, the *Mitwelt* (relationships) and the *Umwelt* (the surrounding

physical world). Psychoanalysis has been all about relationships, but, more recently, as the importance of trauma has been understood, the environment has taken its place among our therapeutic concerns.
27 The population of Vietnam veterans and their children with all its variations cry out for epigenetic study.
28 In its simplest form, this work, done on the giant neurons of the sea slug *Aplysia*, offers a radical reductionist theory of learning and memory.
29 To make things more complex, the inherited transgenerational effects *will* lead to additional psychological effects that are dealt with in the usual manner.

References

Abitz, M., Damgaard, R., Jones, E. G., Laursen, H., Graem, N., & Pakkenberg, B. (2007). Excess of neurons in the human newborn mediodorsal thalamus compared with that of the adult. *Cerebral Cortex, 17*, 11, 2573–2578.

Bachelard, G. (1994). *The poetics of space* (M. Jolas, Trans.). Boston: Beacon Press. (Original work published in 1958.)

Baker, M. (2017). Lines of communication: A previously unappreciated form of cell-to-cell communication may help to speed cancers and infections. *Nature, 549*, 322–324.

Bannister, A., & Kouzarides, T. (2001). Regulation of chromatin by histone modifications. *Cell Research, 21*, 381–395.

Boss, M. (1963). *Psychoanalysis and Daseinanalysis*. New York: Basic Books.

Boulton, M. J. (1996). A comparison of 8- and 11-year-old girls' and boys' participation in specific types of rough-and-tumble play and aggressive fighting: Implications for functional hypotheses. *Aggressive Behavior, 22*, 271–287.

Bourzac, K. (2016). Neuroscience: New nerves for old. *Nature, 540*, S52–S54.

Bowlby, J. (1958). The nature of the child's tie to his mother. *International Journal of Psychoanalysis, 39*, 350–373.

Bowlby, J. (1984). The making and breaking of affectional bonds *The making and breaking of affectional bonds* (pp. 126–160). London: Tavistock. (Original work published in 1979[1977].)

Breckenridge, K. (2000). Physical touch in psychoanalysis: A closet phenomenon? *Psychoanalytic Inquiry, 20*, 2–20.

Breuer, J., & Freud, S. (1955). Studies in hysteria. In J. Strachey (Ed.), *Standard edition* (Vol. II, pp. 1–319). London: Hogarth Press. (Original work published in 1893–1895.)

Burgdorf, J., Kroes, R. A., Beinfeld, M. C., Panksepp, J., & Modskal, J. R. (2010). Uncovering the molecular basis of positive affect using rough-and-tumble play in rats: A role for insulin-like growth factor I. *Neuroscience, 168*, 769–777.

Burgdorf, J., & Panksepp, J. (2001). Tickling induces reward in adolescent rats. *Physiology and Behavior, 72*, 167–173.

Burghardt, G. M. (2005). *The genesis of animal play: Testing the limits*. Cambridge: MIT Press.

Carey, N. (2012). *The epigenetics revolution: How modern biology is rewriting our understanding of genetics, disease, and inheritance*. New York: Columbia University Press.

Carroll, S. B. (2005). *Endless forms most beautiful: The new science of Evo-Devo*. New York: W. W. Norton & Co.

Casement, P. J. (1982). Some pressures on the analysit for physical contact during the reliving of an early trauma. *International Review of Psychoanalysis, 9*, 279–286.

Casement, P. J. (2000). The issue of touch: A retrospective overview. *Psychoanalytic Inquiry, 20*, 160–184.

Celenza, A. (2006). Sexual boundary violations in the office: When is a couch just a couch? *Psychoanalytic Dialogues, 16*, 113–128.

Celenza, A., & Gabbard, G. O. (2003). Analysts who commit sexual boundary violations: A lost cause? *Journal of the American Psychoanalytic Association, 51*, 617–636.

Champagne, F. A. (2008). Epigenetic mechanisms and the transgenerational effects of maternal care. *Frontiers of Neuroendocrinology, 29*, 386–397.

Champagne, F. A. (2010). Epigenetic influence of social experiences across the lifespan. *Developmental Psychobiology, 52*, 299–311.

Champagne, F. A. (2013). Effects of stress across generations: Why sex matters. *Biological Psychiatry, 73*, 2–4.

Churchland, P. M. (2002). *Brain-wise studies in neurophilosophy.* Cambridge: MIT Press.

Cohen, M. C. (1996). Play and game as metaphor for technique. *Journal of the American Academy of Psychoanalysis and Dynamic Psychiatry, 24*, 61–73.

Curley, J. P., & Mashoodh, R. (2010). Parent-of-origin and trans-generational germline influences on behavioral development: The interacting roles of mothers, fathers. and grandparents. *Developmental Psychobiology, 52*, 312–330.

Davidson, R. J. (1998). Anterior electrophysiological asymetries, emotion, and depression: Conceptual and methodological conundrums. *Psychophysiology, 35*, 607–614.

Davidson, R. J., Kabat-Zinn, J., Schumacher, J., Rosenkranz, M., Muller, D., Santorelli, S. F., ... Sheridan, J. F. (2003). Alterations in brain and immune function produced by mindfulness meditation. *Psychosomatic Medicine, 65*, 564–570.

Davies, J. M. (1994). Love in the afternoon: A relational reconsideration of desire and dread in the countertransference. *Psychoanalytic Dialogues, 4*, 153–170.

Davies, J. M. (1996). Dissociation, repression, and reality testing in the countertransference: The controversy over memory and false memory in the psychoanalytic treatment of adult survivors of childhood sexual abuse. *Psychoanalytic Dialogues, 6*, 189–218.

Doidge, N. (2007). *The brain that changes itself.* New York: Viking.

Doidge, N. (2015). *Remarkable discoveries and recoveries from the frontiers of neuroplasticity.* New York: Viking.

Ehrenberg, D. B. (1990). Playfulness in the psychoanalytic relationship. *Contemporary Psychoanalysis, 26*, 74–94.

Erikson, E. (1963). *Childhood and society* (2nd ed.). New York: W. W. Norton & Co. (Original work published in 1950.)

Falk, D. (2011). *The fossil chronicles: How two controversial discoveries changed our view of human evolution.* Berkeley: University of California Press.

Field, T. (2006). *Massage therapy research.* Edinburgh: Churchill Livingstone.

Field, T. (2014). *Touch* (2nd ed.). Cambridge: MIT Press.

Field, T., Deeds, O., Diego, M., Hernandez-Reif, M., Gauler, A., Sullivan, S., ... Nearing, G. (2009). Benefits of combining massage therapy with group interpersonal psychotherapy in prenatally depressed women. *Journal of Bodywork & Movement Therapies, 13*, 297–303.

Field, T., Diego, M., & Hernandez-Reif, M. (2010). Preterm infant massage therapy research: A review. *Infant Behavioral Development, 33*, 115–124.

Field, T., Grizzle, N., Scafidi, F., Abrams, S., Richardson, S., Kuhn, C. M., Schanberg, S. (1996). Massage therapy for infants of depressed mothers. *Infant Behavior and Development, 19*, 107–112.

Field, T. M., Schanberg, S. M., Scafidi, F., Bauer, C. R., Vega-Lahr, N., Garcia, R., Kuhn, C. M. (1986). Tactile/kinesthetic stimulation effects on preterm neonates. *Pediatrics, 77*, 654–658.

Fosshage, J. L. (2000). The meanings of touch in psychoanalysis: A time for reassessment. *Psychoanalytic Inquiry, 20*, 21–43.

Fraga, M. F., Ballestar, E., Paz, M. F., Ropero, S., Setian, F., Ballestar, M. L., ... Esteller, M. (2005). Epigenetic differences arise during the lifetime of monozygotic twins. *Proceedings of the National Academy of Science, 102*, 10604–10960.

Friedman, L. (2005). Is there a special psychoanalytic love? *Journal of the American Psychoanalytic Association, 53*, 349–375.

Gabbard, G. O. (1995). The early history of boundary violations. *Journal of the American Psychoanalytic Association, 43*, 1115–1136.

Gallese, V., Fadiga, L., Fogassi, L., & Rizzolatti, G. (1996). Action recognition in the premotor cortex. *Brain, 119*, 593–609.

Godfrey-Smith, P. (2016). *Other minds: The octopus, the sea, and the deep origins of consciousness*. New York: Farrar, Strauss and Giroux.

Gogtay, N., Giedd, J. N., Lusk, L., Hayashi, K. M., Greenstein, D., Vaituzis, C., ... Thompson, P. M. (2004). Dynamic mapping of human cortical development during childhood through early adulthood. *Proceedings of the National Academy of Science, 101*, 8174–8179.

Goldberg, A. D., Allis, C. D., & Bernstein, E. (2007). Epigenetics: A landscape takes shape. *Cell, 128*, 635–638.

Gould, S. J. (1989). *Wonderful life: The Burgess Shale and the nature of history*. New York: W. W. Norton & Co.

Greenson, R. R. (1967). *The technique and practice of psychoanalysis*. New York: International Universities Press.

Groos, K. (1898). *The play of animals*. New York: Appleton.

Groos, K. (1901). *The play of man*. New York: Heinemann.

Harlow, H. (1958). The nature of love. *American Psychologist, 13*, 673–685.

Hartmann, H. (1958). *Ego psychology and the problem of adaptation* (D. Rapaport, Trans.). New York: International Universities Press (Original work published in 1939.)

Heidegger, M. (2010). *Being and time* (J. Stambaugh & D. J. Schmidt, Trans.). Albany: State University of New York. (Original work published in 1927.)

Heidegger, M. (2015). *The history of Beyng* (W. McNeill & J. Powell, Trans.). Bloomington: Indiana University Press. (Original work published in 1998.)

Heijmans, B. T., Tobi, E. W., Stein, A. D., Putter, H., Blauw, G. J., Susser, E. S., ... Lumey, L. H. (2008). Persistent epigenetic differences associated with prenatal exposure to famine in humans. *Proceedings of the National Academy of Science, 105*, 17046–17049.

Hillerer, K. M., Jacobs, V. R., Fischer, T., & Aigner, L. (2014). The maternal brain: An organ with peripartal plasticity. *Neural Plasticity*. doi:10.1155/2014.

Hoekzema, E., Barba-Müller, E., Pozzobon, C., Picado, M., Lucco, F., Garcia-Garcia, D., ... Vilarroya, O. (2017). Pregnancy leads to long-lasting changes in human brain structure. *Nature Neuroscience, 20*, 287–296. doi:10.1038/nn.4458.

Hofer, M. A. (1990). Early simbiotic processes: Hard evidence from a soft place. In R. S. Glick & B. S. (Eds.), *The role of affect in motivation, development and adaptation, vol I: Pleasure beyond the pleasure principle*. New Haven: Yale University Press.

Hofer, M. A. (2014). The emerging synthesis of development and evolution: A new biology for psychoanalysis. *Neuropsychoanalysis, 16*, 3–22.

Holder, A. (2000). To touch or not to touch: That is the question. *Psychoanalytic Inquiry, 20*, 44–64.

Horton, J. A., Clance, P. R., Sterk-Elifson, C., & Emshoff, J. (1995). Touch in psychotherapy: A survey of patients' experiences. *Psychotherapy, 32*, 443–457.

Husserl, E. (1970). *The crisis of European sciences and transcendental phenomenology* (D. Cairns, Trans.). Evanston: Northwestern University Press. (Original work published in 1937.)

Husserl, E. (1983). *Ideas pertaining to a pure phenomenology and to a phenomenological philosophy: Book one: General introduction to a pure phenomenology* (F. Kersten, Trans.). New York: Springer (Original work published in 1913.)

Inaba, M., Buszczak, M., & Yamashita, Y. M. (2015). Nanotubes mediate niche-stem cell signalling in the *Drosophila* testis. *Nature, 523*, 329–232.

Jablonka, E., & Lamb, M. J. (2014). *Evolution in four dimensions: Genetic, epigenetic, behavioral, and symbolic variation in the history of life* (rev. ed.). Cambridge: MIT Press.

Jaenisch, R., & Bird, A. (2003). Epigenetic regulation of gene expression: How the genome integrates intrinsic and environmental signals. *Nature Genetics Supplement, 33*, 245–254.

Jea, J. J. V., Piaget, J., & Gruber, H. E. (1982). *The essential Piaget: An interpretive reference and guide*. New York: Basic Books.

Jenuwein, T., & Allis, C. D. (2001). Translating the histone code. *Science, 293*, 1074–1080.

Kaati, G., Bygren, L. O., & Edvinsson, S. (2002). Cardiovascular and diabetes mortality determined by nutrition during parents' and grandparents' slow growth period. *European Journal of Human Genetics, 10*, 682–688.

Kaati, G., Bygren, L. O., Pembrey, M. E., & Sjöstrom, M. (2007). Transgenerational response to nutrition, early life circumstances and longevity. *European Journal of Human Genetics, 15*, 784–790.

Kandel, E. R. (2001). The molecular biology of memory storage: A dialogue between genes and synapses. *Science, 294*, 1030–1038.

Kandel, E. R., & Tauc, L. (1965). Mechanism of heterosynaptic facilitation in the giant cell of the abdominal ganglion of *Aplysia depilans*. *Journal of Physiology (London), 181*, 28–47.

Lamarck, J. B. (2012). *Zoological philosophy: An exposition with regard to the natural history of animals*. London: Forgotten Books. (Original work published in 1809.)

Lancaster, J. B., & Lancaster, C. S. (1987). The watershed: Change in parental-investment and family-formation strategies in the course of human evolution. In J. B. Lancaster, J. Altman, A. S. Rossi, & L. R. Sherrod (Eds.), *Parenting across the lifespan: Biosocial dimensions* (pp. 187–205). New York: Aldine.

Landers, M. S., & Sullivan, R. M. (2012). The development and neurobiology of infant attachment and fear. *Developmental Neuroscience, 34*, 101–114.

Latour, B. (1993). *We have never been modern* (C. Porter, Trans.). Cambridge: Harvard University Press. (Original work published in 1991.)

Latour, B., & Woolgar, S. (1986). *Laboratory life the construction of scientific facts*. Princeton: Princeton University Press.

Lazar, S. W., Kerr, C. E., Wasserman, R. H., Gray, J. R., Greve, D. N., Treadway, M. T., … Fischl, B. (2005). Meditation experience is associated with increased cortical thickness. *Neuro-Report, 16*, 1893–1897.

Lear, J. (1998). *Love and its place in nature*. New Haven: Yale University Press. (Original work published in 1990.)

Leffert, M. (2003). Analysis and psychotherapy by telephone: Twenty years of clinical experience. *Journal of the American Psychoanalytic Association, 51*, 101–130.

Leffert, M. (2010). *Contemporary psychoanalytic foundations*. London: Routledge.

Leffert, M. (2013). *The therapeutic situation in the 21st century*. New York: Routledge.

Leffert, M. (2016). *Phenomenology, uncertainty, and care in the therapeutic encounter*. New York: Routledge.

Leffert, M. (2017). *Positive psychoanalysis: Aesthetics, desire, and subjective well-being*. New York: Routledge.

Little, M. I. (1985). Winnicott working in areas where psychotic anxieties predominate: A personal record. *Free Associations, 1,* 9–42.

Loewald, H. W. (1988). *Sublimation: Inquiries into theoretical psychoanalysis.* New Haven: Yale University Press.

Lucas, R. E. (2008). Personality and subjective well-being. In M. Eid & R. J. Larsen (Eds.), *The science of subjective well-being* (pp. 171–194). New York: Guilford Press.

Lucas, R. E., & Diener, E. (2009). Personality and subjective well-being. In E. Diener (Ed.), *The science of well-being: The collected works of Ed Diener* (pp. 75–102). New York: Springer. (Original work published in 2008.)

Maguire, E. A., Woollett, K., & Spiers, H. J. (2006). London taxi drivers and bus drivers: A structural MRI and neuropsychological analysis. *Hippocampus, 16,* 1091–1101.

McLaughlin, J. T. (2000). The problem and place of physical contact in analytic work: Some reflections on handholding in the analytic situation. *Psychoanalytic Inquiry, 20,* 65–81.

Meares, R. (1992). Transference and the play space—Towards a new basic metaphor. *Contemporary Psychoanalysis, 28,* 32–49.

Nacht, S. (1962a). The curative factors in psycho-analysis. *The International Journal of Psychoanalysis, 43,* 206–211.

Nacht, S. (1962b). The curative factors in psycho-analysis—Contributions to discussion. *The International Journal of Psychoanalysis, 43,* 233.

Natterson, J. M. (2003). Love in psychotherapy. *Psychoanalytic Psychology, 20,* 509–521.

Novick, J., & Novick, K. K. (2000). Love in the therapeutic alliance. *Journal of the American Psychoanalytic Association, 48,* 189–218.

Painter, R. C., Osmund, C., Gluckman, P., Hanson, M., Phillips, D. I. W., & Roseboom, T. J. (2008). Transgenerational effects of prenatal exposure to the Dutch famine on neonatal adiposity and health in later life. *BJOG: An International Journal of Obstetrics and Gynecology, 115,* 1243–1249.

Panksepp, J., & Biven, L. (2012). *The archaeology of mind: Neuroevolutionary origins of human emotions.* New York: W. W. Norton & Co.

Pellegrini, A. D., Dupuis, D., & Smith, P. K. (2007). Play in evolution and development. *Developmental Review, 27,* 261–276.

Pellis, S., & Pellis, V. (2009). *The playful brain: Venturing to the limits of neuroscience.* Oxford: Oneworld Oxford.

Pizer, B. (2000). Negotiating analytic holding: Discussion of Patrick Casement's learning from the patient. *Psychoanalytic Inquiry, 20,* 82–107.

Roy, J.-M., Petitot, J., Pachoud, B., & Varela, F. J. (1999). An introduction to naturalizing phenomenology. In J. Petitot, F. J. Varela, B. Pachoud, & J.-M. Roy (Eds.), *Naturalizing phenomenology: Issues in contemporary phenomenology and cognitive science* (pp. 1–80). Stanford: Stanford University Press.

Ruderman, E. G. (2000). Intimate communications: The values and boundaries of touch in the psychoanalytic setting. *Psychoanalytic Inquiry, 20,* 108–123.

Saavedra-Rodriguez, L., & Feig, L. A. (2013). Chronic social instability induces anxiety and defective social interactions accross generations. *Biological Psychiatry, 73,* 44–53.

Sachs, J. (1996). Psychoanalysis and the elements of play. *American Journal of Psychoanalysis, 51,* 39–53.

Schlessinger, H. J., & Appelbaum, A. H. (2000). When words are not enough. *Psychoanalytic Inquiry, 20,* 124–143.

Schore, A. N. (1994). *Affect regulation and the origin of the self.* Hillside: Lawrence Earlbaum Associates.

Scott, E., & Panksepp, J. (2003). Rough-and-tumble play in human children. *Aggressive Behavior, 29,* 539–551.

Segal, H. (1962). The curative factors in psycho-analysis—Contributions to discussion. *The International Journal of Psychoanalysis, 43*, 232–233.

Shane, M., Shane, E., & Gales, M. (2000). Psychoanalysis unbound: A contextual consideration of boundaries from a developmental systems self psychology perspective. *Psychoanalytic Inquiry, 20*, 144–159.

Sisk, C. L., & Foster, D. L. (2004). The neural basis of puberty and adolescence. *Nature Neuroscience, 7*, 1040–1047.

Skolnick, N. J., Ackerman, S. H., Hofer, M. A., & Weiner, H. (1980). Vertical transmission of acquired ulcer susceptibility in the rat. *Science, 208*, 1161–1163.

Slade, A., & Wolf, D. P. (1994). *Children at play: Clinical and developmental approaches to meaning and representation.* New York: Oxford University Press.

Spitz, R. (1965). *The first year of life.* New York: International Universities Press.

Stein, Z., Susser, M., Saenger, G., & Marolla, F. (1975). *Famine and human development: The Dutch hunger winter of 1944/45.* New York: Oxford University Press.

Sullivan, R. M., & Moriceau, S. (2005). Neurobiology of infant attachment. *Developmental Psychobiology, 47*, 230–242.

Tessman, L. H. (2003). *The analyst's analyst within.* Hillsdale: The Analytic Press.

Toronto, E. L. K. (2001). The human touch: An exploration of the role and meaning of physical touch in psychoanalysis. *Psychoanalytic Psychology, 18*, 37–54.

Trevarthen, C. (2009). The function of emotion in infancy: The regulation and communication of rythm, sympathy and meaning in human development. In D. Fosha, D. J. Siegal, & M. Solomon (Eds.), *The healing power of emotion: Affective neuroscience, development and clinical practice* (pp. 55–85). New York: W. W. Norton & Co.

Tversky, A., & Kahneman, D. (1982). Judgment under uncertainty: Heuristics and biases. In D. Kahneman, P. Slovic, & A. Tversky (Eds.), *Judgment under uncertainty: Heuristics and biases* (pp. 3–20). Cambridge: Cambridge University Press. (Original work published in 1974.)

Urry, H. L., Nitschke, J. B., Dolski, I., Jackson, D. C., Dalton, K. M., Mueller, C. J., ... Davidson, R. J. (2004). Making a life worth living: Neural correlates of well-being. *Psychological Science, 15*, 367–372.

Whitelaw, N. C., Chong, S., Morgan, D. K., Nestor, C., Bruxner, T. J., Ashe, A., ... Whitelaw, E. (2010). Reduced levels of two modifiers of epigenetic gene silencing, Dnmt3a and Trim28, cause increased phenotypic noise. *Genome Biology, 11*, R111.

Whitelaw, N. C., & Whitelaw, E. (2006). How lifetimes shape epigenotype within and across generations. *Human Molecular Genetics, 15*, R131–R137.

Winnicott, D. W. (1968). Playing: Its theoretical status in the clinical situation. *International Journal of Psychoanalysis, 49*, 591–599.

Winnicott, D. W. (1972). *Holding and interpretation: Fragment of analysis.* New York: Grove Press.

Youngson, N. A., & Whitelaw, E. (2008). Transgenerational epigenetic effects. *Annual Review of Genomics and Human Genetics, 9*, 233–257.

4
THE ORIGINS OF THE SELF AND ITS CONSCIOUSNESS

The Evo-Devo of human being[1]

Introduction

We are accustomed to treat the idea of the *origins* of the self in a number of ways. We have Jacobson (1964) summarizing the classical position in terms of models based on the flow of "psychic energy" and psychosexual development, Mahler's (Mahler, Pine, & Bergman, 1975) self of separation-individuation, and Bowlby's (1969, 1973) self of attachment. We are somewhat less accustomed to Schore's (Schore, A. N., 2003a, 2003b; Schore, J. R., & Schore, A. N., 2007) neurodevelopmental self or Panksepp's (Panksepp & Biven, 2012) evolutionary self of primary, secondary and tertiary affects, and we are not at all accustomed to the Epigenesis and the Evo-Devo *of* the Self. Beyond discussing some of these newer ontologies of the Self, I want to go on, somewhat speculatively, to discuss its historical origins, going back hundreds of thousands of years and, perhaps, even further.

Another way of thinking about all this is that we are talking about an Evo-Devo, an Archaeology of the Self (keep the historical and individual meanings of the latter in mind). A more user-friendly, folk psychological way of addressing these issues is to ask the simple-seeming question: Who are we and how did we get to be this way? I take the phenomenological position (that I will return to in the next chapter) that any inquiry into the nature and origins of the Self is an inquiry into Human Being and that human beings (*H. sapiens sapiens*) are, by our nature, *Self*-reflective and linguistically competent.

There are two important subtopics here that we need to consider: an Archaeology of Speech and Language and an Archaeology of Consciousness (read Evo-Devo for both). There are some caveats here. There is a vast literature on speech and language that I cannot meaningfully add to: I can only cherry-pick a few references to discuss. There are, however, some interdisciplinary points, specifically involving the Evo-Devo of language that semioticians and linguistic scholars have not yet picked up on that I want to consider. Language, both its acquisition and deployment, is an essential part of what makes us human.[2] The ability to *name* things is an important piece of this. It is a major way (there are other *evolutionarily ancient*, nonverbal ways) we connect with our social world (including the therapeutic situation) and communicate with it and ourselves. It *shapes* the self. I feel on firmer ground concerning the Archaeology of Consciousness, which I have written about in the past (Leffert, 2010). It constitutes an extension into Archaeology of what we talked about in Chapter 2.

This chapter will not offer very much about what you might or might not say to a patient or why you would choose to say it. It is not about Therapeutic Discourse. I am aiming for a speculative, foundational approach concerning what it is and has been like, as hominins,[3] to dwell in our social and physical world. In the language of newspaper writing, it is for the purpose of "deep background." It is about coming to being human, or Human Being, or Dasein. And since we and our patients dwell in the same world, it is hard to see how, learning more about these circumstances could not facilitate what we *do* do in the Therapeutic Situation.

If we think of the birth of the Self we are usually thinking of when and where our awareness of *our* Selves first appears. But is this accurate? Does a newborn who, most likely, cannot be said to be aware of herself constitute a Self, and, if we think not, what on earth is she, then? And if she does constitute a Self, at what point in her ontology can she be said to do so? The argument that she constitutes a Self even before birth is based on an assessment of a Self, made *by an observer*, outside of the Self, where self-awareness, a *property* of the Self, constitutes a mental assessment made *by* the Self *of* herself. Is such an assessment valid? We have, almost accidentally, stumbled into the domain of neurophilosophy, and we will have to consider this issue of Self and Self-awareness at greater length.

The field of study that looks at the Origins of the *Hominin* Self is called Paleoanthropology and the discipline (not yet named) that takes up the Evo-Devo of the brain in particular is Paleoneurology. If we want to address the Evo-Devo and the genetics of the Self and its Origins we will need a number of devices. First, we will need our eyes to look at how an infant *H. sapiens sapiens* develops. Then, we will need two temporal telescopes: one that magnifies our view of events taking place over the last tens of thousands of years and a more powerful one that brings millions of years of Evo-Devo into focus. We will start with the latter. This is a chapter about the birth of a new kind of Bio-Psycho-Social Self and its appearance on the stage of Evo-Devo. It is a Self that is capable of *reflecting* on itself and the world in which she lives. She is called, unsurprisingly, the Autonoetic (self-knowing) Self.

So how *did* we get to be us?

It's a pretty exciting story. First, we need a lesson in hominin genetics. Our direct ancestor, some unknown *Australopithecus* species, appeared in Africa around 4–5 million years ago (mya),[4] splitting off from the Chimpanzees (genus *Pan*). There is debate about the place of a particular *Australopithecus* species, *A. africanus*, on our family tree. It is thought by some (Reardon, 2012) that they split off from the line that would become genus *Homo* 2.5–3 mya while others, Falk and colleagues (2000), believe that they are our direct ancestors. But I get ahead of myself. In 1924, in the northern Transvaal, Raymond Dart and colleagues discovered a skull fragment that was at first thought to be that of a baboon. What was so very unusual about this fossil was that it was found with an endocast of the inside of the skull that offered a model of the creature's brain (Falk, 2011). Examination of the endocast revealed to Dart that he was looking at the brain, not of a baboon, but of some hominin ancestor.[5] "Taung," as he came to be called, was a young hominin who walked the earth between 2.6 and 3 mya and died at age 3 or 4. Taung was thought to represent a new species that Dart christened *Australopithecus africanus*, taken from "austral," meaning southern, and "pithecus," meaning ape, that was found in Africa rather than Java, the sight of the discovery of other early hominin remains. (Although it soon became clear that Taung, while southern, was certainly not an ape, the name stuck.) Examination of the skull revealed most of the structure of the right cerebral hemisphere. It also divulged a number of other things. The position of Taung's *foramen magnum* (the hole in the base of the skull through which the spinal cord exits and enters) strongly suggested that he was bipedal, walking upright rather than using all four limbs as apes do when on the ground. One of the sutures of the skull was incompletely fused (Falk, Zollikofer, Morimoto, & Ponce de Leon, 2012), a feature inconsistent with those of the great apes that fuse shortly after birth and consistent with the developmentally delayed fusion of the skull's sutures and closure of its fontanels of the evolving genus *Homo* whose brains must continue to grow in early life.[6]

Around 3.4 mya, *Australopithecus* experienced the first of two genetic events that led to its evolution into the unusual primate *H. sapiens*. They involved the SRGAP2 gene[7] that drives the development of the neocortex. In a very rare sequence of events, this gene doubled[8] around 3.4 mya and then, about a million years later (2.5 mya), at roughly the point at which the *Australopithecus* and *Homo* lines diverged, this "daughter" gene, SRGAP2B doubled again, producing SRGAP2C[9] the "granddaughter" of the original SRGAP2 gene (Reardon, 2012). As Reardon puts it: "The stage was set. Around 2.5 million years ago, the erroneous duplication of a single gene changed the course of our brains' evolution forever" (p. 10).

Reardon's (2012) conclusions leave unanswered the overriding question: How and why did this particular gene come to double and redouble? We could stick with Darwin's argument of Natural Selection: Such things happen all the time, and natural selection determines which ones will be conserved (that is, selected for, and protected from evolutionary changes that diminish it). This is true in a sort of *general* way. However, if we believe anything we said about Evo-Devo and Epigenetics in the last chapter, then there has to be more to the Natural Selection story. The environment and *A. africanus'* interaction with it must have also been driving the process, intelligent Evo-Devo, if you will: *It's just that we don't yet know how that happens*. However, as we continue to unpack the data of the Dutch Hunger Winter and the Överkalix famines and pursue contemporary as well as archaeological genetics, we will figure it out.

If you find this only a pretty interesting, if complicated, story, what follows is more exciting. SRGAP2 has been highly conserved across mammalian evolution with duplications occurring *only in the human lineage* (Dennis et al., 2012). The appearance of the second doubling corresponded to a number of events in the brain and skull that led to us being who we are. The neurons of our ancestor's neocortex developed more complex, specialized shapes, increasing the number, length, and thickness of their dendritic spines and synapses. These changes enabled higher order, more complex brain function. At the same time that this was going on, infant skulls became more flexible and remained unfused for longer,[10] both of these changes allowing for the development of the larger brains (first doubling in size from 500 to 1000 cm^3 in the first year and, ultimately, reaching 1300 cm^3 in us) that included this advanced neural hardware. Increasing brain size, however, had produced something called the "obstetrical dilemma" (Falk, 2016): the fact that there was a limit to the size of a head that a hominin mother could deliver. Future brain evolution would, therefore, have to involve increases in complexity rather than volume.

Here's how all this worked. The SRGAP2 gene functions in mammals to produce a skull that fuses quickly around a small brain demonstrating less elaborate neuronal architecture. Polleux (Charrier et al., 2012) and Eichler (Dennis et al., 2012) found that the daughter and granddaughter replications of the gene, SRGAP2B and SRGAP2C, inhibit SRGAP2's function, thus leading to a period of increased neoteny. This slowing or delaying of development allowed time for the large brains to grow and for a prolonged period of immaturity allowing for education, in its most global sense, by the parents. Selective pressures caused by the obstetrical dilemma favored the delayed fusion of the Metopic suture (Falk et al., 2012) (also a result of this inhibition), high postnatal growth rates of the brain, and expansion, and reorganization of the frontal lobes of the neocortex. These complex changes in the development of the evolving hominin brain (the Evo-Devo of the brain) involved a conversation between fetal head size and maternal pelvis.

In putting all this together, Falk (2016) describes three trends in the Evo-Devo of, well, us that involve an interaction of the neurological and the behavioral. They occurred under an Evo-Devo umbrella of increasing brain size in which "the increase in both absolute and RBS [relative brain size] during hominin evolution resulted from selection for behaviors that required intelligence" (p. 2). Intelligence is highly conserved across trends in Evo-Devo. The trend to bipedal locomotion with all its skeletal and muscular components began somewhere between 4 and 6–7 mya, well before the first hominin spurt in brain size. Coincident with this first spurt in brain growth occurring about 3.4 mya, primitive stone tools, and animal bones showing cutmarks were found in proximity to *Australopithecus* fossils, *suggesting* a causal relationship between increasing brain size and intelligence.[11] As parts of this trend, the spine and pelvis changed their spatial orientation by 90° and feet became weight bearing rather than grasping appendages. It is possible that advantages in foraging on open ground (a result of climate change in southern Africa) led to the evolution of bipedal locomotion. This change in posture and locomotion also led to delays in development, Neoteny, as compared to ape infants. **This is the first Evo-Devo trend.**

Modern hominin babies conserve this trend in delayed development with their attainment of first-year milestones being far behind that of infant chimpanzees. Now, this is the point where Evo meets Devo. It takes us back to Burghardt's (2005) Surplus Resource Theory (SRT), which was applied to PLAY in the last chapter, but is relevant here as well. For all these *evolutionary* good things to occur, the parents have to be able to provide a *developmentally*, physically, and nutritionally safe space in which they can take place. Trevathan and Rosenberg (2016b) put this aptly in the title of their new edited book: *Costly and Cute: Helpless Infants and Human Evolution.*

As a result of the first trend, hominin infants have lost the ability to cling unsupported to their mothers' bodies at their discretion: "The responsibility for keeping nursing infants attached to caregivers, especially mothers, [thus] shifted from the infants to the caregivers themselves" (Falk, 2016, p. 12). Modern *sapiens sapiens* babies have conserved this failure. This marks an evolutionary reversal, as the ability to cling has been conserved by modern monkeys and apes. By this seemingly circuitous route, we come back to a central pathway in contemporary theories of human development. Because of this inability to cling, the baby must develop ways to signal her needs to her mother and, even if not signaled, the mother must fairly constantly monitor and query her infant about her needs. Since the needs and the monitoring are more complex than those of birds or non-hominin mammals, so must be the signaling and querying. In addition, mothers must also carry about their large (and growing ever-larger) helpless infants (DeSilva, 2016): They get help through the use of slings[12] and the help of others in managing this energetically and socially costly practice. Shared parental carrying tightens social bonds within groups and increases the need for communication between group members. The increasing caloric needs resulting from large brain size and group formation lead to the hunting and gathering of more nutritious foods and, eventually, to increasing caloric content made available through the use of tools (butchering, harvesting) and cooking. From an entirely different perspective, it is at this stage of human Evo-Devo that it might be said that an *ontological* milestone, the achievement of Heidegger's everydayness (*Alltäglichkeit*),[13] has been reached.

Modern babies do not like being set down and will make their displeasure known, often loudly. It seems doubtful that their hominin ancestors were any different, and means were invented (small soft objects, for example) in attempts to sooth. All of this led to the **second Evo-Devo trend** (Falk, 2016) in which infants sought comfort through the use of evolved signals. These signals involved different kinds of crying and babbling that became melodic. The effects of these cries on adults are immensely powerful. We easily distinguish cries indicating something is wrong, which prompts us to anxious, immediate action, from cries indicating the baby is unhappy, which we simply find unbearably irritating. A few weeks ago at the grocery store, I heard a baby chuckling happily behind me. My head automatically (or so it seemed) whipped around with a smile on its face as I made eye contact with the baby: I felt warm and happy.[14] As Trevathen and Rosenberg (2016a) describe the human infant: "They are helpless, dependent creatures who need our care, and they have evolved attractive characteristics and a range of captivating behaviors that are very effective at soliciting and obtaining attention" (p. 1). This signaling would have promoted reciprocal, give-and-take gesturing, vocalizations, and eye contact on the part of the parents. Signaling by both babies and parents became more complex, both as the babies matured and as signaling strategies were shared among social groups, evolving over time. This proto-linguistic communication evolved into conversations (Trevarthen, 1974, 2009) between contemporary infants and their mothers.[15]

As all this was taking place and the Australopiths were efficiently walking around the savannahs of southern Africa with extended lower limbs, pretty much as we do, brain size began to increase in the hominin fossil record. This was the **third Evo-Devo trend** (Falk, 2016) in which brain size increased markedly during the last trimester of pregnancy and the first year of life. This trend allowed our brains to reach sizes 3 to 4 times that of the Australopiths, modern monkeys, and apes.

Increasing hominin brain size over the past 1–2 million years in turn led to architectural reorganization of the brain and increasing cortical lateralization. If increased cytogenesis occurs in some particular parts of the brain whose growth is associated with particular adaptive behaviors, they take the rest of the brain along with it. This raises the fascinating evolutionary question: What might be going on cellularly in the hominin brain when all these good things are happening? Indeed, in a speculative paper, Buckner and Krienen (2013) address this very question. They speculate that the increased size (86 billion neurons) of the human brain led to increased computational capacity.

> What has captured our interest is a peculiar feature of brain scaling [in humans] that might prove critical. The feature concerns how brain scaling [increasing brain size] shifts the predominant circuit organization from one primarily linked to sensory-motor hierarchies to a noncanonical form vital to human thought.
>
> *(p. 650)*

Rapid cortical expansion produced vast areas of neurons untethered by the constraints of the earlier sensory-motor hierarchies of our ancestors. This new freedom allowed for the formation of distributed processing networks, which in turn make possible uniquely human information processing and reasoning.

The first year of life

As psychotherapists and developmental psychologists, we have been very interested in the first year of life. We have come at the first year from a number of different and at times interdisciplinary perspectives. Bowlby's (1958, 1969) work would seem to deserve pride of place here. He described an *attachment behavioral system*, which the young child first develops in order to maintain and secure his connection to his caregivers (an evolutionary response to his loss of the ability to grasp his mother) and the complementary development of a capacity to form internal working models (IWMs). Trevarthen (Bråten & Trevarthen, 2007; Trevarthen, 1974) described what he called stages of *primary and secondary intersubjectivity* as appearing in the first year (*tertiary intersubjectivity* appears in ages 3–6). "*Primary Intersubjective Dialogues* [involve] protoconversations and reciprocal sympathetic imitation … [leading] to more lively *jokes and games* rich in emotions of 'other awareness'" (Bråten & Trevarthen, 2007, p. 22). Secondary intersubjective attunement involves subject-subject-object interactions in which infant and mother jointly inspect objects, emotionally referenced in a process laden with trust.

Meanwhile, A. N. Schore (1994, 2009) was describing what is essentially direct communication between the right preorbital frontal cortexes of mother and infant (left brain communication must await its myelination and the development of protolanguage) through gaze and tactile stimulation. As *he* puts it: "During these bodily based affective communications the attuned mother synchronizes the spatiotemporal patterning of her exogenous sensory stimulation with the infant's spontaneous expressions of his or her endogenous organismic rhythms" (Schore, A. N., 2009, p. 117). Parsons and colleagues (Parsons, Stark, Young, Stein, & Kringelbach, 2013) reach similar conclusions and describe how the maternal orbitofrontal cortex rapidly responds to changing communication cues from her infant.

Finally, we've already (Chapter 3), if briefly, discussed Jaak Panksepp's (Panksepp & Biven, 2012; Panksepp & Watt, 2011) cross-mammalian studies in the development of primary, secondary, and tertiary affective states as they fit into the wider fields of development and affective neuroscience.

So we've talked about the evolutionary part of Evo-Devo, and we've talked about the psychology and the neuroscience of the first year, but we haven't considered one important developmental piece of Evo-Devo. At birth, a human infant's brain has a volume of 500 cm^3; by the end of the first year, it has doubled in size to 1000 cm^3. (This, developmentally, is the increasing computational power that Buckner and Krienen, 2013, spoke about evolutionarily.) This means that the infant brain is literally being built to order.[16] The growth process is interreferential: Interaction drives brain growth and the new brain drives different kinds of interaction with the mother.[17] Brain growth is entirely activity-dependent (Semendeferi & Hanson, 2016) with severe interpersonal and environmental abnormalities in an infant's experiences (widely defined to include those of the autonomic nervous system) leading to abnormal brain structure. This sets the bar pretty high, although not impossibly so, in trying to change this grown-to-order structure through adult psychotherapy or psychoanalysis. We place (sometimes unknowingly) heavy bets on neuroplasticity. Again, the developmental evidence is pressing. Through a process known as *pruning*, the developing brain loses half its synapses before puberty (Chechik, Meilijson, & Ruppin, 1999).[18] We believe the brain starts out with a larger than necessary or efficient number of synapses to offer maximum plasticity and then sheds the ones it no longer needs. It is a case of use them or lose them; if they're not being used, they make for inefficiency in a calorically expensive organ and are pruned away. The process of pruning dovetails with that of procedural learning (Tulving & Schacter, 1990): the development of "how to" circuits. Speculatively, a child locked in a pattern of psychological dysfunction (however we might choose to label it) sheds dendritic spines and synapses associated with normal, healthy psychological function that he is unable to use. Often, pruning is shaped by experiences of unbearable affect leading to deficits in regulation and choices involving emergency shutdowns and disassociations as opposed to open engagement. (This makes subsequent treatment harder). We seek in therapy to broaden the abilities for affective experience (Ogden, 2009), restore regulatory function, and enter into an exploration of emotional trauma. Psychotherapy, if entered into before adolescent pruning, could preserve these dendrites and synapses for use in these processes throughout life.[19]

The unfolding brain of childhood and adolescence satisfyingly follows the two overarching rules of Evo-Devo. Gogtay and associates (2004) used sequential MRIs to three-dimensionally map the developing brain from ages 4 through 21. These "movies" revealed, first, that higher-level growth and function of the cerebral cortexes emerged only *after* the lower-order somatosensory and visual cortical structures whose functions they integrate and regulate. Second, they showed that phylogenetically more ancient structures developed before newer ones. This happily brings us to a subject we have not yet engaged: the Self and the origins of mind.

Some notes on the history of the Self

As psychotherapists, developmental psychologists, and neuroscientists, we already know a great deal about the development of the Self and, as we come to understand its Genetics and Epigenetics as well, its "Evo." We have spent much time trying to describe it. I have argued at length that the Self is not some aspect of mind. It's mental representation, and the IWMs (Bowlby, 1969; Craik, 1943/1952) that constitute this representation is a very different matter entirely. They follow their own path of psychological development, and the neuroscience suggests that the brain's cortical midline structures and Mirror Neuron System (MNS) (Uddin, Iacoboni, Lange, & Keenan, 2007) have much to do with their formation and maintenance. A great deal of time has also been spent pondering the role of consciousness in selfness. It is complicated, as we have seen (Chapter 2 of this volume), by the different kinds of consciousness (Tulving, 1985/2003) known to exist: the anoetic, the noetic, and the autonoetic. The picture is still further complicated by the fact that only a relatively small percentage of thought and mental activity is conscious, the fact that consciousness of any particular thing is fleeting, and that much of what makes us us takes place outside of the domain of consciousness. One would thus expect that Tulving's categories apply to unconsciousness as well. I have also come to suspect, as I think many of us would if we thought about it, that consciousness is not the same in all of us, it has different qualities, and the amounts of time we spend in different states of consciousness vary dramatically. These observations complicate things for those insisting on self-reflective, autonoetic consciousness as being both a necessary and a sufficient condition of our humanity as well as something uniquely ours.

There is evidence pointing towards when *rudimentary* self-awareness appears in human development and of its presence in select species of animals (Gallup, 1968; Lewis, Brooks-Gunn, & Jaskir, 1985). It is called the mirror test, the mirror self-recognition test, or simply the mark test, and, besides us, only higher primates (presumably including our extinct hominin ancestors), some Cetaceans, the African Grey Parrot, and, interestingly, the Crow, are able to pass it. Here's what you do. You first familiarize an individual with a mirror. Then you mark his forehead with some pigment that lacks texture or odor. Then you put him back in front of the mirror. If, after looking at himself in the mirror, he touches or reacts to the spot on his head, he passes the mirror test. We know that human babies generally do this, or do it with increasing frequency, between 18 and 24 months (Lewis et al., 1985) and we know that they can never accomplish it before 15 months. It should not be surprising that myelination of the left cerebral cortex (LB) takes place during this period because the ability would seem to require some LB cognition.

The mirror test is a cognitive developmental milestone. It confers nothing on the individual, but rather serves as an indicator that cognitive developmental accomplishments have taken place.[20] The capacity to construct IWMs has appeared, and self-awareness and self-reflection (autonoetic consciousness) have developed. Full autonoetic consciousness has not yet developed; it appears in *H. sapiens sapiens* at around age 4 (Donald, 2001; Tulving, 2005). This is a *cognitive* development; it is largely independent of attachment. Insecurely attached infants do actually pass the mirror test earlier, perhaps as a result of increased vigilance.

The mirror test is also a phenomenological milestone signifying a change in the toddler's Being. (Phenomenologists and Existentialists have not much concerned themselves with such issues.) Prior to achieving it, toddlers dwell entirely in a state of everydayness, taking up or connecting with things that are "at hand." These include the mother, parts of his or her body, and nearby inanimate objects. Self-awareness and the presence of an internal working model of the Self that incorporates both separateness and togetherness takes the toddler into his first experiences of thrownness, of Existence in the moment. *The toddler knows he is a Self.*

We know a great deal about cognitive psychology and how Self and mind develop in humans, so let's take them for a spin in prehistory. There are different perspectives here. Mithen (1996/1998) dates his inquiry into the prehistory of mind, its *archaeology*, back to the Australopiths who walked the earth 3 mya and to the first of the *Homos* who appeared a million or so years later.

Renfrew (1994) defines cognitive archaeology as the study of ancient ways of thought through the study of ancient remains (studying modern ways of thought through examining the products of tasks offered to children of various ages would be a developmental analog of such studies). Bell (1994) has observed that the study of the prehistoric mind has moved to the center of archaeological interest.

Cognitive science and cognitive development have recently come to archaeology. "A cognitive archaeologist [or a cognitive paleoanthropologist] can study the objects and structures found at archaeological sites with an eye towards answering questions about the knowledge, purposes, practices and skills of the people [or hominins] who produced them" (Segal, 1994, p. 22). In particular, we can study the capacity for thought and feeling that went into the creation of a particular object. Contemporary studies of primates and primitive societies have been used to inform cognitive archaeology, which is fine so long as we remember that they bring strengths and weaknesses to the game.

If we are going to talk even briefly about the historical origins of mind, and if we want to talk about the *development* of mind, then the tale begins with *Homo habilis* around 2 mya in the Olduvai Gorge of Kenya (the most studied paleoanthropological site on Earth) and the so-called Olduvian technology they developed there. A number also of inseparable biological, evolutionary, and sociocultural trends came together at approximately this time and place; attempts at establishing primacy of any one are doomed to failure.

Our starting point is that, based on Olduvian concentrations of scarred broken animal bones, crude tools made of basalt and quartzite, and limited skeletal and cranial remains, *H. habilis* (a.k.a. *handy man*) was largely carnivorous, unlike his more vegetarian Australopith forbears. Also unlike his forbears, this early *Homo* also had, at 640 cm^3, a brain almost double the size of his forbears. There is a trove of information entailed in these intertwined observations. Brains are calorically expensive to run: This larger brain required more energy but offered more computing power. Its caloric requirements could probably not be satisfied by eating uncooked vegetables, probably dictating the dietary change. We really can't say which came first: handy man's new lifestyle requiring a larger brain to pull it off or his new brain requiring a new lifestyle to feed it. Although the archaeological record is expectedly sparse, we do have the collections of large animal bones, crushed and scarred by cutting tools, human teeth, and the teeth and claws of large predators. Assorted crude tools are also present. We also have piles (stockpiles?) of the raw materials, basalt and quartzite (flint, used 2 million years later for more precise toolmaking, was too delicate for handy man), strategically placed within a range of 10 km or so. We know that handy man lacked the technology to hunt and kill the herbivores that made up a significant part of his diet or to defend those kills (or himself) against large predators. (They were forced instead to dine on small animals and the abandoned kills of those same predators.) The rest of the story unfolds from these elements.

How do we know that *H. habilis* was that different from, say, modern chimpanzees that could walk on two legs? Chimps are famous for their ability to use tools and to carry them to perform specific tasks. Calories are at the heart of our story. Although scavenging for high caloric food required only simple tools, other tools had to first be made in order to make *them*.[21] A planned two-stage process signifying noetic and, if a narrative accompanied the plan, some rudimentary form of autonoetic consciousness was required. A cognitive element (Mithen, 1996/1998) involved the ability to maintain sophisticated, shifting territorial maps of the likely locations of kills to scavenge, the behavior and routines of dangerous local carnivores, and the locations of stashes of raw materials, water sources, and safe places to camp. Large-headed infants and their prolonged juvenile period much increased the number of calories needed by *H. habilis* to raise her young and required safe places for them to reside and be educated. In order to do all these things, she had to live in small groups and employ at least some degree of specialization. Lastly, although *H. habilis* lacked the cortical hardware for language, she must have developed some degree of vocal communication supplemented by silent hand signing.

There are also things we can *speculate* about. There must have been some kind of intergenerational education, passing on an understanding of World, the *Umwelt*. Childcare would have been a shared group activity, probably performed by women, as hunting would have been by men. There would have been some gender-specific role differentiation. Cannibalism of some sort, perhaps of the dead, may well have been present: It's not clear how the small groups could have passed up the calories. The making and breaking of affectional bonds would likely have been present in groups and between groups when they congregated.

Phenomenologically, handy man must have spent most of his time in the state of everydayness, taking up things at hand to manage a busy life. There was no time for fallen states; individuals who spent time in them could not long survive. Thrownness must also have been present; life and death moments in the hunt and dealing with predators come to mind.

Let's take all this for a test drive. I have a flint rock that sits on my desk. It's about 6" long, 4" wide, and maybe 3" thick. It is black-brown in color; it looks *old*. I pick it up. It's heavy (it weighs a pound) and my hand fits around the naturally cone-shaped end. This *thing* is a tool. Two flakes were struck off the other end by a hammer stone (another tool) to create a crude point to crush and chop; it is otherwise unfinished. Its simplicity suggests that it was probably made by the man (too heavy a tool for a woman to wield) who used it. The flakes would, similarly unfinished, have been used as cutting or scraping tools. Called a biconical chopper, it was found in Kent, England, in 2009. It is a product of what has been called the Clactonian industry that made tools here 400,000 years ago (ya). There is debate concerning who the toolmakers were: *Homo erectus* or the larger-brained *Homo heidelbergensis*; trying to make such distinctions from scattered 400,000-year-old remains is hard enough, but I would bet on the former. What impresses about the tool is its weight and its crudeness. Is this the best you could do? I ask, and then the limitations of the mind that made it strike me; this person is not at all like me. A final observation is that the struck off face has a kind of smooth softness, not the shiny result of its creation. It looks like *wear*. That would mean a very long period of use, perhaps by more than one generation of hunter-gatherers.

Let's fast forward to 350,000–50,000 ya. I pick up an elliptical flint tool that is around 4" × 2½" × ¾" and weighs 5½ oz. It is a hand ax and it comes from the Dordogne region of France, an area rich in prehistoric human habitation. Unlike the chopper, there is no doubt who made this tool: it was us, or an early archaic us. It is a lovely tool. It has an edge all around and two thumb depressions positioned for chopping or cutting and scraping. It is a delight to hold. It is also a practical tool. A small area of the original surface of the flint nodule is left alone; its removal was not necessary for the design of the tool and was not worth the caloric expenditure. Its elegance and symmetry suggest that it may have been the work of a specialist toolmaker. Along with a flint knife, it could fit comfortably into some kind of fanny pack made of animal hide and, unless needed, would leave its user with two free hands. Unlike the crusher, this kind of tool would require considerable schooling and expertise on the part of the toolmaker. The size of the group would determine whether such specialist toolmakers could be supported on a full-time or part-time basis. Cruder toolmaking would have remained the provenance of the individual, much as it is today.

What we have said about the hand ax says a lot about early *sapiens* (not Neanderthal) society (referred to as the Aurignacian period, *c.*40,000–30,000 ya after a prominent archaeological site in Aurignac, France). It was a society of specialists and task sharing, of art and musical instruments. To survive in ice age Europe, they had to live in larger groups (Mithen, 1994) and Dunbar's (1993) number of 150, the group size of individuals making up tribes in primitive societies of *H. sapiens sapiens* made its appearance. We know about Aurignacian economics. Task sharing involved exchanges of value that speaks to cognitive capacity. Recovering objects like shells in sites at considerable distances from where they could be found speaks to trade and ornamentation that was not found in earlier Homos.

Sapiens had and used a lot more brainpower than handy men to accomplish these social things. To do them—to make these tools, to share tasks, to trade, and wear adornments—a full array of cognitive processes including narrative/reflective, semantic, and procedural knowing, or, to use the older language, formal operational thought must have been present, albeit in less robust forms than we are capable of today. My purpose in this hopefully interesting and certainly brief digression is to demonstrate that the ways of Being that *sapiens sapiens* bring to the consulting room, both as patients and therapists, go back a much longer way that we might have expected. We know a great deal about the rest of the story that connects handy man to us, but we don't have the space here to fill in the dots.[22]

The origins of consciousness

We have already spoken at length about consciousness in Chapter 2, but it seemed appropriate to defer a discussion of its origins until the present chapter. Folk psychology would tell us and we would assume that, once our ancestors reached the *Homo* line, their consciousness was pretty much the same as ours. Like many such assumptions, it does not withstand inspection. A similar assumption about modern *sapiens sapiens* is equally uncertain. Although we all are very likely to possess the same broad categories of consciousness, I have come to believe, as I said in Chapter 2, that how much time we spend in each of them and the *quality* of our being Conscious varies a lot from person to person.[23,24] What I am proposing is that consciousness is uniquely personal and is not available for objective scrutiny. What we find ourselves having to deal with here is only the familiar concept of irreducible subjectivity. We have two questions to address: how consciousness evolved in Homos and how it develops in each of us. We're also curious about the relationship between the two: in other words, it's Evo-Devo.

The phylogeny of consciousness

The writing about the phylogeny of consciousness, now measured in thousands of papers and books, outpaces that on its ontogeny. Writing about and integrating this literature is a difficult task. There is a large body of it (e.g., Feinberg & Mallatt, 2016; Terrace & Metcalfe, 2005) arguing—successfully, I believe—that consciousness *in some forms* exists in mammals and probably all vertebrates; the question remaining is in just what forms. Tulving's (1985/2003) division of consciousness into anoetic, noetic, and autonoetic elements remains the gold standard of the classification of consciousness and memory in Human Beings. He particularly argues that "only human beings possess 'autonoetic' episodic memory and the ability to mentally time travel into the past and into the future and that in that sense they [humans] are unique" (Tulving, 2005, p. 4). (Although still controversial, it is now a safer argument to make than it was when he first made it in 1985.) What he does not get into and we wish that he did, was what exactly he means by Human Being: Is he referring only to *H. sapiens* (brain size 1300 cm^3), or does he include some of our *Homo* ancestors, and if so, which ones? Would he start with Handy Man, (brain size 600 cm^3), the first of our Homo ancestors? Or would it be *H. erectus*, who walked fully upright, whose brain reached a respectable volume of 1000 cm^3, and who made the crusher I have sitting on my desk? Or does he include those strange large-brained (1500 cm^3) creatures *H. Neanderthalenis*, who we supplanted? My guess is he means just us. Other authors, like those writing in the same volume (Terrace & Metcalfe, 2005) as Tulving, devote considerable time to this question. Arguably, it lacks an answer. Much of evolution is gradual. Rudimentary properties appear and then evolve (yes, Epigenetically) into more complex and sophisticated functions, reaching a tipping point, as complex systems do, at which something entirely new appears. If this something new is of great adaptive value, it is greatly conserved. If we think about noetic consciousness in this way, we have no problem parsing its evolution over the various classes of vertebrates (I've already mentioned how the octopus seems to confound even this restriction). Given this, we should similarly have no problem parsing the development of autonoetic consciousness over at least some species of genus *Homo*.

It is essential to recall that if we are unable to *know* what it is like for another person to think and feel, for our children to think and feel, we certainly can't *know* what it's like for other species to think and feel or for other species of men to think and feel. We do, however, have tools with which to approach this problem: scientific inference and empathic inquiry accompanied by a flexible Theory of Mind.

Let me address these points by sending up a trial balloon, a theory of the evolution of consciousness that I am launching for heuristic purposes. An argument

106 Origins of the Self and its consciousness

that I have dipped into over the years (Leffert, 2010, 2013) is whether mental[25] functions are modular or whether they arise as part of a general-purpose system or whether they can be either. I have taken the latter position, but have avoided the term *module* on the grounds that such a plug and play description is overly discreet and that we are rather dealing with *areas of specialization*, basins of attractors perhaps (Leffert, 2008), manifesting various degrees of discreteness. The recent work on the claustrum (Crick & Koch, 2005; Reardon, 2017) (a thin lay of cells residing on the undersurface of the cerebral cortex and known for its high degree of connectedness and interconnectedness to the entire brain) and Baars' (1993/2003) earlier work on what kind of cognitive organization consciousness would entail suggest a general-purpose system of consciousness. It would have to manifest enormous integrative properties connecting all the disparate areas of the brain and its extensions into the body. We comfortably accept the premise that anoetic and noetic consciousness are abilities of the hominin brain. My theory is that, as its size (and the complexity of the neuronal connections within it) increased over the course of evolution, a level of complexity was reached at which autonoetic consciousness, as we know it today, became possible. I would further posit that the appearance of autonoetic consciousness and spoken language are intimately related to each other.

There are two further points we need to mention about autonoetic consciousness: one we know and one we must wonder about. What we know is that the ability to predict the future and plan for it, doing so by weaving together our memories of past events and our semantic knowledge of World, conveys an enormous adaptive advantage, one that *could* have spelled out thriving for us and extinction for the Neanderthals if they lacked it. The other is a question: Does autonoetic consciousness *require* the presence of language (or is it vice versa) to develop? Language, spoken and written, also conveyed massive advantages on its practitioners. Finally, are the two points related? With all these caveats firmly in place, let's try to get a handle on the evolution of mind in the later stages of hominin phylogeny.

The subject begins to get interesting in the transition from the Middle to the Upper Paleolithic:

> Changes in the archaeological record that may reflect the first appearance of *fully modern cognition* [emphasis added] appear after c. 50,000 BP [before the present] with the start of the Upper Paleolithic. Most notably, we see the introduction of bone, antler and ivory technologies, the creation of personal ornaments and art, a greater degree of form imposed onto stone tools, a more rapid turnover of artifact types, greater degrees of hunting specialization and the colonization of arid regions.
>
> *(Mithen, 1994, p. 32)*

Mithen equates this cognitive transition with a shift from highly modular cognition to a much more open general-purpose intelligence,[26] which he posits is connected with the intelligence of modern humans. He also posits that this ability *to transfer knowledge from one context to another* is uniquely human, that is, a property of early *H. sapiens* (the wise men).

The relationship of these changes to questions concerning the relationship of Neanderthal Man to us, the wise guys, was less certain in 1994 than it has become since. A decade's additional research has made a big difference. We are all ambivalently interested in Neanderthals, our larger-brained (1500 cm³ vs. 1300 cm³)[27] cousins, with whom we co-existed in Europe from roughly 50,000 BP to 35,000 BP. Used as an adjective, the name roughly translates today as "dumb brutes," while their large brains (larger than ours) make us imagine special and mysterious mental powers that we lack. Then there is survivor guilt: that *they* disappeared (became extinct) and *we* didn't. Whether we exterminated them or simply survived as the fittest, easily claiming and consuming resources at Neanderthal's expense doesn't matter much in the context of the broad sweep of evolution. Emotionally, we identify our unique survival with the worst of us, not the best, and tap into wellsprings of survivor guilt that also accommodate guilt about modern genocides. Mellars (2005) casts the supplanting of Neanderthals as precipitous, a tipping point in a complex system. The new masters of Europe (us!) manifested some evidence of "abstract notation systems"[28] (p. 12) that suggest symbolic systems, which combined with the decrease in modular cerebral boundaries, we have described as a component of autonoetic consciousness. In articles (2004, 2005) drawing extensively on the paleoanthropological literature, Mellars concludes that systems, appeared in Europe *c.*50,000 BP as a result of our arrival out of Africa and had nothing to do with the Neanderthals. Further evidence for this proposition is the presence of these new capacities in Africa 20,000 to 30,000 years earlier, thus allowing time for the spread of advanced *H. sapiens sapiens* into Europe.

If you are still with me, you can see the obvious problem with this line of reasoning. You might ask something like: Given that we accept your argument about how these abilities got to Europe from Africa rather than arising in Europe, how did they arise in Africa in the first place? The story goes something like this. *H. sapiens*, or anatomically modern humans (AMH), also termed archaic humans arose, in southern Africa about 200,000 ya.[29] Then, around 70,000 ya, something happened. The archaeological record reveals that a group of abilities and talents—advanced stone tools, weapons, sewn clothing, and jewelry—appeared in a fashion contested by different authors.[30] The components of what is referred to as the Upper Paleolithic package were gradually assembled at multiple sites before export to Europe. The spread to Asia and Europe of Humans equipped with the package is known as the "Out of Africa Event" (Dunbar, 2016). Klein (2001) and others (Stringer & Gamble, 1993) however, argue that the appearance of the package in southern Africa was fairly sudden and propose an origin for the change. Analysis of mitochondrial DNA (inherited through the female line) suggests the appearance of a genetic or epigenetic event in a population of roughly 5000 females (that is, women) in southern Africa that enabled the capacities making up the package. It resulted in the appearance of modern humans, *H. sapiens sapiens*, in the archaic population of AMH. Modern humans then began moving north and out of Africa

70,000 ya, migrating first into Asia, and then swinging around, reaching Europe 40–50,000 ya. Lest we dismiss this hypothesis as fanciful (although it does require further study), we should recall that the spontaneous tripling of the SRGAP2 gene was of central importance to the appearance of the *Homo* line 2.5–3 mya (Reardon, 2012). Kinsbourne (2005) observed, for example, that some other as yet unidentified single mutation in the gene controlling how many times cerebral neurons divide could determine increasing cortical size, cognitive capacity, and, potentially, consciousness (the ASPM gene is a proposed candidate). Such qualitative shifts are familiar, unpredictable properties of complex systems (Leffert, 2008) that are then further modified by quantitative change.

We have considered how (Bar-Yosef, 2002; Mithen, 1994) the cognitive changes involved in this evolutionary step could result from a change in the brain's modularity structure. Specifically, Neanderthals (and perhaps archaic humans) were thought to possess domain-specific intelligence in which information concerning social interaction, the environment, and technology was stored and processed in different modules (whether the structure of these modules was anatomical, computational—or, more likely, some combination of both—has not been worked out). The point is that there was very little connectivity or sharing of information between modules. Individual modules *could* have possessed their own *situational consciousness* that was not transferable. Modern human brains, however, were posited to have an open architecture that facilitated integration of diverse categories of information and an open consciousness.

We know that procedural consciousness and noetic consciousness were in advanced states of development in the early wise wise guys (*H. sapiens sapiens*). It is hard to imagine how the complex tasks required to Be in Heidegger's (1927/2010) world of thrownness and everydayness, of *Eigenwelt* and *Mitwelt* and *Umwelt*, could be carried on by procedural and noetic cognition alone. It is equally hard to imagine how one could survive in ice age Europe in the complex ways that we wise men did without our possessing mental time travel.[31] One has to believe in the equation:

Symbolic Reasoning + Mental Time Travel + Theory of Mind + Self-Reflection = Autonoetic Consciousness

The autonoetically conscious *Homo* must be able to deploy his consciousness in two particular ways. One involves the ability to voluntarily escape the consciously experienced (Kinsbourne, 2005) present into mental time travel and episodic memory in order to plan. This is a shift from everydayness to thrownness. The other is the capacity to experience the uncertainties of life and its projections into the future and incorporate them into the short- and long-term planning of activities. This involves both the conscious weighing of possibilities and the capacity to develop Heuristics and Biases (Tversky & Kahneman, 1974/1982).

The questions we now have to ask, to paraphrase the one we asked about the vegetative patient, Kate Bainbridge, in Chapter 2 (Is she conscious?) is not whether they were conscious or not but instead: How conscious were these early Europeans and when did they become conscious like us?

As one gets into questions about the phylogeny of autonoetic consciousness it appears that many authors (e.g., Terrace & Metcalfe, 2005) are willing to locate this consciousness in humans but deny its presence in non-human primates. They argue that the autonoetic seeming activities of primates like the great apes can actually be explained in terms of noetic consciousness. Their willingness derives in part from the ability to do research on living sapiens and apes. They are less willing to speculate about the presence of autonoetic consciousness in our hominin or *Homo* ancestors. The problem that remains is that however one chooses to avoid these questions, one cannot eradicate them; they *have* answers even if our tools for ascertaining them are currently limited.

We can identify some parameters of consciousness. It seems impossible that grammatical language could exist in the absence of autonoetic consciousness. If the modularity hypothesis fails, as we have seen that it does, then we cannot identify autonoetic consciousness itself with putative apparatuses of consciousness such as the claustrum, and we are left with the global hypotheses that autonoetic consciousness is a property of the neural net of the Self. We now have to turn to the work of Julian Jaynes (1977), the theory of the origins of consciousness he proposed, and what might, or might not follow from it.

Before proceeding, I must again offer the caveat that, in trying to understand the wise guys in these distant times, we are relying on conjecture and inference to develop a narrative. Narratives are stories, and as the Postmoderns tell us, many stories of variable standing always exist to describe any circumscribed series of events. Jaynes' work,[32] published in 1977, had the benefit of Sperry's (Sperry, 1969; Sperry, Gazzaniga, & Bogen, 1969) split-brain studies of patients with intractable epilepsy who underwent commissurotomy and were then evaluated neurocognitively. He did not have the benefit of Tulving's (1983, 1985/2003) elucidation of different systems of memory and consciousness. In talking about consciousness, Jaynes says he is talking about *subjective consciousness*, by which he means something like Autonoetic Consciousness. To summarize his hypothesis, he posits that while writing appeared in roughly 3000 BCE, Autonoetic Consciousness was neither present nor required. Autonoetic consciousness, he posits, appeared around 1200 BCE,[33] an idea that paleoanthropologists would find shocking. He supports his hypothesis in part by drawing on the *Iliad* (Homer, 1998), an epic poem that was chanted by poets in an auditory trance starting around 1200 BCE and written down about 900–850 BCE when the Greek alphabet was first developed. (How *this* happened is still another conundrum.) By being very careful about language, trying to define words like *psyche* in terms of their original early Greek meaning (breath, blood, life substance lost in death) rather than their later *c.*300 BCE meaning (soul), he describes the characters as lacking a Self, of lacking autonoetic consciousness, of operating in response to what they hear in their heads, what they call the voices of the Gods. His argument rests on two things: "*the lack of mental language and the initiation of action by the gods*" (p. 79); the characters of the *Iliad* do not think or feel, they are directed to act.

What we call Noetic and Anoetic Memory in these times resided,[34] he posits, in the right cerebral hemisphere (with significant subcortical contributions to the latter), and consciousness, in the form of hallucinated voices experienced as providing direction or commands of Gods, was communicated (perhaps "shouted" is a better term) to the left hemisphere by the right across the cerebral commissures.

His hypothesis is that the Cerebral Hemispheres were functionally split in these times—he refers to a "bicameral mind"—and that the pressure of complex social events, larger and larger populations interacting with each other (hearing different voices), often in conflict, led to the collapse of the barrier, producing the "single mind" we have today. The hypothesis, itself, is not implausible. We would question the dates and whether we are looking at qualitative or gradual, quantitative change. I have posited variabilities in consciousness both among individuals and in a single individual over time, so it might be that people now slip in and out of these proposed bicameral states.

Before going on to what other authors have to say about the origins of Autonoetic Consciousness, I'd like to offer an alternative narrative concerning the nature and social role of texts like the *Iliad* in ancient Greece and ancient society. The *Iliad* was chanted by the priest-poets, the *aiodoi*, in an oral tradition that preceded but did not end with the appearance of textual writing. These performances were designed to drive the audience into an altered state of consciousness taking them back cognitively to at least Neolithic times and probably even further (think religious hymns). Human beings have continued to seek out such experiences in both religious and entertainment venues, enhanced at times by mind-altering substances, and to derive great satisfaction and meaning from them. What was, in effect, the elimination of the individual as a center of reason in the *Iliad* could easily represent a trope in common usage at the time to enhance these effects. Jaynes (1977) even knows this when he observes, "the function of meter in poetry is to drive the electrical activity of the brain and most certainly to *relax the normal emotional inhibitions* [emphasis added] of both chanter and listener" (p. 73).

If Jaynes (1977) is an outlier, Humphrey (1976/1988) has exerted a seminal influence on researchers studying the origins or consciousness and its relation to *social intelligence*. Social intelligence, or Machiavellian intelligence (Whiten & Byrne, 1988), stands in contradistinction to technological intelligence, the stuff of gadgets, intelligence testing, running rats through mazes, and studying prehistoric tools. Machiavellian intelligence involves mental time travel; planning a course of action in dealing with people that will lead to a sought-after interpersonal result. Social intelligence, the stuff of how individuals relate to each other, requires some very different cognitive functions compared to those required by technological intelligence.

Humphrey (1976/1988) first argues that since, in the day-to-day practice of living, we in effect mostly get by with what Heidegger (1927/2010) calls our Everydayness (*Alltäglichkeit*), then there would seem to be little need for creative intelligence (thrownness), the kind of intelligence we use to perform creative tasks, use to do philosophy, and that can be demonstrated in primates and humans in the research lab. The question is then: If we (men, chimpanzees, and apes) seem to be able to get around without this intelligence much of the time, why have it in the first place? Humphrey's answer is that it is *socially* necessary and that social groups cannot exist without it. It is necessary because one thing we do know, from personal experience, is that *life in the large social groups in which we wise guys live is complex and highly problematic.* Just how necessary it has been for the maintenance of these groups over the course of hominin evolution (Dunbar, 2016) we will get to in a moment. We also know that there are great benefits, Machiavellian benefits, to be had by each individual member of a group in both preserving the structure of the group *and* exploiting and outmaneuvering others within it. Accumulated knowledge (semantic memory) is not enough. Adding to Humphrey, social intelligence requires, and rewards complex calculation and things like mental time travel.[35]

Socializing takes a lot of time. "If the social is to be of any net biological benefit the improvement in subsistence techniques which it makes possible must more than compensate for the lost time" (Humphrey, 1976/1988, p. 21). When our hominin ancestors moved out into the savannahs from the jungles millions of years ago, technical knowledge began to pay new dividends. This pressure from the environment led to the need "to give children an even better schooling creat[ing] a social system of unprecedented complexity—and with it unprecedented challenge to intelligence" (p. 22).

Mithen (1996/1998) offers a summary of Humphrey's views:

> Consciousness evolved as a cognitive trick to allow an individual to predict the social behaviour of other members of his or her group [mental time travel]. Humphrey suggested that it evolved to enable us to use our minds as models for those of other people.
>
> (p. 166)[36]

If we accept all these good things about the evolution of consciousness, we have to integrate them with what we already know. The first is that consciousness involved the assembly of a number of components: Theory of Mind, Mental Time Travel, Episodic Memory, and Self-Reflection. The second is that nothing evolves in its fully realized form, so this "cognitive trick" must have first appeared in rudimentary form, developing, and perhaps adding components over time. The third is that we know, from studying humans in the present, that even if we buy what I would call the Social Hypothesis of Consciousness, and even if consciousness is the guide to social and physical action, still, many of the nuts and bolts of such actions are carried out *unconsciously* (e.g., Nisbett & Wilson, 1977; Tversky & Kahneman, 1974/1982). This last point is really only a restatement of past arguments (Leffert, 2016) concerning how conscious and unconscious cognition interact. Perhaps the most interesting question in paleoanthropology is just when and in whom did all this occur. I will take a stab at this, and it can obviously only *be* a stab, but I want to defer doing so for just a moment. I particularly want to talk about the work of Merlin Donald (1991) and Robin Dunbar (2016).

Donald (1991) and Dunbar (2016) are painstakingly careful in offering an evidence-based discussion of the origins of mind. Both authors look at transitions in hominin cognitive evolution, with Dunbar hanging it on the phylogeny while

Donald hangs the phylogeny on points of *qualitative cognitive change*. Their accounts are complementary and innovative. As Donald put it in 1991: "There are no existing classifications of ape or human culture that are based primarily on cognitive considerations" (p. 148). (Such a shift in classification was what Renfrew had been talking about in 1994.) Dunbar describes a consensus, by 2016, that what moves brain evolution and increasing cortical size in primates is the evolution of ever more complex social behaviors, which in turn correlate with increasing social group size, ultimately reaching *Dunbar's Number* (Dunbar, 1993) of 150 *H. sapiens sapiens*. "Orbitofrontal cortex volume determines mentalizing competences and mentalizing competences determine the size of the social network" (Dunbar, 2016, p. 65). This social brain hypothesis also can be used *to precisely predict group size*. Drawing on what we have already said, the corollary to these two premises is that brain size can only increase if a species can increase its food intake to supply the extra energy needed to run larger brains.[37] While other more familiar aspects of behavior such as toolmaking correlate with brain size, *they turn out to be consequences of having a large brain rather than the evolutionary causes of it*.

If we are going to think about the activities of the social brain that are certainly on the road to consciousness, then we have to consider a different component of time budgets: social time. Monkeys and Apes, for example, spend about 20% of their time in social one-on-one mutual grooming. Grooming triggers endorphin release, which is essential for social bonding. The 20% is limited by other time budget requirements and, as a result limit the size of a group that can be socially bonded to 50 individuals (Dunbar, 2016). How to get past the two-person limit? Humans (and presumably *Homos*), it turns out, engage in a particular group behavior, laughter, that also releases endorphins and allows for larger group bonding and lesser amounts of social time needed to maintain an increasing group size. Laughter's contagiousness facilitates the process. As group size continues to increase, laughter alone is no longer enough to maintain expanding group size, reaching a limit of 110 for Neanderthal bands. Dunbar suggests that *making* music (e.g., communal singing and dancing, modern day rock concerts) would be a more effective alternative that has been shown in contemporary humans to trigger an endorphin surge (much greater than that achieved by simply *listening* to music and on a par with that achieved by people working or competing in groups). Music reduces the percentage of the time budget necessary for social bonding.

When we reach a group size of 150 we face the same requirements for increasing social time to maintain the larger groups and the increasing caloric needs of the wise guys. The music of the Neanderthals, as posited by Dunbar (2016), would not have been enough, and, at this evolutionary point, language could have appeared to fill the gap. (I want to bracket the discussion of language development here, deferring it to the discussion of language p. 117.) This was an evolutionary shift in which sapiens replaced Neanderthals as the high point of hominin evolution. One might well ask how it took place.

Dunbar (2016) provides high quality social data analysis (as opposed to opinion offered as fact) about the evolution or archaic humans and the rise of AMH. He does not have much interest in the origins of consciousness in humans or the different kinds of consciousness that we understand and are interested in. What he does talk about is intentionality and language. Dunbar seems to use *intentionality* as a sort of placeholder for consciousness.

There are some caveats here. Intentionality, or conscious social behavior, is solidly backed by *unconscious* processes. We have Tversky and Kahneman's (1974/1982) work on decision-making made unconsciously through the use of Heuristics and Biases, Nisbett and Wilson's (1977) now classic study of how human decision-making is made unconsciously while it is *experienced* as being made consciously. Finally, we come to Christakis and Fowler's (2009)[38] studies of the behavior of social networks that has particular relevance here. They look at how individuals are connected in these networks by degree of separation. Groups of individuals cohere up to three degrees of separation. Beyond that, individuals can maintain only very casual connections to each other, like traders moving through a settlement or chatting with a bank teller. According to Christakis and Fowler's calculations, how big is this basic social group bordered by three degrees of separation? Guess what—it just so happens to be 150, Dunbar's number. Information, which they call *contagion*, passes from member to member unconsciously: socially based beliefs, fashions, and trends just seem to appear in our heads. (Contagion can spread to link large collections of groups behind some shared idea or belief system like nations or political parties.) The point is that a lot of the business that members of groups of 150 carry on with each other can be carried out unconsciously.

Donald's (2001) ideas about cognition, representation, speech, and consciousness can add something to our thinking. He labels a transition in these capacities from apes to hominins and from Australopiths to humans, but doesn't peg the cognitive evolution he posits to particular human species. He notes an obvious evolutionary distinction between linguistic and prelinguistic mental representation and that consciousness is profoundly shaped by both language and society. Donald does not believe in what he calls a "line in the sand" theory of consciousness. That is, he grants "a modicum of consciousness to any creature that can achieve an independent mental model of the world, one that *transcends its immediate environment* [emphasis added]" (p. 123) and manifests an agenda for navigating it.

Having said all this, we do have to step up to the plate and offer a hypothesis as to when autonoetic, self-reflective, consciousness appeared in the course of hominin evolution. (It can only *be* a hypothesis because we can only infer, we cannot [yet] know.) I am going to posit that this form of consciousness first appeared as Humphrey's (1976/1988) "cognitive trick" with the advent of archaic Anatomically Modern Humans in southern Africa around 200,000 ya. I base this on the appearance of a modern sized brain (1300 cm^3) with the new larger frontal and prefrontal cerebral cortex and increased number of granular cells necessary for "crunching" the data that consciousness required. I cannot speculate about what happened for the next 130,000 years, but I will posit that 70,000 ya ago in southern Africa and 40–50,000 ya in Europe, either as a result of gradual quantitative changes becoming qualitative or of spontaneous mutation, full autonoetic consciousness appeared. It is entirely possible that the change was Epigenetic, a response to the complex social environment we have been talking about, operating in the same way as the Epigenetic processes we have discussed in the preceding chapter. I will further posit that it necessarily appeared to power the Upper Paleolithic package. To briefly reprise the contents of the package, they include:

1 increased diversity and standardization of artifact types;
2 rapid increase in rates of artifact evolution and rate of geographical transfer;
3 first shaping of bone, ivory and shell into small precise tools;
4 first appearance of art and personal ornamentation;
5 first appearance of architectural design of living space;
6 oldest evidence for the transport of raw materials over long distances;
7 earliest evidence for the appearance of ceremony (religious?) in art and elaborate graves;
8 earliest evidence of ability to live in the coldest parts of Eurasia;
9 first evidence for human population density reaching that of historic hunter-gatherers; and
10 first evidence of fishing and other ways to extract calories from nature.

(Paraphrased from Murray, Wise, & Graham, 2017, pp. 386–387)

This is mostly about technology and custom as understood from *physical evidence*. Our interest lies, however, in the social and intellectual capacities that are evidenced in these abilities (Dunbar, 2016) and the kind of intellectual power and consciousness that are required to carry them out. In short, I believe that to do these things, *you have to be autonoetically conscious* (some of the time). We can say that modern ethological evidence supports such conclusions, conclusions also drawn, as we have seen, by Tulving (2005).

So, in the face of all this, how are we to understand Jaynes (1977)? Is there nothing there or do we need to understand his contribution in a different way? First off, the neuroscience does not support Jaynes' concept of a silent Left Brain controlled by a Godlike Right Brain shouting at it across the cerebral commissures. It raises the specter of squads of automatons being ordered around by a shared public address system and does not allow for the advanced LB conscious activity necessary for language development. I would suggest something in between. Let's posit that, prior to 1200 BCE or so, both hemispheres were active simultaneously. LB self-reflective thought and speech was going on, supplemented by the RB's periodically shouting at it. Then something happened. Perhaps it was that the reality of needing to function in increasingly complex social structures (Dunbar, 2016) overpowered this cognitive system with its direct, conscious communication between the hemispheres and needed to shut it down, replacing it with the unconscious interhemispheric communication we have today. We can even imagine a mechanism for this. There are LB to RB inhibitory fibers in the corpus callosum (Hoppe, 1977) that are thought to function in repression. It is entirely reasonable to speculate (this is speculation and not proof) that the increase in social and technological activities (explicit and semantic memory) in the serially organized LB reached a tipping point around 3200 ya. This increasing activity drove the inhibitory fibers of the corpus callosum to shut down the conscious connection and leave autonoetic consciousness to function independently in the LB. This would have been the last (so far, anyway) transition in human consciousness.

Ontogeny of consciousness

> The evidence from developmental psychology appears conclusive: the ease with which children learn about language, other minds and biology appears to derive from a cognitive foundation of innate content-rich mental modules. Such modules appear to be universally shared by all humans.
>
> (Mithen, 1996/1998, p. 57)

During development, this modularity morphs into an open brain architecture.[39]

At the start, we can offer a number of hypotheses about the development of consciousness in the infant and young child. We have evidence that (Bråten & Trevarthen, 2007) infants are *aware* (will visually track a moving finger) within moments of birth: We will defer for the moment any speculation concerning what sort of consciousness that awareness might represent. We also have a number of developmental milestones present in these early years that must relate to a developing consciousness. By the end of the first year of life, the brain has doubled in size from 500 cm^3 at birth to 1000 cm^3. While the Right Cerebral Hemisphere is up and functioning at birth, the Left Cerebral Hemisphere begins myelination and sending axons across the cerebral commissures to the right hemisphere in the second year; these processes reach a peak at 18 months and continue to 24 months. If the Right Brain is involved in emotional experience and the operation of the autonomic nervous system (Schore, A. N., 2009, 2011), one of the functions of the Left Brain when it comes on line is the *modulation* (I prefer this term to the harsher *regulation*) of RB function. During the same 18–24 month period, the young toddler develops the ability to perform the mirror test. A not much studied component of early development is the appearance of a Theory of Mind (Baron-Cohen, Tager-Flusberg, & Cohen, 2000). It is thought to *begin* to develop towards the end of the first year as a part of secondary intersubjectivity (Bråten & Trevarthen): the subject-subject-object interactions that occur when infant and mother jointly inspect objects. Advancing motor and language skills are also well-documented for this period. These accomplishments do not appear out of nowhere. We would rather speculate that new functions first appear as kernels or subsystems (Nelson, 2005) whose development and recombination with other subsystems lead to the appearance of new functions. There remains, however, some point in time where such quantitative changes become qualitative. We are left to examine how the advent of consciousnesses fits into this picture.

There is a consensus (Donald, 2001; Nelson, 2005; Tulving, 2005) that by 4 years of age human beings have established autonoetic consciousness. Its emergence follows a process of social and emotional interaction along with increasing brain size and all the increasing synaptic complexity that this involves. Again, Humphrey's (1976/1988) cognitive trick adds complexity to ontogeny and morphs into true consciousness.

I have in the past (Leffert, 2013) described an experience I had in a coffee shop. A father walked in. Holding his hand was a 2-year-old *H. sapiens sapiens* who we'll call Jerry.[40] The father straps Jerry into a toddler high-chair and goes to the nearby counter while keeping an eye on him the whole time. He returns to the table with a coffee for himself and a juice box for Jerry. Jerry is actively looking around the coffee shop; then a very interesting thing happens. *Without ceasing his observations* or looking at either his father or the juice box, he picks up the latter and thrusts it out to the former. Without comment, the father takes the juice box, pierces it with one of these pointy straws and hands it to his son, who takes it, also without comment, and proceeds to drink the juice while still studying the room and the people in it. What exactly went on here?

I described this episode in the past to demonstrate secure attachment (which it does). We now have a second hat to put on that plays with rather than replaces the first; the hat of an anthropological ontologist. So what does the situation tell us about Jerry's cognitive development and maybe his consciousness? Let's deconstruct it.[41] First, he knows what the juice box is and the *procedure* for getting at the juice. He wants to drink the juice, or at least some of it. He also knows he is incapable of performing the procedure and that his father is. Jerry is displaying semantic consciousness and semantic memory. His thinking he wants to drink the juice displays first-order intentionality (Dennett, 1988). His thrusting the juice box at his father means he wants his father to give him the juice to drink and has this procedure for getting him to do so. This is second order intentionality. But it is also true that Jerry wants his father to *believe* that he wants him to get the juice ready for him. This is third order intentionality. This is what Jerry is capable of at this point in his life, but Dennett describes higher levels of intentionality in an increasingly complex back and forth sequence. Mithen (1996/1998) posits that chimps are capable of third order, Neanderthals of fourth order, and us wise guys of fifth order intentionality. It is the latter that is required, they posit, for autonoetic consciousness.

Putting our clinician/developmentalist hat back on we would have to say Jerry has a Theory of Mind and the rudiments of tertiary intersubjectivity (Bråten & Trevarthen, 2007), "entailing prediction and a sense of verbal or narrative self and other in first-order modes of symbolic communication" (p. 23). He also is demonstrating mental time travel (playing out the sequence of events that, in the future, will get him his juice), a component of autonoetic consciousness. What we are seeing is the ontogeny of Humphrey's (1976/1988) cognitive "trick." It should be noted that, although Jerry and his father carry out the interaction of their intersubjectivities silently, they do so by mutual choice (*perhaps* this is early fourth order intentionality) and *could* have done so verbally *had they wished* to.

Perhaps the final capacity to appear by age 4 that makes up the "consciousness package" is the shift in the child from liking a parent to read stories to them to being able to tell stories themselves. This capacity includes the ability to tell the stories that they have loved having parents read to them, or the stories they have watched on social media, or being able to relate stories about what has happened to them. The latter include events of the day or events of sufficient emotional force to remain in intermediate or long-term memory. And, with the advent of the latter, comes perforce the need to keep some narrative memories out of consciousness.

Speech and language

Language, that is, syntactical and grammatical speech, belongs in our account of autonoetic consciousness because the two have a complex and interreferential relationship. It is hard to imagine how one could exist in the absence of the other. Dunbar (2016) also notes "we need to draw a clear distinction between speech (as a form of vocalization) and language (as grammatically ordered utterance)" (p. 239). It is the latter, its phylogeny and ontogeny, that we will primarily be talking about. Speech, although lacking the *structure* of language, does combine vocalizations with content, the two conveying named things (semantic memory) for which the names are accepted by a particular group and may also have agreed on emotional content. It is accompanied by amplifying gestures. Speech involves third order intentionality (I want you to know x and I want you to know that I know it). Third order intentionality would be entirely adequate for a group of Neanderthals to organize a hunt or to maintain their social group size of 110.

Adults use language to convey conscious experience to other living things.[42] During the first year of life, infants have only protolanguage (cries, gurgles, and their ever-more-differentiated refinements and imitations of others) to convey what they are experiencing, making their experience knowable to us in only general terms. Prelinguistic cognition developmentally lacking the laterality of adult cognition must, inevitably, be all that accompanies it. The vast changes in hardware, body, brain, and perceptual apparatus during that year, along with the infant's own uniquely personal mental development, make her first year a rocky one. We must remember that all of these processes *are impacted by social experiences* (the *Mitwelt* and the *Umwelt*: a Heideggerian way of talking about Erikson), as is our adult consciousness.

It is easy to forget, in our inquiries into the advent of language, that it is an example of procedural as well as semantic knowledge and that the way language is used differs profoundly among individuals and among the social groups of which they are members. This issue, which is of little interest to researchers investigating the ontogeny and phylogeny of language, should be of great interest to us as clinicians. In the last analysis, Henry Higgins was correct.

Phylogeny of language

"Of the numerous behaviors proposed as the prime mover of brain evolution the only one that is unique and universal in humans is symbolic grammatical language, although when it originated remains an open question" (Falk, 2016, p. 3). Whatever we might want to say about the origins of human language, we cannot avoid the observations that it is the result of a qualitative change in building blocks *already present* in the *sapien* brain, *derived from our genes*, or their epigenetic expression. We also have to posit (Clowry, 2014) that our brains evolved to embody a capacity for a universal grammar. Clowry's question of whether "our brains evolved to embody a knowledge of universal grammar or that language has evolved to fit the functional constraints imposed by the brain" (p. 220) is unanswerable. Given these considerations, perhaps we should begin our discussion with the FOXP2 gene.

FOXP2 is a gene that encodes a transcription factor. Transcription factors affect the expression of suites of genes by binding to the noncoding portions of their targets on the double helix. In its different forms or *alleles*, FOXP2 is intimately involved in vocalization in both birds and mammals (White, 2013) and is highly conserved with only minor variations between families or species. Studies of Zebra Finches show that FOXP2 is not only involved in the anatomical development of the machinery of song, but also operates on an ongoing, real time basis as the birds sing. Human FOXP2 is differentiated from that of our closest living relatives, chimpanzees, by only two amino acid substitutions (Krauss et al., 2007). The discovery of FOXP2 (Hurst, Baraitser, Auger, Graham, & Norell, 1990) arose out of the study of a speech disturbance in half the members of an extended family, called the KE family, where it appears as an autosomal dominant. The affected FOXP2 gene in the family differed from the normal human gene by a single point mutation (Enard et al., 2002): Two intact FOXP2 genes were found to be necessary for normal speech and language. Speech vocalizations of affected family members with only one intact FOXP2 gene are severely impaired, demonstrating a difficulty in controlling the complex sequential movement of the orofacial muscles necessary for speech. However, both peripheral control of this musculature and the ability to perform activities such as suckling, chewing, and blinking are unimpaired; the problem lies in the brain rather than in motorneurons and their targeted musculature. Language fMRI patterns (Liégois et al., 2003) in unaffected members of the KE family showed normal left-sided dominance of Broca's speech area of the cerebral cortex, while affected members showed underactivation of Broca's area as well as other language-related areas. They also showed a more general decrease in cortical laterality. As Vargha-Khadem and colleagues (Vargha-Khadem, Watkins, Alcock, Fletcher, & Passingham, 1995) describe the KE family:

> Affected members suffer from a specific impairment in *grammar*, [emphasis added] namely, a selective inability to generate syntactic rules such as those for tense, number and gender ... Our initial and present investigations of the same (KE) family indicate that the affected members' disorder transcends the generation of morphosynatactic rules to include impaired processing and expression of other areas of grammar, grossly defective articulation of speech sounds, and, further, a severe extra-linguistic orofacial dyspraxia. In addition, the affected family members have both verbal and performance quotient [IQ]

scores that are on average 18–19 points below those of the unaffected members.

(p. 930)

So what makes this interesting to us in a discussion of the phylogeny of language? In a controversial paper, Krauss and colleagues (2007) sequenced the DNA of two Neanderthals in which they found a FOXP2 gene identical to that found in modern humans. They posit that the human allele of FOXP2, the gene associated with fully modern language ability, was probably inherited by both AMH *and* Neanderthals from their last common ancestor 300,000 to 400,000 ya. This seems to suggest, in this fascinating and ongoing argument that Neanderthals, our closest extinct relative, *spoke and thought as we do*,[43] which titillates our survivor guilt by portraying them as the mystical flower-children of prehistory (Papagianni & Morse, 2015).

There is considerable literature (Benítez-Burraco, Longa, Lorenzo, & Uriagereka, 2008; Coop, Bullaughey, Luca, & Przewoski, 2008; Jablonka & Lamb, 2014) contesting Krauss and colleagues' (2007) conclusion about the presence in Neanderthals of the FOXP2 allele found in modern humans. Dunbar (2016), approaching the question from an interpersonal direction, argues that singing, chanting, and speech would have been enough for a social group of 110 (Neanderthals) to cohere but not enough for a group of 150 (*H. sapiens sapiens*). What Neanderthals *did* have (and needed), and paleoanthropological evidence supports it, was the physical, neurological, and social capacities to support speech (Evans, 2015), prelinguistic communication with limited syntax and grammar. The latter could have been rich in nouns and verbs, allowing a social group to be together or to plan and carry out a hunt.

Verbal communication in mammals and birds has always served two purposes: the exchange of information and the enhancement of social cohesion. This is as true for a flock of finches awakening in a tree as it is for a scientist delivering a Nobel lecture. Unfortunately, the science does not support our linguistic wishes concerning our closest extinct relatives. Verbal communication including speech is not language, and neither the anatomy, nor the functional neuroanatomy necessary for it existed before the advent of archaic AMH. The general feeling (Evans, 2015), and it is really a well-educated guess, is that archaic modern humans did not have language but that it appeared along with the other, documentable components of the Upper Paleolithic package either before or perhaps as a result of the Out of Africa migration beginning about 70,000 ya. The MNS serves as a platform for both the evolution and the development of language (Corballis, 2010) in human beings (Fadiga & Craighero, 2007). The central role of the MNS in language supports the gestural hypothesis: that is, that language evolved from primate communications through gestures, both mediated by the MNS. "This mechanism is, in fact, of great evolutionary importance since it is supposed to be at the basis of the way in which primates understand actions made by their conspecifics" (Fadiga & Craighero, p. 101). In particular, it is a region of the left inferior frontal cortex, a part of the MNS that processes gestural information coming from the other: the area in chimpanzees that corresponds to Broca's region in humans. The multifaceted communication requirements of *H. sapiens sapiens*, including the need to communicate complex environmental information in present and past tenses, episodic memories, and mental time travel, required a formalization, and a grammaticalization of speech. We see the same forces at work in human development.

Ontogeny of language

"Neonates begin to learn the building blocks of language by perceiving the statistical and prosodic regularities of their native languages, which creates neural networks for higher-order linguistic computations" (Falk, 2016, p. 7). Although "six-month-olds can distinguish the approximately 800 consonants and vowels in all of the world's languages … by the end of their first year their perception has become selectively tuned to the roughly 40 speech sounds [present] in their native language" (pp. 7–8). Our knowledge of infant brain maturation (Schore, A. N., 1994) tells us that the prosodic is a matter of Right Brain development, while the semantic and grammatical elements of language are matters of the Left Brain, beginning to come on line as its myelination begins to occur in the second year.

The development of language is a vast subject beyond the scope of the few words I can say about it here. Our understanding of language acquisition (Kuhl, 2000; Poeppel, Emmorey, Hickok, & Pylkänen, 2012) has changed dramatically in recent years. What I want to do is to pick up the threads of the above arguments concerning the phylogeny of speech and language and apply them to the appearance of language in contemporary *sapien* children. I have argued, as does Terrace (2005), that "Language is uniquely human and that its grammatical structure distinguishes it from all other forms of animal communication" (p. 85). As psychoanalysts studying child development from the dual perspectives of attachment and conflict theory, we have not integrated the parallel track of language development and its attendant neuroanatomical and neurophysiological maturation. This is all, ultimately, about the phylogeny and ontology of the Autonoetic Self. I am not, for even a moment, creating still another self to add to the one I have already pushed you to adopt. I have been talking instead about how the Bio-Psycho-Social Self came, phylogenically and ontogenetically, to be able to reflect on itself and the world that it inhabits. In other words, it is how Dasein (Heidegger, 1927/2010) came to be.

Essential prelinguistic developments growing out of the brain's maturation and verbal-social interactions during the infant's first year of life (Kuhl, 2000) pave the way for the later advent of language. They also shape the nature of an individual's unique version of linguistic competence. The strategies used by developing infants to assemble the building blocks of language have neither been predicted nor understood by the now classical linguistic theories of the last half of the 20th century.

"Any theory of language acquisition has to specify how infants parse the auditory world to make the critical units of language available" (Kuhl, 2000, p. 11851). Segmenting speech is a formidable task, with infants able to parse the basic units of language; they discriminate only between auditory stimuli arising in different phonetic categories. This observation did not imply an inborn knowledge of the phonetic units themselves, only an ability to distinguish among them when they appear on the acoustic horizon. It has been shown that, "by simply listening to language, infants acquire sophisticated information about its properties" (p. 11852). Kuhl talks about a three-step process in which infants first detect and abstract patterns of language input, then operate statistically to detect distributional and probabilistic patterns contained in ambient language and, finally, as a result, find their perceptions altered by experience to enhance subsequent perceptions and vocalizations of ambient language. A shift occurs for an infant in the first year of life from universal perception to language-specific perception that paves the way for language acquisition.[44]

"Historically, language input was seen as a trigger for selecting among innately specified options" (Kuhl, 2000, p. 11854). It is now understood that language addressed *to* infants, rather than an innate unfolding, plays a much more important role in language development. *Reception* (of language) *shapes expression*. The format of this language is the same the world over: It is called *Motherese*, and infants have been shown to prefer it to adult-directed language. Motherese acoustically exaggerates phonetic units to help infants learn. Mothers speak it with many different voices to resemble other adults in an infant's life. Motherese is also used to teach language to the infant: "See the ___, what's this?" It comprises unconsciously made modifications in adult speech. The MNSs of mother and infant offer nonlinguistic support for its deployment. Motherese is powerfully and comfortingly regressive when it is used by adult couples to talk to each other. The *innate* ability to speak Motherese is a component of the maternal toolbox available to the good enough mother. In the adult clinical situation, one can listen carefully for variations in language that point to partial failures of the less than good enough mother to teach her child to speak.

Again, we can notice (if we listen) these things in our adult patients. An adult patient who has been severely traumatized may manage it by using childhood names for intense emotions. A person, then, is not intensely angry, she is *crabby*: a person who is making no sense is not irrational, he is *cuckoo*.

As a child ends her second year, there is a sea change in the literature on language development and the research behind it. Interest shifts from neurodevelopment (Hoff, 2009) to concerns of educators and speech pathologists. It is organized around children reaching various milestones of speech and the techniques of therapy used to help them if they don't. By age 5, children have mastered the phonology of their language and the 40 or so phonemes that comprise it. Children first acquire accent and dialect from their caregivers. Unlike phonetics, they are not permanent but continue to be shaped by an individual's social milieu.

Children develop surprisingly vast vocabularies. Anglin and colleagues (Anglin, Miller, & Wakefield, 1993) studied what amounted to word recognition, in first, third, and fifth graders, garnered by orally administered multiple choice tests asking the children to choose the best definition for each word. They found that the average first grader knew 10,000 words. By the third grade, this had risen to 20,000 words, and, by the fifth grade, the number was 40,000, much more than we might have supposed. Ability to maintain conversations through related conversational turns increases throughout childhood. Whereas fifth graders maintain conversations through factual connections, 12th graders, and adults were more likely to respond to connections related to feelings or attitudes.

These numbers leave unanswered questions about word usage and conversational style, starting in childhood, and moving on to adulthood. The popular literature (e.g., Tannen, 1990) is now replete with descriptions of how men and woman have different conversational styles, resulting in an ease of misconception when they speak to each other.

As clinicians, we probably don't think often enough about the patterns of language manifested by our patients: their chosen vocabulary, frequency of word usage, and grammatical style. These choices can reveal a lot about a patient's development. They also change over the course of life. As children and parents start out with similar conversational styles, we would expect spouses' ways of communicating to become similar as relationships extend over time. It is also useful to monitor a patient's language over time to see if they take up our own terms for things or the expressions we may use (the reverse may also occur). There are certainly no rules here, but we can use what we observe about language as one more tool for understanding our patients.

To sum up

This has become a sprawling and rather disparate chapter. It began with the idea of wanting to say something more about the origins of consciousness that, rather than belonging in Chapter 2, should be informed by the study of Epigenetics and Evo-Devo to be found in Chapter 3. In the writing, it soon became clear that "origins" had to involve both Phylogeny and Ontology and that this was a broad undertaking that would need a chapter of its own rather than a chapter section. The length of this chapter is evidence of just how impossible the original plan would have been. What it reveals is how the origins of consciousness are inextricably a part of the Self, both its Phylogeny and Ontology, and neither could be considered without thinking about language.

We have talked more expansively than expected about the Self and its consciousness. But then, still another, in retrospect obvious, problem arose. Language is a fundamental aspect of the Autonoetic Self, and it is doubtful that Autonoetic consciousness could exist in the absence of language. So to fully understand consciousness and the Self we had to look at both the Phylogeny and the Ontogeny of language as they relate to the above.

This was not a clinical chapter; it brought with it no cases to discuss. I *have* attempted to flag places at which this basic science discourse raised points of inquiry that have some relevance to the clinical situation, issues that we have generally not thought about as we have listened to and interacted with our patients and which we now might want to explore. Attending to the totality of a patient's was such a point.

We will shift gears in the next chapter as we turn to Existentialism and Phenomenology and how they play out in the clinical situation, a discussion I began in 2016. We will see how they expand our understanding of psychopathology. Perhaps we will also be able to link them to the Phylogenical and Ontological material we have been exploring here.

Notes

1 This chapter started out life as a section of the last chapter on Evo-Devo and Epigenetics. It rapidly became clear, however, that the material that needed to be covered was too diverse and went way beyond the subject matter of that chapter: It both merited and required a chapter of its own.
2 Although the terms *language* and *speech* are often used interchangeably, they are different. Speech refers to communication through symbolic verbal utterance, while language is verbal utterance organized by the rules of grammar and syntax.
3 The taxonomy is a bit murky here, but I am using the term *hominin* to refer to the clade that originated when our direct ancestors split off from the Chimpanzees somewhere around 5 to 7 million years ago (mya). (Some authors, to the contrary, use the term *hominins* to refer to some members of the clade.)
4 Dates and exact places on the evolutionary tree are still the subject of debate and uncertainty, as are ideas in psychoanalysis for that matter.
5 The fragment also revealed very humanlike (as opposed to apelike dentition).
6 Recent measurements of Taung's endocast (Falk & Clarke, 2007) making use of modern computer enhanced technology revealed a brain size of 382 cm^3 with a projected adult brain size of 406 cm^3. (Our adult brain size is 1300 cm^3.)
7 Slit-Robo-Rho GTPase-activating protein 2 (Dennis et al., 2012).
8 Doubling is a process whereby a gene produces a copy of itself that then sits next to it in the DNA gene sequence. Like what you get with a copy machine, the copy is not exact and wouldn't function effectively on its own (Reardon, 2012), but it *does* effect the function of the original gene in game-changing ways. Doubling is an exciting and rare genetic event.
9 To add a final piece to the story, about a million years ago, SGRP2C doubled to produce SGRP2D, a great-granddaughter (Dennis et al., 2012).
10 This is true in particular for the Metopic or MS suture (Falk et al., 2012).
11 We have good reason to believe that trends in Evo-Devo that increase the complexity of neuronal connections, that is, the number of neuronal processes (axons and dendrites) and synapses present in the brain, correlate with increasing intelligence.
12 Prior to the invention of slings, nurslings were held, balanced on hips, or set down *nearby*. The latter practice, common in modern times, was not seen with monkey or ape mothers.
13 I have offered (Leffert, 2016, 2017) my own reading of Heidegger's ontology in which I posit three states of being: *everydayness*, in which an individual's self-consciousness is subordinated to the group and the everyday tasks of life that are "at hand": *thrownness*, in which the individual is fully and consciously engaged with both being alive and the reality of death: and *fallen*, in which there is no engagement but only fear of death and trying to deny its inevitability.
14 It is easy to see how a mother plagued by her own developmental deficits would not experience such a response, perhaps she would feel inadequate instead, and this crucial feedback would have been lost to her infant.
15 Note that *Trevathen* and *Trevarthen* are different authors, not the result of a typo.

124 Origins of the Self and its consciousness

16 It's worth bearing in mind that while the familiar developmental processes of the first year of life are proceeding, brain growth is literally exploding under our very eyes to make them possible.
17 This process is probably already going on in utero during the brain's third trimester growth spurt; the communication here is through sounds and rhythms, the respective autonomic nervous systems of mother and infant, and through changes in the composition of blood plasma that crosses the placental barrier.
18 A similar, less understood pruning occurs at the end of the first year.
19 Remember that our neurons need to live as long as we do; unlike the Self's other cells, they do not replenish themselves through cell division over the course of life.
20 It cannot be a coincidence that the neonatal brain has more than doubled in size while these processes are going on.
21 A hammer stone had to first be made to shape the choppers and cutters/scrapers used to process carcasses.
22 Mithen's (2006) *After the Ice: A Global Human History 20,000–5000 BC* is a good place to start to do so.
23 Take the color blue for example. If our hardware is intact (e.g., no cataracts, not color blind), we all see the color blue, but do we experience it, do we know it, in the same way? We can't answer this question (Dennett's [1991] concept of *qualia* or "hard feels" attempts to do so), but given how experience influences everything in our lives, we might expect that the answer is "no."
24 Indeed, we do have objective evidence for the uniqueness of consciousness: that what we perceive depends on what we have perceived and how we have processed it. Von Senden (1932/1960) studied patients who had congenital cataracts removed surgically and were able to see for the first time. What he found was that such patients did not naturally see: they had to learn from experience *how* to see (they naturally "saw" only flashes of light and color). In addition, if the surgery was performed after the onset of adolescence (post-pruning) they never *could* learn and "saw" only the uncharacterizeable flashes of light and color.
25 By *mental* I mean simply a particular kind of property pertaining to the whole Bio-Psycho-Social Self *and nothing more*.
26 In the Middle Paleolithic for example, there were in place advanced technologies for working flint. These technologies were not present in working bone or antler; this lack of transfer speaks to a high level of modularity. In cognitive terms, we are speaking about limitations in the transferability of procedural (working the stone) and noetic (having a plan for the stone tool one is making) knowing.
27 This number is perhaps less relevant in that much of it involves a large *occipital* cortex involved in visual perception and perhaps adapted to the low-light ice age conditions of Northern Europe.
28 See Marshack (1991) for striking illustrations of stone and bone fragments from the Upper Paleolithic demonstrating diverse notation and counting systems.
29 There is now evidence for the presence of a number of different *Homo* species located across Africa at this time.
30 Indeed, McBrearty and Brooks (2000), in their provocatively titled paper "The Revolution that Wasn't...," argue that these abilities arose in southern Africa starting around 100,000 ya and took 20,000 or 30,000 years to assemble.
31 Neanderthals lived a simpler life and, as a result, were periodically thrown out of their European territories by Climate Change.
32 A confession of sorts: I was an uncritical reader of Jaynes (1977) when his work first came out and found his thinking radically innovative.
33 He also posits that the rudiments of speech began to appear around the Middle to Upper Paleolithic shift, but did not emerge as true grammatical language until the advent of autonoetic consciousness.
34 Where they reside now is something of an open question. We understand that the Right Brain knows things in very different ways than the Left (Leffert, 2010), but it knows

them as well and we could argue that, although Jaynes (1977) did not understand it that way, Right Brain consciousness functioned then much as it does now.
35 Humphrey's (1976/1988) argument allows for the fact, as we know from personal experience, that some players are better at this than others.
36 Note that Humphrey's view is *not* an argument against consciousness being an emergent property of mind but only that it did not emerge in the fully developed form by which we know it today.
37 Dunbar (2016) uses a concept of *time budgets*, a sort of time and motion study of the various tasks that a species has to perform, measuring group size, foraging capacity, and social behavior, in order to determine if those extra calories are available to a given species. For example, calculations show that *A. africanus* would need to spend 44% of its time foraging while the larger-brained *H. ergaster* would need to forage 49% of the time and the still larger-brained *H. erectus* required 51%. At this rate, Neanderthals would require an untenable 78% and the only solution to the problem would be to modify the way in which calories were obtained (e.g., hunting larger prey, cooking food) to drive down the percentages.
38 The work of these three groups of authors is discussed in Chapter 2 of this volume and in greater detail in Leffert (2013) and (2016).
39 As we know as clinicians, attachment, or conflictual issues arising in problematic, or failed parental relationships can impact this integration in many ways. Arguably, this is what we see in an adult suffering from Borderline Personality Disorder. Although we usually don't formulate our thinking about these problems in this way, we and our patients might benefit from our doing so. We could, for instance, monitor our patients' and our own ease of informational transfer across different kinds of problem-solving.
40 I'm telling it this way to highlight two very different ways we can think about what's going on.
41 This little sentence slips in the fact that we will be using a Post-Structural philosophical tool to explore a neurodevelopmental process.
42 Other adults, but also children, and animals with whom they are involved.
43 In their defense, Krauss and colleagues have acknowledged that, although FOXP2 is the only gene we have found to be associated with speech and language, this should not be taken to mean that the latter are not complex genetic processes. What we *can* say is that an intact FOXP2 is a necessary prerequisite for speech and language: whether it is also sufficient remains to be seen.
44 This neuro-socio-developmental process cannot be explained, contrary to past attempts to do so, in terms of classic Skinnerian reinforcement.

References

Anglin, J. M., Miller, G. A., & Wakefield, K. C. (1993). Vocabulary development: A morphological analysis. *Monographs of the Society for Research in Child Development* (Vol. 58). New York: Wiley.

Baars, B. J. (2003). How does a serial, integrated, and very limited stream of consciousness emerge from a nervous system that is mostly unconscious, distributed, parallel and of enormous capacity? In B. J. Baars, W. P. Banks, & J. B. Newman (Eds.), *Essential sources in the scientific study of consciousness* (pp. 1123–1129). Cambridge: MIT Press (Original work published in 1993.)

Bar-Yosef, O. (2002). The Upper Paleolithic revolution. *Annual Review of Anthropology, 31*, 363–393.

Baron-Cohen, S., Tager-Flusberg, H., & Cohen, D. J. (2000). *Understanding other minds: Prespectives from developmental cognitive science* (2nd ed.). Oxford: Oxford University Press.

Bell, J. A. (1994). Interpretation and testability in theories about prehistoric thinking. In C. Renfrew & E. W. Zubrow (Eds.), *The ancient mind: Elements of cognitive archaeology* (pp. 15–21). Cambridge: Cambridge University Press.

Benítez-Burraco, A., Longa, V. M., Lorenzo, G., & Uriagereka, J. (2008). Also sprach Neandertalis … Or did she? *Biolinguistics, 2*, 225–232.
Bowlby, J. (1958). The nature of the child's tie to his mother: *International Journal of Psycho-Analysis, 39*, 350–373.
Bowlby, J. (1969). *Attachment and loss volume 1: Attachment.* New York Basic Books.
Bowlby, J. (1973). *Separation: Anxiety and anger, attachment and loss* (Vol. 2). New York: Basic Books.
Bråten, S., & Trevarthen, C. (2007). Prologue: From infant intersubjectivity and participant movements to simulation and conversation in cultural common sense. In S. Bråten (Ed.), *On being moved: From mirror neurons to empathy* (Vol. 68, pp. 21–34). Amsterdam: John Benjamins Publishing Company.
Buckner, R. L., & Krienen, F. M. (2013). The evolution of distributed association networks in the human brain. *Trends in Cognitive Sciences, 17*, 648–665.
Burghardt, G. M. (2005). *The genesis of animal play: Testing the limits.* Cambridge: MIT Press.
Charrier, C., Joshi, K., Coutinho-Budd, J., Kim, J., Lambert, N., de Marchena, J., … Polleux, F. (2012). Inhibition of SRGAP2 function by its human-specific paralogs induces neoteny during spine maturation. *Cell, 149*, 4, 923–935.
Chechik, G., Meilijson, I., & Ruppin, E. (1999). Neuronal regulation: A mechanism for synaptic pruning during brain maturation. *Neural Computation, 11*, 2061–2080.
Christakis, N. A., & Fowler, J. H. (2009). *Connected: The surprising power of our social networks and how they shape our lives.* New York: Little, Brown and Company.
Clowry, G. J. (2014). Seeking clues in brain development to explain the extraordinary evolution of language in humans. *Language Sciences, 46*, 220–231.
Coop, G., Bullaughey, K., Luca, F., & Przewoski, M. (2008). The timing of selection at the human *FOXP2* gene. *Molecular Biology and Evolution, 25*, 1257–1259.
Corballis, M. C. (2010). Mirror neurons and the evolution of language. *Brain & Language, 112*, 25–35.
Craik, K. (1952). *The nature of explanation.* Cambridge: Cambridge University Press. (Original work published in 1943.)
Crick, F. C., & Koch, C. (2005). What is the function of the claustrum? *Philosophical Transactions of the Royal Society Biological Sciences, 360*, 1271–1279.
Dennett, D. C. (1988). The intentional stance in theory and practice. In R. Byrne & A. Whiten (Eds.), *Machiavellian intelligence: Social expertise and the evolution of intellect in monkeys, apes, and man* (pp. 180–202). Oxford: Oxford University Press.
Dennett, D. C. (1991). *Consciousness explained.* New York: Little, Brown and Company.
Dennis, M. Y., Nuttle, X., Sudmant, P. H., Antonacci, F., Graves, T. A., Nefedov, M., … Eichler, E. E. (2012). Evolution of human-specific neural SRGAP2 genes by incomplete segmental duplication. *Cell, 149*, 4, 912–922.
DeSilva, J. M. (2016). Brains, birth, bipedalism, and the mosaic evolution of the helpless human infant. In W. R. Trevathan & K. R. Rosenberg (Eds.), *Costly and cute: Helpless infants and human evolution* (pp. 67–86). Albuquerque: University of New Mexico Press.
Donald, M. (1991). *Origins of the modern mind: Three stages in the evolution of culture and cognition.* Cambridge: Harvard University Press.
Donald, M. (2001). *A mind so rare: The evolution of human consciousness.* New York: W. W. Norton & Co.
Dunbar, R. (1993). Coevolution of neocortex size, group size and language in humans. *Behavioral and Brain Sciences, 16*, 681–694.
Dunbar, R. (2016). *Human evolution: Our brains and behavior.* Oxford: Oxford University Press.
Enard, W., Przewoski, M., Fisher, S. E., Lal, C. S. L., Wiebe, V., Kitano, T., … Pääbo, S. (2002). Molecular evolution of *FOXP2*, a gene involved in speech and language. *Nature, 418*, 869–872.

Evans, V. (2015). *The crucible of language: How language and mind create meaning.* Cambridge: Cambridge University Press.

Fadiga, L., & Craighero, L. (2007). Cues on the origin of language: From electrophysiological data on mirror neurons and motor representations. In S. Bråten (Ed.), *On being moved: From mirror neurons to empathy* (pp. 101–110). Amsterdam: John Benjamins Publishing Company.

Falk, D. (2011). *The fossil chronicles: How two controversial discoveries changed our view of human evolution.* Berkeley: University of California Press.

Falk, D. (2016). Evolution of brain and culture: The neurological and cognitive journey for *Australopithicus* to Albert Einstein. *Journal of Anthropological Sciences, 94,* 1–14.

Falk, D., & Clarke, R. (2007). Brief communication: New reconstruction of the Taung endocast. *American Journal of Physical Anthropology, 134,* 529–534.

Falk, D., Redmond Jr., J. C., Guyer, J., Conroy, G. C., Recheis, W., Weber, G. W., & Seidler, H. (2000). Early hominid brain evolution: A new look at old endocasts. *Journal of Human Evolution, 38,* 695–717.

Falk, D., Zollikofer, C. P. E., Morimoto, N., & Ponce de Leon, M. S. (2012). Metopic suture of Taung (*australopithicus africanus*) and its implications for hominin brain evolution. *Proceedings of the National Academy of Science, 109,* 8467–8470.

Feinberg, T. E., & Mallatt, J. M. (2016). *The ancient origins of consciousness: How the brain created experience.* Cambridge: MIT Press.

Gallup Jr., G. G. (1968). Mirror image stimulation. *Psychological Bulletin, 70,* 782–793.

Gogtay, N., Giedd, J. N., Lusk, L., Hayashi, K. M., Greenstein, D., Vaituzis, C., … Thompson, P. M. (2004). Dynamic mapping of human cortical development during childhood through early adulthood. *Proceedings of the National Academy of Science, 101,* 8174–8179.

Heidegger, M. (2010). *Being and time* (J. Stambaugh & D. J. Schmidt, Trans.). Albany: State University of New York. (Original work published in 1927.)

Hoff, E. (2009). *Language development* (4th ed.). Belmont, California: Wadsworth.

Homer (1998). *The Iliad* (R. Fagles, Trans.). New York: Penguin Books.

Hoppe, K. D. (1977). Split brains and psychoanalysis. *Psychoanalytic Quarterly, 46,* 220–244.

Humphrey, N. K. (1988). The social function of intellect. In R. Byrne & A. Whiten (Eds.), *Machiavellian intelligence: Social expertise and the evolution of intellect in monkeys, apes, and humans* (pp. 13–26). Oxford: Oxford University Press. (Original work published in 1976.)

Hurst, J. A., Baraitser, M., Auger, E., Graham, F., & Norell, S. (1990). An extended family with a dominantly inherited speech disorder. *Developmental Medicine and Child Neurology, 32,* 352–355.

Jablonka, E., & Lamb, M. J. (2014). *Evolution in four dimensions: Genetic, epigenetic, behavioral, and symbolic variation in the history of life* (rev. ed.). Cambridge: MIT Press.

Jacobson, E. (1964). *The self and the object world.* New York: International Universities Press.

Jaynes, J. (1977). *The origins of consciousness in the breakdown of the bicameral mind.* Boston: Houghton Mifflin Company.

Kinsbourne, M. (2005). A continuum of self-consciousness that emerges in phylogeny and ontogeny. In H. S. Terrace & J. Metcalfe (Eds.), *The missing link in cognition: Origins of self-reflective consciousness* (pp. 142–156). Oxford: Oxford University Press.

Klein, R. G. (2001). Southern Africa and modern human origins. *Journal of Anthropological Research, 57,* 1–16.

Krauss, J., Lalueza-Fox, C., Orlando, L., Enard, W., Green, R. E., Burbano, H. A., … Pääbo, S. (2007). The derived FOXP2 variant of modern humans was shared with Neandertals. *Current Biology, 17,* 1908–1912.

Kuhl, P. K. (2000). A new view of language acquisition. *Proceedings of the National Academy of Science, 97,* 11850–11857.

Leffert, M. (2008). Complexity and postmodernism in contemporary theory of psychoanalytic change. *Journal of the American Academy of Psychoanalysis and Dynamic Psychiatry, 36,* 517–542.

Leffert, M. (2010). *Contemporary psychoanalytic foundations.* London: Routledge.

Leffert, M. (2013). *The therapeutic situation in the 21st century.* New York: Routledge.

Leffert, M. (2016). *Phenomenology, uncertainty, and care in the therapeutic encounter.* New York: Routledge.

Leffert, M. (2017). *Positive psychoanalysis: Aesthetics, desire, and subjective well-being.* New York: Routledge.

Lewis, M., Brooks-Gunn, J., & Jaskir, J. (1985). Individual differences in visual self-recognition as a function of mother-infant attachment relationship. *Developmental Psychobiology, 21,* 1181–1187.

Liégois, F., Baldeweg, T., Connelly, A., Gadian, D. G., Mishkin, M., & Vargha-Khadem, F. (2003). Language fmri abnormalities associated with *FOXP2* gene mutation. *Nature Neuroscience, 6,* 1230–1237.

Mahler, M. S., Pine, F., & Bergman, A. (1975). *The psychological birth of the human infant: Symbiosis and individuation.* New York: Basic Books.

Marshack, A. (1991). *The roots of civilization.* Mt. Kisco, New York: Moyer Bell Limited.

McBrearty, S., & Brooks, A. S. (2000). The revolution that wasn't: A new interpretation of the origin of modern human behavior. *Journal of Human Evolution, 39,* 453–563.

Mellars, P. (2004). Neanderthals and the modern colonization of Europe. *Nature, 432,* 461–465.

Mellars, P. (2005). The impossible coincidence. A single-species model for the origins of modern human behavior in Europe. *Evolutionary Anthropology, 14,* 12–27.

Mithen, S. (1994). From domain specific to generalized intelligence: A cognitive interpretation of the Middle/Upper Paleolithic transition. In C. Renfrew & E. W. Zubrow (Eds.), *The ancient mind: Elements of cognitive archaeology* (pp. 29–39). Cambridge: Cambridge University Press.

Mithen, S. (1998). *The prehistory of the mind: A search for the origins of art, religion, and science.* London: Orion House. (Original work published in 1996.)

Mithen, S. (2006). *After the ice: A global human history 20,000–5000 BC.* Cambridge: Harvard University Press.

Murray, E. A., Wise, S. P., & Graham, K. S. (2017). *The evolution of memory systems: Ancestors, anatomy, and adaptations.* Oxford: Oxford University Press.

Nelson, K. (2005). Emerging levels of consciousness in early human development. In H. S. Terrace & J. Metcalfe (Eds.), *The missing link in cognition: Origins of self-reflective consciousness* (pp. 116–141). Oxford: Oxford University Press.

Nisbett, R. E., & Wilson, T. (1977). Telling more than we can know: Verbal reports on mental processes. *Psychological Review, 84,* 231–259.

Ogden, P. (2009). Emotion, mindfulness and movement: Expanding the regulatory boundaries of the window of affect tolerance. In D. Fosha, D. J. Siegal, & M. F. Solomon (Eds.), *The healing power of emotion: Affective neuroscience, development, and clinical practice* (pp. 204–231). New York: W. W. Norton & Co.

Panksepp, J., & Biven, L. (2012). *The archaeology of mind: Neuroevolutionary origins of human emotions.* New York: W. W. Norton & Co.

Panksepp, J., & Watt, D. (2011). What is basic about basic emotions? Lasting lessons from affective neuroscience. *Emotion Review, 3,* 1–10.

Papagianni, D., & Morse, M. A. (2015). *The Neanderthals rediscovered: How modern science is rewriting their history.* London: Thames & Hudson.

Parsons, C. E., Stark, E. A., Young, K. S., Stein, A. D., & Kringelbach, M. L. (2013). Understanding the human parental brain: A critical role of the orbitofrontal cortex. *Social Neuroscience, 8,* 525–543.

Poeppel, D., Emmorey, K., Hickok, G., & Pylkänen, L. (2012). Toward a new neurobiology of language. *The Journal of Neuroscience, 32,* 14125–14131.

Reardon, S. (2012). The humanity switch. *NewScientist, 214,* 10–11.

Reardon, S. (2017). Giant neuron encircles entire brain of a mouse. *Nature, 543,* 14–15.

Renfrew, C. (1994). Towards a cognitive archaeology. In C. Renfrew & E. W. Zubrow (Eds.), *The ancient mind: Elements of cognitive archaeology* (pp. 3–12). Cambridge: Cambridge University Press.

Schore, A. N. (1994). *Affect regulation and the origin of the self.* Hillside: Lawrence Earlbaum Associates.

Schore, A. N. (2003a). *Affect dysregulation and disorders of the self.* New York: W. W. Norton & Co.

Schore, A. N. (2003b). *Affect regulation and the repair of the self.* New York: W. W. Norton & Co.

Schore, A. N. (2009). Right-brain affect regulation: An essential mechanism of development, trauma, dissociation, and psychotherapy. In D. Fosha, D. J. Siegal, & M. F. Solomon (Eds.), *The healing power of emotion: Affective neuroscience, development, and clinical practice* (pp. 112–144). New York: W. W. Norton & Co.

Schore, A. N. (2011). The right brain implicit self lies at the core of psychoanalysis. *Psychoanalytic Dialogues, 21,* 75–100.

Schore, J. R., & Schore, A. N. (2007). Modern attachment theory: The central role of affect regulation in development and treatment. *Clinical Social Work Journal, 36,* 9–20.

Segal, E. M. (1994). Archaeology and cognitive science. In C. Renfrew & E. W. Zubrow (Eds.), *The ancient mind: Elements of cognitive archaeology* (pp. 22–28). Cambridge: Cambridge University Press.

Semendeferi, K., & Hanson, K. L. (2016). Plastic and heterogenous: Postnatal developmental changes in the human brain. In W. R. Trevathan & K. R. Rosenberg (Eds.), *Costly and cute: Helpless infants and human evolution* (pp. 133–147). Santa Fe: University of New Mexico Press.

Sperry, R. W. (1969). A modified concept of consciousness. *Psychological Review, 76,* 532–536.

Sperry, R. W., Gazzaniga, M. S., & Bogen, J. E. (1969). The neocortical commissures: Syndromes of hemisphere disconnection. In P. J. Vinken & G. W. Bruyn (Eds.), *Handbook of clinical neurology* (Vol. 4). Amsterdam: North Holland Publishing Company.

Stringer, C., & Gamble, C. (1993). *In search of the Neanderthals.* London: Thames & Hudson.

Tannen, D. (1990). *You just don't understand: Men and women in conversation.* New York: Morrow.

Terrace, H. S. (2005). Metacognition and the evolution of language. In H. S. Terrace & J. Metcalfe (Eds.), *The missing link in cognition: Origins of self-reflective consciousness* (pp. 84–115). Oxford: Oxford University Press.

Terrace, H. S., & Metcalfe, J. (Eds.). (2005). *The missing link in cognition: Origins of self-reflective consciousness.* Oxford: Oxford University Press.

Trevarthen, C. (1974). Conversation with a two month old. *New Scientist, 2,* 230–235.

Trevarthen, C. (2009). The function of emotion in infancy: The regulation and communication of rythm, sympathy and meaning in human development. In D. Fosha, D. J. Siegal, & M. Solomon (Eds.), *The healing power of emotion: Affective neuroscience, development & clinical practice* (pp. 55–85). New York: W. W. Norton & Co.

Trevathan, W. R., & Rosenberg, K. R. (2016a). Human evolution and the helpless infant. In W. R. Trevathan & K. R. Rosenberg (Eds.), *Costly and cute: Helpless infants and human evolution* (pp. 1–28). Santa Fe: University of New Mexico Press.

Trevathan, W. R., & Rosenberg, K. R. (Eds.). (2016b). *Costly and cute: Helpless infants and human evolution.* Albuquerque: University of New Mexico Press.

Tulving, E. (1983). *Elements of episodic memory.* Oxford: Clarendon Press.

Tulving, E. (2003). Memory and consciousness. In B. J. Baars, W. P. Banks, & J. B. Newman (Eds.), *Essential sources in the scientific study of consciousness* (pp. 575–591). Cambridge: MIT Press. (Original work published in 1985.)

Tulving, E. (2005). Episodic memory and autonoesis: Uniquely human? In H. S. Terrace & J. Metcalfe (Eds.), *The missing link in cognition: Origins of self-reflective consciousness* (pp. 3–56). Oxford: Oxford University Press.

Tulving, E., & Schacter, D. L. (1990). Priming and human memory systems. *Science, 247,* 302–306.

Tversky, A., & Kahneman, D. (1982). Judgment under uncertainty: Heuristics and biases. In D. Kahneman, P. Slovic, & A. Tversky (Eds.), *Judgment under uncertainty: Heuristics and biases* (pp. 3–20). Cambridge: Cambridge University Press. (Original work published in 1974.)

Uddin, L. Q., Iacoboni, M., Lange, C., & Keenan, J. P. (2007). The self and social cognition: The role of cortical midline structures and mirror neurons. *Trends in Cognitive Sciences, 11,* 153–157.

Vargha-Khadem, F., Watkins, K., Alcock, K., Fletcher, P., & Passingham, R. (1995). Praxic and nonverbal cognitive deficits in a large family with a genetically transmitted speech and language disorder. *Proceedings of the National Academy of Science, 92,* 930–933.

von Senden, M. (1960). *Space and sight: The perception of space and shape in the congenitally blind before and after operation* (S. Schweppe, Trans.). London: Metheun & Co. (Original work published in 1932.)

White, S. A. (2013). FoxP2 and vocalization. In C. Lefebvre, B. Comrie, & H. Cohen (Eds.), *New perspectives on the origins of language* (pp. 211–235). Amsterdam: John Benjamins Publishing Company.

Whiten, A., & Byrne, R. (1988). The Machiavellian intelligence hypothesis. In A. Whiten & R. Byrne (Eds.), *Machiavellian intelligence: Social expertise and the evolution of intellect in monkeys, apes, and humans* (pp. 1–9). Oxford: Oxford University Press.

5
BEING AND NOTHINGNESS OR TO BE OR NOT TO BE

Introduction

In the previous three chapters we talked about how we Human Beings came to be: our Evo-Devo, the confluence of Phylogeny and Ontology, and our paleoanthropology, how we progressed from the Southern Apes to the Wise Guys. That process culminated in the appearance in *H. sapiens sapiens* of Autonoetic Consciousness. In this chapter, we will turn from Evo-Devo to Existentialism and Phenomenology to discuss the failures of the Self, the diseases of Being, their origins, and their treatment. *It is the Self that remains the subject of this new discourse.* A comprehensive account of these issues cannot fit within the confines of a single chapter; it is meant to be a meaningful introduction to what will be taken up in a subsequent volume.

Authors (myself included) have struggled to draw a distinction between Phenomenology and Existentialism. It now seems to me that they are simply coming at the same problem of Being in two different ways: each necessary but not in itself sufficient. Phenomenology is a branch of ontological study; it amounts to a scientific inquiry into the nature of human existence. Existentialism offers a complementary inquiry into the human psychology of Being. The work of Medard Boss, *Psychoanalysis and Daseinanalysis* (1963), provides a rare clinical bridge between the two.

If we are engaged in an Evo-Devo grounded Existentialist enterprise (an interesting conjunction in and of itself), we must draw on a number of bodies of literature in order to do so. One is the Existentialist *Philosophy* of the 1930s and 1940s, and another is the Existentialist *Psychoanalysis* of the 1950s and 1960s, centered around the work of Rollo May (May, Angel, & Ellenberger, 1958) and his colleagues (Leffert, 2016, Chapters 2 and 3). Both fell out of favor among the great majority of psychotherapists and psychoanalysts,[1] certainly by the late 1970s, for unclear reasons having more to do with the politics of theory than clinical failure. They were replaced by the "next big thing," Self-Psychology, without any sense at all that the latter might owe some debt to the former. Towards the end of the 20th century, there was a resurrection of these ideas in a Phenomenological psychotherapy growing out of the Intersubjective School with its impetus provided by Robert Stolorow and his colleagues (Stolorow, 2011; Stolorow & Atwood, 1992; Stolorow, Orange, & Atwood, 2002). This is a bottoms-up, patient to theory, not a top-down, theory to patient approach, primarily referencing the works of Martin Heidegger (Heidegger, 1975/1982, 1987/2001, 1927/2010; Leffert, 2016). As useful as it has proven to be, it didn't quite capture the Existentialist slant on Human Being that I am taking up here.

Although it involves a different and at times unfamiliar language, dealing with this problem of Existence is the essence of the task facing us as psychotherapists. I would posit that we all should be thinking Existentiality about our patients. Paradoxically, most people (and I include here a majority of people who are not also our patients) are mostly oblivious to the problem: They are only reminded of it by the death of a friend or loved one, a failure in living, or when sociocultural, or personal circumstances render life problematic. Indeed, most people, most of the time, live happily in a state of Everydayness where a regression to the absurd or the fallen (to draw together Existentialism and Phenomenology) may lead to a depression and can bring them to consult us.

Existentialist psychoanalysis offers a critique of the idea of a dynamic unconscious defined by repression, which, combined with confirming data drawn from the neurosciences, I have been (Leffert, 2010, 2013) and remain sympathetic to. It has also offered a critique of the concept of psychological depth, a critique that most psychoanalytically oriented psychotherapists find uncongenial. There is some misunderstanding here. Existentialism *is* critical of the concept of unconscious psychic depth and the notion of buried (that is repressed) things, but that does not mean it is exclusively rooted in a conscious present. What we have instead of depth is *historicity* and the dynamic past that influences present action and feeling but is subject to analytic inquiry.

An area of Existentialist thought and its clinical applications that has mostly fallen out of favor has to do with the central idea that the Self dwells in an *absurd* World and is, at times, overwhelmed by it. What we all do clinically, in whatever manner we do it, and with whatever language we use to describe it, is to access and treat that absurdity and the way a patient unknowingly replicates it. Stoltzfus (2003) offers a useful working definition:

> The absurd describes the state of mind of individuals who are conscious of a discrepancy between desire and reality: the desire for freedom, happiness, and immortality, and the knowledge that life imposes limits on desire even as death announces finitude.
>
> (p. 1)[2]

Death in an absurd world is an issue, which Camus (1942/1989, 1942/1991) was much taken up with: among clinicians, Yalom (1980, 1989/2012) is perhaps the lone author to continue to write about death and its clinical ramifications.

If the Absurd is a principle subject of existential inquiry, it leads us to cognitive and emotional issues that are better explored phenomenologically, as the things themselves (Husserl, 1937/1970, 1913/1983). They must be thought of as fully deployed (Heidegger, 1975/1982), rather than metapsychologically conceived of as things rooted in an unavailable unconscious concealed by repression. Consciousness (Autonoetic Consciousness, actually) is central to existentialist thought and is also seen as the peak of Evo-Devo in the history of Human Beings (Donald, 2001; Humphrey, 1992/1999, 2011). Unfortunately, consciousness receives short shrift in many psychoanalytic circles; much of psychoanalysis is based on trying to see *past* conscious mental activity in the search for putatively dynamically unconscious wishes, fears, and so on. A misunderstanding of this divergence may well have been at the root of existentialism's fall from therapeutic interest.[3]

The term Existential has come into such common, such everyday usage that it has lost its meaning. People will call an artist or a writer an Existentialist as if it is a term like *radical* or *philosophical* that is immediately understood. What does it mean, then? Jean-Paul Sartre (1997/2007), who got in on the ground floor, says quite simply that it is "the belief that existence precedes essence; or, if you prefer, that *subjectivity* [emphasis added] must be our point of departure" (p. 20). He goes on to clarify this with the example that the existence of man [*sic*] precedes his essence that a man first comes into existence and then, subjectively, defines himself. Man is what he wills himself to be after he is *thrown* into existence (we see Heidegger here). Existentialism as a philosophical point of view seeks to understand the psychology of the human condition. The cognitive issues that it addresses are being and nothingness, life and death, living and dying. The emotions, the *feelings* (as opposed to affective products of metapsychology) that it tackles are anxiety, despair, misery, hopelessness, and depression, not in any order of importance. The question we also have to ask is whether these various things are parts of the human condition or, instead, diseases of Human Being, and hence subject to treatment. I opt for the latter with the proviso that at times natural or cultural disasters trump the individual.[4] I have already (Leffert, 2017) had something to say about the latter and we will deal with it again here.

Camus and Hemingway

Beyond the kitschy chapter title, I want to suggest two different although related Existential failures in Human Being with the tension between them, their *différance*, defining the contemporary psychoanalytic enterprise. I'm going to first draw on the work of two 20th century authors, Camus (1942/1989, 1942/1991) and Hemingway (1926/2006), to define this workspace,[5] and then proceed to an extended case illustration. Although they are not often spoken of in the same breath today, there is a small but determined literature (Stoltzfus, 2003) on how Camus read and was influenced by Hemingway, the hard-boiled American detective fiction of the 1930s, and Faulkner. As Sartre (1946) put it, "They both took from Faulkner the method of reflecting different aspects of the same event, through the monologues of different sensitivities" (p. 114). They both, broadly speaking, drew their characters from life (Blume, 2017; Kaplan, 2016) and are, I would posit, writing philosophy, and clinical psychology as well as literature. It is precisely their differing sensibilities that interest us as therapists and that we listen for clinically with our patients. This is why we need to pay particular attention to the differing narratives of the same event that patients tell us over the course of a therapy.

What I want to begin with here is how *they* began their first books, *The Stranger* and *The Sun Also Rises*.[6] These beginnings are equivalent to our patients' beginnings, their first words to us, usually spoken over the phone when they request an appointment. In *The Stranger* (Camus, 1942/1989), Meursault (whose surname alone we only learn a third of the way through the book) begins his story with a number of facts, his *Maman* (Momma or Mommy) died today. Or was it yesterday, maybe? He just doesn't know. (His not knowing is the first thing that strikes us, even before his mother's death.) Meanwhile, 27 years earlier (Hemingway, 1926/2006), Jacob Barnes, Jake, whose name we shortly find out, told us that Robert Cohn had been the middleweight boxing champion of Princeton. He assures us that this meant nothing to either Cohn or himself. (So why tell us? Again, this may be the first thing that strikes us.) The way that Meursault tells us that he has lost his Maman reveals that there is something very wrong with his connection to his world (and to his mother), and we can soon figure out that there is something very wrong, an emptiness, inside of *him*, his *Eigenwelt* (Heidegger, 1927/2010). Jake, on the other hand, offers us a few short punching sentences that tell us about Robert Cohn and his success, a character incidental to Jake's issue:[7] trying to adapt to what the world has made him and finding it impossible. Their writing is remarkably similar— "the same short, brutal sentences, the same lack of psychological analysis" (Sartre, 1946, p. 114)— although the similarities are obscured by their so different sensibilities. While both narratives stay in the present, this should not be taken to mean that there is no past (a misunderstanding of Existentialism), *only that it is not commented on*. Both protagonists are fallen, but it is Jake's sensitivities in place of Meursault's otherness that make it easier to ache for him. If there are previously unlooked for similarities in Hemingway and Camus, they are to be found between the poles of the *différance* of their sensitivities. Meursault tells his story dissociatively, with a degree of depersonalization. Jake, to the contrary, is engaged with life, so much so that we may fail to notice that the people he interacts with are not. Our exploration of these problems constitutes the essence of the Existentialist enterprise in psychoanalysis. (As we have seen, not just in the previous chapters, there are many psychoanalytic enterprises and this is but one of them.)

Both authors write in what Hemingway described as an *iceberg style* (1932/1960) and what would come to be called the Iceberg Theory or the theory of omission (Smith, 1983). Its dual premises are that the bulk of a text remains unexpressed, beneath the surface, and that the author *communicates* as much by what he leaves unsaid, as by what he does say. This is a point of view that we, as psychotherapists, could be expected to be much in sympathy with.) In the immortal words of Joe Friday, "Just the facts, Ma'am." But *which* facts, and in *what* order? The theory would seem to suggest that the decisions about what goes in and what is omitted are consciously made when we know that that can be only partly true of such decisions. Listening to our patients in order to hear what's in the spaces, what's unsaid, is very much what we *do* as psychotherapists. Both the Iceberg Theory and clinical listening are consistent with Heideggerian ontology in which all is deployed (in place of an undeployed unconscious) but much can be hidden or secret.

What Camus' and Hemingway's protagonists struggle with is their fallen experience of the meaninglessness of life and whether it is even possible to recover meaning. Camus and Hemingway (the authors) struggle with the question of whether this is a problem that goes beyond their protagonists' suffering, a problem that exists in the very essence of the human condition. We, as therapists, implicitly, or explicitly take a very different position, that they are diseases of Being with which particular individuals are afflicted.[8] The pursuit of Meaning and the cure of meaninglessness (Leffert, 2016, Chapter 6) are aspects of our psychoanalytic enterprise (Leffert, 2017, Chapter 2).

In the past, I have been critical of attempting to psychoanalyze authors (Leffert, 2017, Chapter 4) by analyzing the characters in their books. Although such analyses offer material for endlessly satisfying debate and, after all, in the end, harm no one, they lack any sort of ontological standing. A different sort of analysis that looks at how an author constructed a work of fiction and what he is saying *is* valid. What I am offering here is what might be called a phenomenological report on Camus' and Hemingway's protagonists and the territory they are trying to navigate that returns to "the things themselves" (Husserl, 1925/1977), their fully deployed selves, and the partially deployed worlds they inhabit. We are interested in their Being and the diseases (to emphasize their gravity) of the Self with which they are afflicted. The sociocultural environment of France—that of the Lost Generation in the 1920s in Jake's case and that of France's impotence in the 1930s and the Nazi occupation of the 1940s in Meursault's—dominates both books. The authors, through their work, are speaking to their *contemporaries*, and to understand the meaning of what they wrote we must stay within *that contemporary context*. The dilemmas of their protagonists are described entirely in terms of the then present; they are portrayed as ahistorical, yet we know that such cannot be the case.

I am, however, after bigger game. I want to use these accounts to lead into an Existential account of Human Being and—a difficult task—to inform this account with what we learned about our origins, our Phylogeny and Ontology, in the last chapter. We are interested in a conversation that seeks to deconstruct the absurd. So what, exactly, is it that is desired and unobtainable for Jake and Meursault?

In a previous volume, *Positive Psychoanalysis: Aesthetics, Desire, and Subjective Well-Being* (SWB) (Leffert, 2017), I discussed a major deficiency in psychoanalytic discourse, how to correct it and, finally, how to apply it to the therapeutic situation. The work of Ed Diener (2009a, 2009b, 2009c) on SWB is of particular relevance here. It involves the things, freedoms, and happiness that go into well-being: I took up the therapeutic questions of how some individuals find them unattainable for internal *or* external reasons and what might be done to restore well-being. Some preliminary work done by Bitwas-Diener and Diener (2001), suggested that environment might not be the implacable factor it has been thought to be. They studied individuals living in circumstances of great adversity in the slums of Calcutta and found, in contrast to Camus' and Hemingway's characters, that states of SWB were to be had by some even there. This leads us to a discussion of Human Being in the face of the absurd, which goes beyond Conflict Theory, Intersubjectivity, and Relational Theory. The Existentialists suggest that the ultimate absurdity is life itself, in which we are present for a time, *exist* for a time, seek meaning, and then die, and *cease to exist*.

The First World War left both victor and vanquished, France and Germany, in states of despair and exhaustion. It was, by all metrics, an absurd war. That absurdity continued in France through the Second World War. It continued for a time in Germany where it produced an *apparent* (to the Germans of the 1930s) solution: the rise of Hitler and the Nazi state, then, a second severer collapse and failure, that, this time, was somehow constructive. It was left to the members of the Existentialist movement in France during the nihilism of the 1930s[9] and the German occupation of the 1940s to document and attempt to make sense of their situation. *The Stranger* was one of many attempts to do so.

Let's begin with a look at our two protagonists: Meursault and Jake.

Meursault the antihero

The first thing about *The Stranger* that you must remember, *and the one that is most often forgotten*, is its context. *The Stranger* is a central text of the existentialist movement of 1930s France, but it was published in a Nazi-occupied France in 1942 in the face of that period's intellectual oppression. It had to get past Nazi censors. The second is that it is not a book about colonial Algeria or Algerians in spite of at times being mistaken for such by contemporary Post-Colonial authors (e.g., Daoud, 2013/2015). The third is that although a novel, it is also an early text of a new philosophical discipline: Existentialism. Camus observed in his *Notebooks* (1962/1963) that if you want to do philosophy, write novels and *The Stranger* must be read with that in mind. *The Stranger* is unusual in that an essay, *The Myth of Sisyphus* (Camus, 1942/1991), was written as a kind of study guide for us and published more or less simultaneously by this then mostly unknown 29-year-old Algerian author.

As Meursault describes it (and just why he bothers to describe it given his listless connection to his world, remains unstated), he is living his life once removed from the world of people and things, in a state of depersonalization and derealization: The metaphors living a dream, living in a fog, or experiencing life as observed behind a glass wall come to mind. The novel is divided into two parts. It begins with his telling us that his mother has died and his travel arrangements to attend the funeral. He had placed her, against her will, in an old people's home 3 years before. It is in Marengo, 80 km from Algiers where he still inhabits the apartment that he had previously shared with her. There is a journey and a lengthy series of funeral scenes under a blazing Algerian sun. He is at some pains to avoid any interchange, particularly of feelings, with the people he encounters; his disassociation is noticed and reverberates in the novel's second part. Upon his return, he takes a girl he has met to a movie and then sleeps with her; she is surprised when he tells her of his mother's death because he had acted as if nothing has happened. The story evolves with *apparent* pointlessness, sketching human vignettes as it goes, culminating with Meursault's shooting and killing a man, an Arab, while he remains in his depersonalized state. Part 2 is the story of the trial. What seems strange is that they would even bother trying a Frenchman for the murder of an Arab in 1930s Algeria. And, indeed, the trial has little to do with the murder, beyond first ascertaining that he did it. What the trial involves is a series of witnesses describing Meursault's lack of feeling or focus, the absence of grief during his vigil over his mothers' body and the ensuing funeral procession and funeral activities. He is being tried for his *disassociation*. The prosecutor sums up the case, not in terms of the murder, but in terms of Meursault's total emptiness: He lacks a "soul" and any human feeling to put into it. He cannot think, feel, or speak *anything* about her death or the murder except about the physical discomfort, and the heat of the sun at the funeral. *This* is his crime. This is the information that is presented as evidence of his guilt.

The story he tells us is bounded by his mother's death at the beginning and his impending execution via guillotine for this meaningless murder that is about to happen at the end. Looking forward to the execution somehow restores meaning and happiness to Meursault's life and, if a large crowd is present at the execution, one that will greet him with hate, it will help him to feel less alone. The execution also seems to constitute some sort of reconnection to his mother. This engagement in a restorative death sounds like a Heideggerian return to thrownness, similar to the concept of a restorative death via suicide, a concept popular in the coffee houses of *fin de siècle* Vienna (Janik & Toulmin, 1973/1996; Johnston, 1972). Here we are aided by The *Myth of Sisyphus*, which tells us that Camus knew Heidegger's work and used it in support of his own ideas about anxiety, nothingness, and death.

This is a strange story. Meursault's lack of engagement and what he implies (the iceberg) in the manner in which he tells it makes it hard to feel sympathy for him and impossible to empathize with him. A question to ask is: Do we actually see patients like this, and how do they appear to us? As May (1958a) puts it, can we experience "the instantaneous encounter with another person who comes alive to us on a very different level from what we know *about* him" (p. 37) when meeting a patient like Meursault? Let's come back to this after we talk about Jake.

Jake the damned

Jake is a very different customer. He also tells his story in short, punchy sentences, but they are in bright colors: Meursault has only a bright yellow sun, blue water, and washed-out gray everywhere else. Recall also that *The Sun Also Rises* is a contemporaneous work: It is set in 1925; the characters are patterned after real people living the story (Blume, 2017). Reading it today we must try to grasp how it was understood and felt long ago by its 1925 Anglophone readers. Please forget the talk about it being The Great American Novel (despite the fact that this point *can* be argued). Jake, although lost, is profoundly present in the life he struggles to make sense of while many of the characters he meets, the members of his circle, are Meursaultlike. Jake very soon picks up a passing prostitute, Georgette, to share a meal with so he doesn't have to eat alone. She offers sex, and he casually tells her he can't because he is "sick," that he was "hurt" in the war. To anyone but Georgette, this is a profound and shocking disclosure in 1925 that he offers us in an exercise in understatement. To have one's genitals destroyed or damaged beyond use is the most dreaded of war wounds; scarcely a soldier exists who has not thought of it. It was also something not to be spoken of. To *casually* offer it up as an understatement would have stopped 1925 readers in their tracks, an exercise even in lascivious horror. For Jake, as any *1925* reader could understand and empathize with, this loss produced a hole in the self, one that could not be filled.

Jake and his crowd set out on a trip to the festival of San Fermin at Pamplona to watch the running of the bulls and the bull fighting. This journey is the ostensible *raison d'être* for this book as the journey and funeral cortege were for *The Stranger*. It is implied that this journey will solve the different Existential problems with which members of the group are afflicted. It of course does nothing of the kind. A man running before the bulls is gored and killed. It is a pointless death, just as Meursault's shooting his Arab was pointless and Jake's wounding was pointless.

Hemingway's story lives between the two epigraphs that he conveniently provides us with: Gertrude Stein's observation, "You are all a lost generation" and the passage from Ecclesiastes: "One generation passeth away, and another generation cometh: but the earth abideth forever. *The sun also ariseth,* [emphasis added] and the sun goeth down..." (Eccles. 1:4–5 King James Version). The first is at once an existential pronouncement: Jake and his crowd are lost while the second is more complicated: the day will always begin again, but with opportunity, or a situation reminiscent of Prometheus or Sisyphus?

Camus, in place of an epigraph, offers us instead a whole essay on the absurd, *The Myth of Sisyphus*. In it, he gets right to the point. If life is absurd, is the only logical response to commit suicide? (Meursault's actions could be described as a form of suicide and his elation as a positive answer to this question.) Camus ultimately concludes that meaning is subjectively constructed and is to be found even in the absurd, a conclusion beyond Jake.

Clinical issues

Jake and Meursault manifest comparable degrees of damage, but different diseases of Being. They manifest different iterations of the absurd. This language might seem strange, even meaningless, to some psychotherapists and psychoanalysts. The clinical question we want to come back to is whether or not and how often we see patients like these.

Meursault exhibits an existential failure that, although I have rarely encountered it in so extreme a form, is by no means uncommon. Shifting our frame of reference for a moment, the description of his symptoms fits comfortably within the categories of the *Diagnostic and Statistical Manual of Mental Disorders, 5th Edition (DSM-5)*: He meets the criteria for the Dissociative Disorders, specifically Depersonalization/Derealization Disorder (F48.1). The old term Schizoid is also of use here (Guntrip, 1971). We understand these conditions as often arising clinically out of severe trauma, although nothing we are told about Meursault meets any of the DSM criteria for post-traumatic stress disorder (PTSD). We have, in recent years, become very interested in Trauma, Trauma having to do with real world events, not inner fantasies and their elaborations. Meursault (like Jake) offers us very little information about how he got to be himself. We are left to infer (looking in the spaces for the rest of the iceberg) that some Trauma or Traumas led Meursault to fall out of the world, and it is in this fallen state that we encounter him when he hears of his *Maman's* death.

Jake has suffered a wound to the Self that does not heal. Unlike Meursault, he perceives the damage clearly but has concluded, we would in the *21st century* say erroneously, that *nothing* can be done about it. As we understand the term, Jake's situation is absurd. We *could* describe, using older language, his having suffered a narcissistic injury, or, going back to still older language, a castration, or an Oedipal defeat; both languages fail to address the extent of the *trauma* or its grounding in a real world that acted disastrously on the Self and became meaningless. This is not about fantasy. This is part of a quiet shift in clinical thinking that includes an emphasis on World (*Mitwelt + Umwelt*) acting on the Self rather than trying to see around or through it to get at an Unconscious with its incumbent fantasies, which has been (and often still is) thought to be the real business of psychoanalysis. Jake has suffered a major trauma but does he now (in 1925) suffer from PTSD (DSM F43.10)? There is no mention of any of the symptoms of PTSD in the narrative called *The Sun Also Rises*. Jake offers the absolute minimum of information to tell us what happened (he is sick because of the war) and how it affects his life (he cannot have a relationship with Brett, the woman he loves, because he cannot perform sexually). But, given that this is an iceberg narrative in which what is left out and subject to inference is as important as what is stated, it would not be surprising to hear that he *did* suffer from flashbacks, nightmares, sleep disturbances, intrusive memories, and the other symptoms in the PTSD package. This descriptive language is more clinically relevant than is metapsychological speculation.

Erikson (1950/1953, 1950/1963) offers us psychoanalytic ways of understanding both of their conditions that does not involve a return to theory. He speaks in terms of failing to meet developmental challenges encountered in the world throughout the life cycle, developmental failures leading to identity diffusion, and the suggestion that life crises can be weathered by a healthy personality in ways that Jake and Meursault could not weather theirs. Erikson's language is more Existentialist-friendly.

If we think in terms of the British School—Winnicott (1972, 1975); Guntrip (1971); Fairbairn (1952/2013); and even Kahn (1983), who was a sufferer as well as a practitioner—we encounter another psychoanalytic language that is much more

140 Being, nothingness or to be or not to be

congenial to our attempts to understand people like Meursault and Jake in Existentialist terms. We need not be reductionists in our thinking here (this proviso should apply to all clinical thinking). By making them into potential patients, we do not lessen their essential humanity; they are still people, lost souls struggling (or not) to find a place in the world.

So let's talk about a patient. The most dramatic example of a Meursaultlike patient I have encountered in my own practice was Bill,[10] a young man I treated in the 1970s and whose case I described at some length in a very different context (Leffert, 2017, Chapter 4). Bill had served in the Coast Guard during the Vietnam War. He was stationed far from combat at a small (population 70, give or take) base in the South China Sea. He had, in some fashion that he never understood, offended one of the men at the base a couple of months after he arrived, and he had been shunned by all of the enlisted men for the rest of his 1 year tour-of-duty on the island. He would sit alone in the mess hall: If he tried to sit next to someone, they would move away. No one spoke to him. He was never threatened with any sort of physical harm. For Bill, this was a severe trauma (*he* met the criteria for PTSD) and, driven by social anxiety, he withdrew from the world. (A different person might simply have ordered in a supply of books and journals and proceeded to have a wonderful vacation.) When I knew him, he lived alone in a Volkswagen Microbus, avoiding people and social contacts whenever possible. He was referred to me by the Veteran's Administration: I did not consider at the time how hard it *must* have been for him to come and see me for the first time, and I did not know then to welcome him as I would such a patient now. I could find nothing in his history or childhood to explain the severity of his reactions or the fact that they did not heal over time (in 1975, I knew nowhere else to look). He was on good terms with his still-living parents whom he enjoyed visiting for several days every few months (they would have been happy to have him live with them; he could not live with anyone). I could infer that his mother was deeply concerned about him, but the family did not seem to speak much about feelings.

So what was wrong with Bill, and what could be done about it? Psychoanalytic language is not much help here and, although descriptively he had suffered a trauma, this also did not help us much.

What Bill was suffering from was just the kind of Existential failure we have been talking about. His life in the South China Sea was absurd. At the time, all I had to offer him was genetic interpretations that were useless, encouragement, and an attempt, mostly unsuccessful, to get him to take small steps to reengage his world. All that 1970s talk therapy could do was to convey the fact that I wanted to care for him (Leffert, 2016, Chapter 6) even if I could not, at the time, formulate that I did, and to provide a vehicle for establishing and maintaining a healing relationship. When I wrote about him last (Leffert, 2017, Chapter 4), I suggested a mode of therapy designed to move this so impaired man back into the world: an Existential therapy. It would have involved physically taking him out into the world[11] that he had so fearfully left and talking with him about the process. What I would also have done (and would still do) would be to get him involved in aesthetic activities as a viewer or a participant, using aesthetics to directly treat his Existential withdrawal. In patients with a less severe form of Bill's condition, I would offer these remedies in smaller, less physical doses, and would expect psychotherapy or psychoanalysis to offer more than just a substrate for a healing relationship.

The Existentialist approach

What I am proposing for treating Bill is what I would call a knowledgeable as opposed to an ignorant rejection of theory. Here's what I mean. An out-of-hand rejection of theory, of metapsychology, would suggest that, in the century or so that psychoanalysis has been around, analysts have learned nothing about the human condition and made no use of whatever knowledge they did possess. The various metapsychologies do teach us something about the human condition in bits and pieces, and a thorough acquaintance with them is a desirable outcome of a psychoanalytic education. A clinical misuse of this information would be to listen to a patient's associations (as opposed to engaging him in discourse (Leffert, 2010, 2013, 2016, 2017), which I strongly recommend) until ascertaining a more than passing resemblance to one of these points of view, and then interpreting everything that follows in that light. As an example of what I mean, a colleague is the second analyst at bat in the treatment of a patient he describes as a "poster child" for an Oedipal neurosis. After many years without clinical progress, he reformulates his understanding of the patient as suffering from a narcissistic disorder. Progress is then made but—and it's a big *but*—it's not clear whether this is a metapsychological success or a result of the patient finally having an analyst actually listen to him and care for him. The change in perspective also rekindled the analyst's enthusiasm for the work with his patient. I suspect this to be more generally true and to account for why analytic patients get better in spite of their analyst's theories.

This brings us to the question of what I am offering instead. Do not believe for a moment that I am suggesting that I am the first person to raise these issues. As Rollo May (1958b) put it a half-century ago: "many psychiatrists and psychologists in Europe and others in this country have been asking themselves disquieting questions and others are aware of gnawing doubts which arise from the same half-suppressed and unasked questions" (p. 3). The problem as May put it then was the mounting numbers of patients suffering with anxiety that "*will not be quieted by theoretical formulae* [emphasis added]" (p. 3). We have beautiful theories but, when we meet a patient, are we meeting him as he is or as a projection of those selfsame theories? To rephrase the question in a different language are we simply employing a Representativeness Heuristic (Kahneman, Slovic, & Tversky, 1982)? The complimentary question is when a patient tells us about his world, how do we know if this is "really" the world he lives in? These questions, according to May, were taken up by an Existential-Analytic movement in Europe (Binswanger, 1958; Boss, 1963) derived from the Phenomenology of Martin Heidegger (1987/2001, 1927/2010).[12]

May (1958b) further posits that the Existential movement arose in clinical psychoanalysis and psychotherapy to be *more* rather than *less* scientific.[13] Its practitioners believed that then traditional scientific methods (in mid-century) did not do justice to the therapeutic situation and, in fact, concealed more than they revealed. What exactly is it that we do need to do justice to?[14] If we treat this as a phenomenological question that can be answered by *observation*, then it is the human condition as it is manifested in both clinical and social situations. What we are interested in looking at and treating is damage to the Self and it Being, damage to Dasein. Framing it in these terms makes it sound esoteric, and you are to be forgiven if it seems impossible to intuitively grasp these ideas. Remember the definition of the Self I have insisted on. What I am talking about then is simply damage to the whole person and how she is in the world. Let me offer an illustration.

Sam, a cardiologist, was in his late 60s when he first came to see me.[15] He was the only child of a cold depressed mother and a passive, ne'er-do-well father, both deceased, who distanced themselves from him even more when, as a teenager, he told them he was gay. Many years ago, he had served as a combat medic in Vietnam. Without manifesting any signs of trauma, he transitioned smoothly into civilian life. He found that he had acquired a taste for medical work and, using his veteran's educational benefits, went to college and on to medical school and a residency in internal medicine. All *seemed* well. He then began to suffer lower back pain. Diagnostic findings were equivocal but, on the advice of his orthopedic surgeon, he tried several weeks of bed rest, which sort of helped and sort of didn't. As the years passed, other somatic conditions appeared for which no diagnoses could be found. After a minor injury, he developed pain in his right shoulder that persisted and intensified long after whatever questionable injury he had sustained would have been expected to heal. Chronic abdominal pain, presenting at times with severe acute episodes, eventually led to an exploratory laparotomy performed at the Mayo Clinic; it revealed nothing. The severity and unpredictability of the pain was unbearable and led to an early and unhappy retirement. Through all of this, Sam had adamantly refused psychological interventions, insisting that there was something "really wrong" with him and a diagnosis was just around the corner (Annie singing "The Sun'll Come Out Tomorrow" at the height of the Great Depression popped into my head). Finally, depressed and at his wit's end, he took the advice of a colleague I had successfully treated and grudgingly came in to see me. Ten minutes into his story, I knew that I did not have endless time to listen and understand (sometimes excuses for doing nothing) if I were to interest him in therapy I would have to do so quickly—besides, I had served as a Navy psychiatrist in the Vietnam era, and brought to the table some knowledge of the disease Sam was suffering from.

In getting Sam to tell me about himself through discourse rather than mostly silent listening, two things emerged. *I* observed that he had nothing to say about his combat service, treating it as a non-psychological event, and *he* observed that I was deeply interested in talking with him but not particularly talking about the etiology of his pain. The reason for my lack of curiosity was twofold: I trusted the work-ups he had had, and I thought I had a pretty good idea what was going on with his pain. I thought that, existentially speaking, Sam was a lot like Jake, only *his* wound involved his total body. In other words, Sam was suffering from PTSD. His body's absurd response to the psychological damage he had endured in Vietnam had destroyed his work life. However, a solid and supportive relationship with a strong, loving partner, Robert—who was no stranger to such problems in his work as an Emergency Room physician—had helped him to weather the series of storms that had finally overcome him. I also knew something about the neuroscience of pain (Gatchel, Peng, Peters, Fuchs, & Turk, 2007; Giordano, 2010; Ramachandran & Blakeslee, 1998). In people suffering from debilitating chronic pain, it is often the case that the injury that gave rise to the pain had physically healed long ago (this was the case with Sam's spine and shoulder problems), or that there never was any *physical* injury in the first place (his abdominal symptoms fell into this category). In either case, the Bio-Psycho-Social Self eventually hardwires the pain into its neural circuitry so that pain becomes the only way the Self can "know" (again, *connaissance* works so much better here) the affected parts of its body.

There is a psychodiagnostic/psychotherapeutic literature (Gatchel et al., 2007; Luyten, von Houdenhove, Lemma, Target, & Fonagy, 2012) (beyond the Existential Literature that I am developing) on Sam's problems. In it, Sam would be thought to suffer from a functional somatic disorder (FSD). FSDs are a heterogeneous group of diseases, differing in their etiologies and the parts of the Self that they affect. Luyten and colleagues describe a mentalization-based approach to these disabling bio-psycho-social disorders.[16]

Mentalization is the process in which we develop feelings and thoughts with which to make sense of ourselves and the social world in which we exist (note the phenomenological language). A particular sort of failure involves an inability to mentalize bodily states. Mentalization is profoundly interreferential and intersubjective. It is involved in being-in-the-world. It is a clinically useful concept in that it helps *us* to mentalize what it is like for patients who lack these capacities in some area and to empathize with that lack. *Our* mentalization can also teach our patients to mentalize a problem area where it has been absent. Authors writing about mentalization (e.g., Bateman & Fonagy, 2013) often imply that it is globally absent, whereas its absence tends to be more focal. Sam's failure in mentalization applied to his experiences in Vietnam and to his subsequent somatic symptoms. Careful inquiry revealed that he was not adequately mentalizing his symptoms, the parts of the body in which they seemed to be taking place, or his behavior connected with trying to relieve them. In his attempts to physically lessen his symptoms, it emerged that Sam was over-exercising to the point of collapse, making his pain worse. Secondary failures in mentalization occur in situations in which these abilities are present but may not be employed for conflictual reasons: Primary failures occur when those abilities are absent in some situation. Although these authors seem to be unaware of it, their approach to mentalization and the construction of meaning is essentially an Existential one. *A failure in mentalization is an existential failure*: Meursault and Jake both suffered from such failures.

Luyten and colleagues (2012) argue that "FSD probably result from negative vicious cycles involving person-environment interactions.... The model [they] propose distinguishes between predisposing, precipitating and perpetuating factors" (p. 123) (as would a proposed model for understanding the origins of *any* disease process). Predisposing factors involve an interaction of genetic-biological and environmental factors, their Evo-Devo, with the former involving inherited failures in brain and body. Precipitating factors are broadly described as "Stress." Stress overwhelms an individual's *allostasis* leading to a state of allostatic load "mediated by dysfunctions of the hypothalamus-pituitary-adrenal (HPA) [circuit], the main human stress system" (p. 123).

Secure attachment plays a key role in a developing individual's ability to manage stress and maintain allostasis, while insecure attachment carries with it an increased vulnerability to stress (Luyten et al., 2012). In the face of stress, we all seek proximity to attachment figures or their descendants, present in the world or internalized. Unsurprisingly, oxytocin, the "intimacy hormone," (Panksepp & Biven, 2012) plays a role in this process.

FSD patients usually manifest insecure attachment histories involving severe adversity in early life (Heim et al., 2009). (Sam displayed a history of insecure attachment to his distant, radically unavailable mother.) When faced with stress, they employ secondary attachment strategies and mentalizing impairments; both of which are pathological. (These *may also* appear as a *consequence* of FSD (Luyten et al., 2012), a distinction that does not change the clinical situation or our approach.) There are two such secondary strategies. *Attachment deactivation strategies* attempt to regulate stress by denying attachment needs. These people appear autonomous and resilient but are actually vulnerable and insecure. Although deactivation strategies appear to work in the short run, they are associated with high interpersonal and metabolic costs. Suppression of distress increases the allostatic load and ultimately leads to a worsening of symptoms and deep loneliness. *Attachment hyperactivation strategies* involve anxious demands for support and clinging behavior that lead to deep bilateral resentments. The anxious clinging blocks mental exploration and makes these patients "insight-resistant."

These secondary attachment strategies interact with mentalizing impairments that perpetuate symptoms and relational problems. Focal impairments in mentalization include an inability to equate physical sensations with negative emotional states (Luyten et al., 2012) or to understand them as cues that particular behaviors are causing a worsening physical condition (Sam's over-exercising), or that they are failing to monitor their therapeutic behaviors. For example, a patient described a peculiar numbness of his forehead whenever the subject of physical abuse arose (it emerged that he had once been hit in the head with a belt buckle). Many of these impairments and the behaviors that follow from them act to perpetuate FSDs. The very old psychoanalytic concept of secondary gain also applies here. It goes without saying that well-functioning mentalization is one of the best everyday tools *at hand* for stress regulation, and hence the treatment of FSDs rests heavily on facilitating its development. The goal is to help patients to see the way they employ secondary attachment strategies, follow them back to their traumatic origins, and help the patient learn to mentalize present and past stress.

Before we go on, I want to resolve a point of possible confusion. In this chapter, I have seemingly been speaking in many tongues, describing the human condition and our understanding of it in many different ways. Existential psychology is an umbrella under which these various ways of viewing that condition and the various modalities of therapeutic action we have been discussing congenially coexist.

The severe, chronic debilitating pain with which Sam was afflicted is refractory to psychotherapy alone, even to the approach described by Luyten and colleagues (Luyten et al., 2012). One must look elsewhere for the tools required to mobilize the necessary *neuroplasticity* (Doidge, 2007) needed to treat this symptom. The Mayo Clinic's Pain Rehabilitation Center, for example, offers an intensive 3-week bio-psycho-social program that aims to restore function and does not use medication. (I understood that this was an Existential therapy although I doubted that they did). Sam was willing (he was willing to *try* anything at this point), if skeptical. We faced a tactical problem. The program at Mayo teaches its patients how to look past their pain, to see something else and, in the process, the Self (my words) returns to pre-PTSD ways of knowing itself and knowing the world, or it establishes new ones. The problem facing us was that the psychotherapy needed to do the opposite, to get into the issues that had driven the pain. The answer I came up with was to do that part of the therapy first, telling Sam that it would have little effect on the pain (or that it might even worsen it), *then* send him off to Mayo, and, finally, do the rest of the psychotherapy while strengthening what he had learned at Mayo. And that's what we did.

The reason that I pursued Sam's experiences as a combat medic was that, from my own experiences as a Navy psychiatrist treating Vietnam-era Marines, I knew that they had to have been traumatic and related to his symptoms, *a connection that Sam could not initially mentalize*. Without this extra-therapeutic knowledge, it might have taken much longer to get to it. (Another patient comes to mind who had been punched and slapped by his parents and siblings. It took years of non-specific therapeutic work for him to formulate meaning around these experiences, to be able to mentalize them, so that he could tell me *and himself* about them.) The problem was not that Sam was using denial or disavowal to distance himself from the traumas but rather that he was unable to mentalize them, the process that would allow him to know and speak about of them.[17] I had read about the 1968 Tet offensive mounted by the Viet Cong and North Vietnamese Army in the old imperial city of Huê (Bowden, 2017). When I talked to him about outnumbered companies of marines being fed into what amounted to a meat grinder of Viet Cong troops he was able to piece together his feelings and experiences there, trying to save friends who died in his arms.

In addition to his inability to mentalize these traumas, Sam made use of secondary attachment deactivation strategies that became the subjects of focused clinical work. We were able to observe how they were expressed in his relationship with me; moving away when he found the material threatening and then working to regain his connection with me. I would hesitate to call this transference in that in involved the mechanics rather than the content of this part of the therapeutic relationship. This work lessened his anxiety but did not, as expected, much affect his FSD. With increasing abilities to mentalize his traumatic experiences and his body's symptoms, he became able to lessen his reliance on attachment deactivation strategies and to turn to Robert for increasing closeness. Had we not first addressed these issues, he would not have been able to learn or employ the pain management strategies that the specialists at Mayo had developed.

My goal upon his return was to reinforce his newly learned techniques for looking past his pain and not letting his mind go to or dwell on it. On the surface, this might seem to be the opposite of what we do analytically; it is not. As I've previously written (Leffert, 2016), work on a painful and unformulated past is eventually completed: It is necessary to not leave the patient there but to get her back to the present, separating herself from the traumas (we do know that spending *too much* time with traumas makes a patient worse, not better). We moved into working through a final separation from his parents, which led to his being able to take pleasure being with Robert's warm, supportive family, and his now adult nieces and nephews.

The absurd and the emotions that accompany it

An Existentialist approach to the psychoanalytic therapies focuses on an absurdity of Being with which an individual Self can be afflicted. To start at the beginning, *Merriam-Webster's Collegiate Dictionary* (2004) defines the *absurd* as "having no rational or orderly relationship to human life—MEANINGLESSNESS" or "the state or condition in which human beings exist in an irrational and meaningless universe and in which human life has no ultimate meaning" (p. 5). I would insert *subjective* as a modifier of universe and add that absurdity entails a discrepancy between Desire and Reality. Existentialism and Phenomenology both teach that we avoid absurdity by making our own meaning. This is the missing piece of what we must do to help our patients that is not covered by psychoanalytic schools of thought that pursue theoretically driven clinical goals.

Absurdity, then, is the opposite of meaning; both are entangled with emotions. For the Existentialist, meaning entails freedom, and absurdity its opposite. The freedom we are talking about is a *psychological* freedom. This is not much different from what we as psychoanalysts have understood for a long time, except that we have understood these as states of mind, governed by conflict, or inhibition that can, for good, or ill, fly in the face of one's external situation: the *Umwelt* and the *Mitwelt*.[18]

Sam's absurdity was that so many of his friends had died in his arms and he had lived. Perhaps in celebration of them, he was mostly disabled, and yet, no biophysiological cause could be found for any of it.

Absurdity exhausts; it drains and diminishes life. While it can lead to anxiety and depression, it also produces emotional states that we don't think much about. The most prominent of these is despair. A search of PEP-Web returns only 30 articles with *despair* in their titles, where it proves to be mostly a placeholder for *bad depression*.

It is rather—and Luyten and colleagues (2012) would, I think, agree—a bio-psycho-social state of being, unique in its own right. It is a judgment of hopelessness concerning the relations of Self and World and an experienced impossibility of improving them. Misery is a follow-on state. Despair very much equates with the Heideggerian (1975/1982) *fallen* state of Being. Medard Boss's (1963) patient, whom he calls Dr. Cobling,[19] was certainly in a profound state of despair when she first came to see him. Her despair was very much related to her work as a physician, its meaninglessness (*for her*) and its sadomasochistic self-destructiveness, which she was unable to mentalize. When he recommended to her that she stop work, she readily complied (what had seemed *im*possible became *possible*), and the despair was immediately much ameliorated.

Returning to our two fictional characters, Meursault uses being thrown into death as a subjective way of restoring meaning to his life; *he* is satisfied with this result, even though we could be pardoned for being somewhat dubious. The title, *The Stranger*, expresses our dubiousness. Jake, as he ends his story in a taxi with the (for him) impossibly unavailable Brett, has failed to even engage his Existential problem: how to have a meaningful life in the absence of a part of himself. The title of the book, *The Sun Also Rises*, and the epigraph from the Book of Ecclesiastes from which it is drawn, poignantly express that failure.

Traditional psychoanalytic thought of whatever ilk has viewed negative emotions as intrapsychic responses to World explained by particular metapsychological formulations. They can, for example, be seen as responses to conflict, relational, or interpersonal problems. Recent work in the neurosciences (Panksepp & Biven, 2012; Panksepp & Watt, 2011) has described the wired-in basis for these emotions as comprising seven primary emotional states, but not their meaning or what the Self makes of them (Leffert, 2017, Chapter 2). In keeping with what *we* have been saying, we would understand these emotions as States of Being, subject to an existential exploration that includes their historicity. Historical narration is very much a process of mentalization that includes an emotional component.

This chapter has offered a necessarily abbreviated account (it will be the subject of a subsequent volume) of Existential problems in Being and how they can be approached therapeutically. It, and the previous two, have looked at dramatically different aspects of Human Being. The final task is the interesting if complex one of fitting them together: We will turn to it now in the next and final chapter.

Notes

1 Irwin Yalom (e.g., 1980) stands out as a stark exception to this trend.
2 This statement with an implied "fallen" owes an unmentioned debt to Heidegger.
3 In some schools of psychoanalysis it never was of interest. I trained analytically in the 1970s at what I would call a progressive Freudian institute that was beginning to integrate object relations theory (not clinical practice) into its curriculum where existentialist ideas were never mentioned. For that matter, the same can be said of the institute I am now affiliated with, 40 years later.
4 One might think of trying to do analysis in Nazi-occupied Vienna or in Houston when it was struck by hurricane Harvey. At the same time, some individuals, Viktor Frankl

(1959/2006) for example, were capable of existential survival in the face of the most awful of circumstances.
5   In choosing the term *workspace*, I mean to signal that the neuroscience of conscious Being-in-the-Moment (Dehaene & Naccache, 2001) is a fundamental part of this discourse.
6   I am going to assume (with all the risks that such a procedure entails) at least some broad familiarity with these two texts on the part of my readers that will allow them to follow my arguments. If not, the works are easily obtainable, short, and well worth the trouble.
7   In Phenomenological (Leffert, 2016) terms we are talking about Dasein's problem, a concept that was also being formulated in the late 1920s (Heidegger, 1927/2010).
8   Social conditions leading to cultural failure can overwhelm an individual's coping strategies and bring about plagues of meaninglessness. The First World War was such an experience for Hemingway, as was the Nazi occupation of France for Camus. Whether we are now entering such a period is a question worthy of consideration.
9   Gertrude Stein's signifier "You are a lost generation" was actually hijacked by Hemingway to describe the expat community, mostly made up of the Americans and British living in Paris between the wars. She rather meant it to apply to all of the people displaced and rendered absurd by the war.
10 Let me stress that, when I treated Bill, I was decades away from understanding him in the way I want to tell you about.
11 In cases where resources were not a problem I would have worked with a cotherapist or hired him a personal assistant.
12 For an account of these developments, see Leffert, 2016, Chapters 2 and 3.
13 Science as we now understand it (Latour, 1991/1993), is comprised of inseparable objective and social elements, both involving Uncertainty.
14 To put it in a nutshell, it is the fundamental *non-linearity* and *multiplicity* of even the most "objective" of the sciences.
15 This is not the sort of case that we have talked and written about for decades. It is, however, very much the sort of patients that I see today. The question is (and I have no answer to it): Have patients always been like this but we just didn't see it or is the World different now? Going over my practice from this point of view, I see things I didn't see in the past and suspect that things have always been like this.
16 It takes only a moment's thought to recognize that all of the conditions that bring our patients to us are bio-psycho-social disorders.
17 This failure of construction has already been explored as a failure of memory and mentalization in the face of trauma by other authors (Bateman & Fonagy, 2013; Fonagy, 1999).
18 Frankl (1959/2006) talks about being able to find personal meaning and feel free even while imprisoned in a Nazi concentration camp.
19 For a discussion of this interesting case, see Leffert, 2013, especially Chapters 2 and 3.

References

A. P. A. (2014). *Diagnostic and statistical manual of mental disorders, DSM* (5th ed.). New York: C B S.
Bateman, A., & Fonagy, P. (2013). Mentalization-based treatment. *Psychoanalytic Inquiry, 33*, 595–613.
Binswanger, L. (1958). The existential analysis school of thought (E. Angel, Trans.). In R. May, E. Angel, & H. F. Ellenberger (Eds.), *Existence* (pp. 191–213). New York: Simon & Schuster.
Bitwas-Diener, R., & Diener, E. (2001). Making the best of a bad situation: Satisfaction in the slums of Calcutta. *Journal of Happiness Studies, 55*, 329–352.

Blume, L. M. M. (2017). *Everybody behaves badly: The true story behind Hemingway's masterpiece The Sun Also Rises*. Boston: Houghton Mifflin Harcourt.
Boss, M. (1963). *Psychoanalysis and Daseinanalysis*. New York: Basic Books.
Bowden, M. (2017). *Huê 1968: A turning point of the American War in Vietnam*. New York: Atlantic Monthly Press.
Camus, A. (1963). *Notebooks 1935–1942* (P. Thody, Trans.). Chicago: Ivan R. Dee. (Original work published in 1962.)
Camus, A. (1989). *The stranger* (M. Ward, Trans.). New York: Vintage Books. (Original work published in 1942.)
Camus, A. (1991). *The myth of Sisyphus and other essays* (J. O'Brien, Trans.). New York: Vintage Books. (Original work published in 1942.)
Daoud, K. (2015). *The Meursault investigation: A novel* (J. Cullen, Trans.). New York: Other Press. (Original work published in 2013.)
Dehaene, S., & Naccache, L. (2001). Towards a cognitive neuroscience of consciousness: Basic evidence and a workspace framework. *Cognition, 79*, 1–37.
Diener, E. (Ed.). (2009a). *The science of well-being: The collected works of Ed Diener*. New York: Springer.
Diener, E. (Ed.). (2009b). *Culture and well-being: The collected works of Ed Diener*. New York: Springer.
Diener, E. (Ed.). (2009c). *Assessing well-being: The collected works of Ed Diener*. New York: Springer.
Doidge, N. (2007). *The brain that changes itself*. New York: Viking.
Donald, M. (2001). *A mind so rare: The evolution of human consciousness*. New York: W. W. Norton & Co.
Erikson, E. (1953). Growth and crisis of the healthy personality. In C. Kluckhohn & H. A. Murray (Eds.), *Personality in nature, society, and culture* (pp. 185–225). New York: Alfred A. Knopf. (Original work published in 1950.)
Erikson, E. (1963). *Childhood and society* (2nd ed.). New York: W. W. Norton & Co (Original work published in 1950.)
Fairbairn, W. R. D. (2013). *Psychoanalytic studies of the personality*. London: Routledge. (Original work published in 1952.)
Fonagy, P. (1999). Memory and therapeutic action. *The International Journal of Psychoanalysis, 80*, 215–224.
Frankl, V. E. (2006). *Man's search for meaning* (I. Lasch, Trans.). Boston: Beacon Press. (Original work published in 1959.)
Gatchel, R. J., Peng, Y. B., Peters, M. L., Fuchs, P. N., & Turk, D. C. (2007). The biopsychosocial approach to chronic pain: Scientific advances and future directions. *Psychological Bulletin, 133*, 581–624.
Giordano, J. (2010). The neuroscience of pain, and a neuroethics of pain care. *Neuroethics, 3*, 89–94.
Guntrip, H. (1971). *Psychoanalytic theory, therapy and the self: A basic guide to human personality in Freud, Erikson, Klein, Sullivan, Fairbairn, Hartman, Jacobson, and Winnicott*. New York: Basic Books.
Heidegger, M. (1982). *The basic problems of phenomenology* (rev. ed., A. Hofstadter, Trans.). Bloomington: Indiana University Press. (Original work published in 1975.)
Heidegger, M. (2001). *Zollikon seminars: Protocols-conversations-letters* (F. Mayr & R. Askay, Trans.). Evanston: Northwestern University Press. (Original work published in 1987.)
Heidegger, M. (2010). *Being and time* (J. Stambaugh & D. J. Schmidt, Trans.). Albany: State University of New York. (Original work published in 1927.)

Heim, C., Nater, U. M., Maloney, E., Boneva, E., Jones, R., & Reeves, J. F. (2009). Childhood trauma and risk for chronic fatigue syndrome: Association with neuroendocrine dysfunction. *Archives of General Psychiatry, 66,* 72–80.

Hemingway, E. (1960). *Death in the afternoon.* New York: Charles Schribner's Sons. (Original work published in 1932.)

Hemingway, E. (2006). *The sun also rises.* New York: Charles Scribner's. (Original work published in 1926.)

Humphrey, N. (1999). *A history of the mind: Evolution and the birth of consciousness.* New York: Springer. (Original work published in 1992.)

Humphrey, N. (2011). *Soul dust: The magic of consciousness.* Princeton: Princeton University Press.

Husserl, E. (1970). *The crisis of European sciences and transcendental phenomenology* (D. Cairns, Trans.). Evanston: Northwestern University Press. (Original work published in 1937.)

Husserl, E. (1977). *Phenomenological psychology: Lectures, summer semester; 1925* (J. Scanlon, Trans.). The Hague: Martinus Nijoff. (Original work published in 1925.)

Husserl, E. (1983). *Ideas pertaining to a pure phenomenology and to a phenomenological philosophy: Book one: General introduction to a pure phenomenology* (F. Kersten, Trans.). New York: Springer (Original work published in 1913.)

Janik, A., & Toulmin, S. (1996). *Wittgenstein's Vienna.* Chicago: Ivar R. Dee. (Original work published in 1973.)

Johnston, W. M. (1972). *The Austrian mind: An intellectual and social history 1848–1938.* Berkeley: University of California Press.

Kahn, M. M. R. (1983). *Hidden selves: Between theory and practice in psychoanalysis.* New York: International Universities Press.

Kahneman, D., Slovic, P., & Tversky, A. (Eds.). (1982). *Judgement under uncertainty: Heuristics and biases.* Cambridge: Cambridge University Press.

Kaplan, A. (2016). *Looking for The Stranger: Albert Camus and the life of a literary classic.* Chicago: University of Chicago Press.

Latour, B. (1993). *We have never been modern* (C. Porter, Trans.). Cambridge: Harvard University Press. (Original work published in 1991.)

Leffert, M. (2010). *Contemporary psychoanalytic foundations.* London: Routledge.

Leffert, M. (2013). *The therapeutic situation in the 21st century.* New York: Routledge.

Leffert, M. (2016). *Phenomenology, uncertainty, and care in the therapeutic encounter.* New York: Routledge.

Leffert, M. (2017). *Positive psychoanalysis: Aesthetics, desire, and subjective well-being.* New York: Routledge.

Luyten, P., von Houdenhove, B., Lemma, A., Target, M., & Fonagy, P. (2012). A mentalization-based approach to the understanding and treatment of functional somatic disorders. *Psychoanalytic Psychotherapy, 26,* 121–140.

May, R. (1958a). Contributions of existential psychotherapy. In R. May, E. Angel, & H. F. Ellenberger (Eds.), *Existence* (pp. 37–91). New York: Simon & Schuster.

May, R. (1958b). The origins and significance of the existential movement in psychology. In R. May, E. Angel, & H. F. Ellenberger (Eds.), *Existence* (pp. 3–36). New York: Simon & Schuster.

May, R., Angel, E., & Ellenberger, H. F. (Eds.). (1958). *Existence.* New York: Simon & Schuster.

Merriam-Webster's collegiate dictionary (11th ed.). (2004). Springfield: Merriam-Webster, Inc.

Panksepp, J., & Biven, L. (2012). *The archaeology of mind: Neuroevolutionary origins of human emotions.* New York: W. W. Norton & Co.

Panksepp, J., & Watt, D. (2011). What is basic about basic emotions? Lasting lessons from affective neuroscience. *Emotion Review, 3*, 1–10.

Ramachandran, V. S., & Blakeslee, S. (1998). *Phantoms in the brain: Probing the mysteries of the mind.* New York: Harper Perennial.

Sartre, J.-P. (1946). American novelists in French eyes. *Atlantic Monthly, 178*, 114–118.

Sartre, J.-P. (2007). *Existentialism is a humanism.* New Haven: Yale University Press. (Original work published in 1997.)

Smith, P. (1983). Hemingway's early manuscripts: The theory and practice of omission. *Journal of Modern Literature, 10*, 268–288.

Stolorow, R. D. (2011). *World, affectivity, trauma.* New York: Routledge.

Stolorow, R. D., & Atwood, G. E. (1992). *Contexts of being.* Hillsdale: The Analytic Press.

Stolorow, R. D., Orange, D., & Atwood, G. E. (2002). *Worlds of experience: Interweaving philosophical and clinical dimensions in psychoanalysis.* New York: Basic Books.

Stoltzfus, B. (2003). Camus and Hemingway: The solidarity of rebellion. *The International Fiction Review, 30*(1).

Winnicott, D. W. (1972). *Holding and interpretation: Fragment of analysis.* New York: Grove Press.

Winnicott, D. W. (1975). *Through paediatrics to psycho-analysis.* New York: Basic Books.

Yalom, I. D. (1980). *Existential psychotherapy.* New York: Basic Books.

Yalom, I. D. (2012). *Love's executioner: And other tails of psychotherapy.* New York: Basic Books. (Original work published in 1989.)

6
COMMON GROUND

Introduction

Over the course of this book, we have been confronted with two different threads of Human Ontology—Paleoanthropology and Existentialism—and are now left to find a way to braid them together. To accomplish this, we need to find bridges between the two. Their seeming to manifest an unequal clinical relevance further complicates this task.

Evo-Devo, broadly defined as an interreferential braiding of Evolution and Development, forms a basis for the beginning of our integrations as it encompasses both disciplines. Neuroscience and, in particular, Consciousness Studies offers relatively unexplored connections to both Paleoanthropology and Existentialism, a first bridge. The appearance of Autonoetic Consciousness in hominin evolution and development is a major event with far reaching consequences; it is a tipping point producing a qualitative change in Being-in-the-World. Existentialism recognizes this singular importance of Consciousness is a foundation for what makes us human but it need not dismiss the richness and preponderance of unconsciousness mental processes in Human Being. Such a dismissal while a part of early phenomenology (Husserl, 1913/1983, 1931/1999) was more a critique of the Freudian unconscious than it was an ontological statement. In particular, phenomenologists were highly critical of what follows from an embrace of the topographic model: that unconscious mental processes were not fully deployed and that repression was a barrier to deployment. Many of us, to phrase it in an unfamiliar way, believe that a major task of clinical psychoanalysis is to increase deployment and that the therapeutic task is to get past what is conscious in order to explore unconscious processes. Classical psychoanalysis privileges the exploration of a discrete, psychodynamic unconscious. The Existential psychoanalysts of the 1950s and 1960s dismissed this view of clinical process. Relational theorists, without expressing any particular interest in Existentialism, attempted to correct this prejudice while Intersubjectivists followed a path that, within a decade, led them to Existentialism and Phenomenology. In particular, if something conscious was repressed, some part of it had ceased to exist. The Existential and later phenomenological position is that *all* mental processes are *fully* deployed and that consciousness (or unconsciousness) is simply a changing aspect of that deployment. The Iceberg Theory could be considered an expression of this position.

The origins of consciousness have been the object of speculation by paleoanthropologists but have been largely shunned by neuroscientists, who much prefer the hard science and accompanying neuroanatomical investigations that can be performed on living mammals, birds, and humans. Although their preference for hard science over informed speculation is understandable, it leaves unaddressed important questions about our Evo-Devo,[1] particularly our first question: Where do we come from and when did we arrive?

A second bridge involves what Paleoanthropology and Existentialism have to say about death. The appearance of consciousness as part of the Upper Paleolithic package and the increased understanding of the human condition that went into it forced our ancestors to deal with the concept of individual death (and the terror that it had for us). Some of the techniques they developed are still in use. Roughly 50,000 years later Phenomenology and Existentialism developed as attempts to manage the terror by an increased understanding of the human condition.

One could (and can) easily spend one's professional life as a psychoanalytic psychotherapist knowing little or nothing about either thread (I did so for the first 30 years of mine). So why even bother? Let's leave that question for a moment while we ask it about Interdisciplinary Studies. Many of us have been writing about how Interdisciplinary Studies enlighten psychoanalysis for some time (again, some thankfully decreasing number of us still have no such interests, attempting to use psychoanalysis as a sufficient means of explaining the human condition, using it in an attempt to answer the questions: Where are we, and where do we come from?). If we were to summarize these interdisciplinary contributions in a few words, it would be to say they inform a shift in our thinking about the nature of the Self from some sort of mental representation to that of a particular Mind possessing unique characteristics, to, finally, the existence of the Bio-Psycho-Social Self. The major interdisciplinary thread that has come to interest psychotherapists is neuroscience, with the work of Kandel (2006) and Doidge (2007, 2015) having much to do with the advent of that interest. It has, over the past 20 years or so, become respectable for psychoanalysts to do neuroscience and for neuroscientists to focus their interests on psychoanalysis.

We have, more recently (Leffert, 2016), been able to say similar things about the threads of Psychoanalysis and Existentialism and Phenomenology.

Paleoanthropology[2] and Existentialism teach us about the same things from radically different perspectives: how we became Human Beings and what is the nature of the human condition. It is very easy to argue the negative: How could these things *not* help us to be better psychotherapists? (I'm looking at the

350,000-year-old chert chopper sitting on my desk that I told you about in Chapter 4 and trying to imagine my British ancestors that made and used it.) Can we perform our work *without* being students of the human condition and what it means to be a Human Being? (The alternative, an alternative that May [1958] wrote critically about, is to apprentice oneself to some particular theoretical school and then spend one's professional life observing how Human Beings fit into it.) Consciousness is central to this inquiry into what makes us Human Beings.

Consciousness and the Evo-Devo of the Self

In the Book of Deuteronomy there is a particular *Parshe* or portion entitled *Re'eh* (pronounced "re-ay"). Speaking to Moses and the Israelites, God says: "I set before you this day a blessing and a curse." He [sic] goes on to assign them a difficult task with catastrophic results if it is not fulfilled. They are to cross the river Jordan and go into a new land; they are to possess it and dwell in it. I will argue that Autonoetic Consciousness is just such a new land and that it imposes upon us new and at times difficult tasks. It is a land we reached (*evolved* to) less than 70,000 years ago and that each of us *develops* into between the ages 4 and 6. Let me begin by offering a graphical representation of ourselves, the Bio-Psycho-Social Selves that inhabit it.

Imagine, figuratively, a Bio-Psycho-Social Self sitting in World. We can think of it as a sphere wearing a cap. It is not homogenous. The cap part represents *consciousness* and the rest of the Self is unconscious (not *The Unconscious*, just unconscious). Consciousness is constantly shifting as is its composition of different parts or fragments[3] of the Self. Although we have to use lines to draw our representation of the Self, these lines all represent semipermeable membranes whose permeability can vary over time and from place to place. The outer lines are comprised of the organs of sensory perception and the skin, the part of the Self that is its container. The graphical representation does not distinguish physical and mental;[4] they both are contents of the sphere and its hat that change with time. There is no exact spatial representation for what it is best to call the Conscience.[5] It and the Self's collection of memory, Heuristics and Biases (Kahneman, 2011) develop out of conscious and unconscious contact with World, and we might think of Conscience as being concentrated but not limited to the cap and nearby areas of the rest of the Self. Conscious and Conscience, along with their origins and maintenance, are profoundly social.

Autonoetic Consciousness appeared/appears in two different contexts: evolutionarily in *H. sapiens sapiens* and developmentally in our children. I have used the purposefully evocative term *awakening* for this process of coming-to.

The evolution of consciousness

Let's first look into the evolution of consciousness. I can tell you roughly when, how, and why it evolved. The best "when" arguments would mostly (we can't drop the qualifier) date the advent of Consciousness to sometime after the Middle to Upper Paleolithic transition and probably coincident with the development of the Upper Paleolithic package we talked about in Chapter 4. Whether Consciousness facilitated the development of the package or was simply a part of it is unclear. We are, of course, talking about the appearance of *H. sapiens sapiens* in southern Africa *c.*70,000 years ago (ya) and their showing up in Europe 40–50,000 ya.[6] They were the first primates to possess full Autonoetic Consciousness, although rudimentary compartmentalized Consciousness is thought by some to have existed in Neanderthals and must have existed in *H. sapiens*.

Noetic and Anoetic Consciousness are present in Mammals and Birds as well as Human Beings and their ancestors (Tulving, 1985/2003, 2005). The individual frames of Noetic Consciousness may have come faster and faster and, eventually, like early motion pictures, blurred into a continuous autonoetic stream; jerky at first and becoming gradually smoother. Alternatively, narratives may first have appeared noetically (I know that story) and then found to also include the self. The origins of consciousness follow two biological principles of change: Incremental elements of quantitative change eventually become qualitative and, in evolutionary biology, structure and function begin as rudimentary elements that evolve through a process of adaptation into fully realized new parts of the Self. Fully developed features do not simply appear. There is *some* evidence that the evolution of a neural structure encircling and connecting all of the brain and called the claustrum (Crick & Koch, 2005) had a lot to do with the coming of Consciousness.

A short answer to the question of why consciousness evolved involves the increasing complexity of life: making a living in an increasingly complex *Mitwelt* and *Umwelt* (the world of relationships and the physical world). As Baars (1993/2003) observed, bottom-up researchers into the design of the most powerful Artificial Intelligence (AI) systems had concluded that a system capable of solving very complex problems required the interaction of a slow, serial, and integrated [conscious] system with a fast, mostly parallelly organized distributed processing [unconscious] system. The complexity of the *Umwelt* involved surviving, reproducing, and thriving in the intermittent ice ages of Europe, which, even in that distant time, struck us as ecological disasters. Larger groups of hominins would have a survival advantage. Dunbar (2016) has much to say about group size. He first looked broadly at how individuals met their caloric needs (something many of us take for granted even though much of the world still goes hungry). It turns out that the larger brains of *H. sapiens sapiens* burned more calories than did those of our smaller-brained ancestors. Dunbar posited that larger group size correlated with a superior ability to fulfill the caloric needs of its members. Based on the relationship of social and cognitive capacities to brain size, Dunbar calculated how many people an individual could maintain contact with, that is, group size. The number increased with hominin evolution, reaching 110 in Neanderthals, and then 150 in us. He also posited that, at least for us, these groups formed connections with each other into tribes having looser social and economic ties. Christakis and Fowler (2009), studying *us* in the present, determined that our social network size was also 150 with overlapping networks and loose connections across larger and much larger groups.

Consciousness was a feature of these large brains that made larger group size possible. In addition to bringing narrative memory, future time travel that allowed planning purposeful activity, and at-will access to semantic knowledge to the table, it also made possible a new kind of knowledge and intelligence, and the behavior that went along with it. Membership in these comparatively large groups also brought with it a number of requirements. One needed to be able to function socially and be able to maintain *at least* some kind of minimal relationship with the other 149 group members. This involves a kind of social understanding of these group members as individuals, how they will react, and how to treat them so as to get them to do what you want. This ability is termed Machiavellian intelligence (Humphrey, N. K., 1976/1988), and we alone of the living primates possess it. In Existential terms, it is certainly a form of relational knowing. Machiavellian intelligence is accompanied by and is facilitated by an awareness that others like us, including strangers, think and feel and act much as we do. This is called a Theory of Mind (Baron-Cohen, Tager-Flusberg, & Cohen, 2000) and, again, we humans alone possess it (Premack, 1988). N. Humphrey (1992/1999) puts it rather well:

> For it is consciousness, with its power to make the vanishing instant of physical time live on as the felt moment of sensation that makes it LIKE SOMETHING TO BE OURSELVES—and so sweetens and enriches the being of the external world FOR US.
>
> (p. 228)

The development of consciousness

Autonoetic Consciousness appears in human children somewhere around ages 4 or 5 (Tulving, 2005). As Nelson and Fivush (2004) put it, "autobiographical memory [a marker of consciousness] emerges[7] gradually across the preschool years through processes of social interaction and cognitive development" (p. 486). There is great interest and some controversy (Tulving) concerning this developmental milestone in the interdisciplinary literature. Researchers who study child development have, however, tended to implicitly think of the childhood brain, after Left Brain myelination occurring from 18–24 months (Schore, 2009), as an anatomically stable entity. As we have already discussed, nothing could be farther from the truth: The brains of children change structurally and functionally on a daily basis. Subjectively, this experience must be very much like living in a house that is under constant renovation: New rooms are being added, new equipment is always being installed, and old equipment is being hauled away. Every day. We could learn a lot about Consciousness if we were to make use of fMRIs and PET scans to study what changes in the brain of a child when this new capacity appears.

We are ready to offer the first answer to the question: Why, as psychoanalytic psychotherapists, do we need to know any of this? Let's first consider a research study that demonstrates what we mean by the development of episodic memory and the Autonoetic Consciousness that goes with it. Gopnik and Graff (1988)[8] studied the way 3-, 4-, and 5-year-olds remember things. They had children in each age group learn about the contents of a drawer in one of three ways. One group was shown the drawer. The second group was told the contents without seeing them. The third group was given clues from which the drawer's contents could be inferred. The researchers then asked the children to tell them two things. One was what were the contents of the drawer. The second was how did they know: Had they seen it, been told it, or inferred it. The first question tested acquired semantic knowledge, but to answer the second question the children would have had to recollect *how* they found out the drawer's contents and *this would be an episodic memory*. With regard to the first question, Gopnik and Graf found no age differences in the children's responses, even with tests of delayed recall. The second question was different. It turned out that, while the 5-year-olds mostly remembered how they had found out about the drawer's contents, the 3-year-olds' responses were no better than chance. The 5-year-olds had developed narrative memory, and this requires the capacity for self-reflection.

These research findings are at once problematic for psychoanalysts and psychotherapists who are accustomed to working with adults' presumed narrative memories of events that happened to them as very young children, frequently before the age of 5.[9,10] This early childhood research—straight from the horse's mouth if you will—has told us that these adult memories of such early events cannot be what they appear to be and can have only had a limited relationship to actual events. This observation is of particular importance for the therapeutic recovery in adult psychotherapies of childhood memories of trauma, particularly sexual abuse. In a recent edited volume (Sandler & Fonagy, 1997), noted authors discuss the veracity of such reports in their adult patients but *do not consider age of occurrence as a factor relevant to their discussions*. Analysts and psychotherapists have, in recent years, become much more interested in Trauma. With that interest has come a departure from earlier psychoanalytic thought that considered Trauma the outcome of childhood fantasy. We now understand that Trauma refers to actual events that, in some form, happened to the child. We have, following Fonagy's (1999) example, hypothesized that there are "individuals whose experience has led to a disruption of the entire memory system. Such individuals are most common amongst those with persistent and pervasive experiences of *trauma* [emphasis added]" (p. 220). However, we already know that, although this formulation may fit the effects of Trauma on the memory systems of children older than the age of 5, it cannot apply to younger children because the memory system in question *simply doesn't exist* at that time. Before we dismiss these putative memories out-of-hand, we should ask, since they are so frequent: If they are not autonoetic memories, just what are they?

Gopnik and Graf's (1988) work tells us that the only thing they can be are semantic memories for these events as facts with a superimposed *later* narrative context.

Over the past few decades, memory researchers (e.g., Schacter, 1996, 2001)[11] have completely rewritten our theories of memory. What we had been calling relatively stable, archived *memories* are, in fact, fluid *acts of recall*, each a unique never-to-be-repeated construction. These "memories" vary situationally and interpersonally and the act of recall itself can corrupt stored memory data. Working with our patients' memories, although necessary, is thus a dicey business. Although we don't have autonoetic memory before age 5, the noetic and anoetic memory systems are functional at age 3 or before.[12] What, then, exactly *are* these autonoetic-seeming early memories if they are not autonoetic? The answer is that they are *retrospective, episodic constructions* that combine information, semantic memory, from early anoetic and noetic memory systems with later thoughts, feelings, and autonoetic memories.[13] This doesn't mean that we shouldn't work with them clinically, but rather that we should understand just what we are working with—present day accounts of the past—and treat them as ways of understanding the Self as we currently encounter it. The developmental research on memory thus, requires a reappraisal of Trauma, as it has been psychoanalytically perceived.

Consciousness and its discontents

The title of this section is meant as an acknowledgment that, in *Civilization and Its Discontents* (Freud, 1930/1961) and *Totem and Taboo* (Freud, 1913/1953), Freud was very much onto these problems a century ago. He was, however, hampered in his speculations by an astigmatism resulting from the limitations of his vision to libido theory and ego psychology.

The paleoanthropological baseline

Going back to the paleoanthropological baseline, *H. sapiens sapiens* in Europe 50,000 ya, Consciousness gave us at-will access to a vast amount of semantic (general information) and social knowledge that allowed us to make our way in the world. It was an enormously powerful tool that dramatically expanded our lives and, at least as significantly, the quality of those lives. There were, however, problems. Two sorts of information gave our ancestors[14] difficulty and, with their new cognitive tool, the ability to *reflect on this information* for good *and* ill. The first of these involved our perceptions of the behavior of the world, the *Umwelt*, specifically its propensity to both respond predictably to our manipulations and to change suddenly in incomprehensible and unpredictable ways. The larger the change, the more likely it was to be incomprehensible[15] and to affect the life of an individual and the group to which she belonged. Extreme weather, eclipses, seasons, and natural disasters had such an impact on early humans. Their effects on us have not changed all that much: to be on the ground for any of them is to experience dysphoria ranging from anxiety to fear and finally to terror. The greatest among this group of *unknowables* and the second sort of information to cause us difficulty was a consciousness of *death*. Death represents *the* singular problem of existence for *H. sapiens sapiens*, it also bridges the two threads, Evolution and Existentialism.

In reaching the paleoanthropological baseline, *H. sapiens sapiens* had developed the tools and capacities necessary to meet their physical needs *most of the time*. This meant that, although *some* time still needed to be devoted to safeguarding those physical needs, there was at least some time available for reflection on the wider issues of life that we now, as psychotherapists and philosophers, spend much of our time thinking about. Changing perspectives for a moment, Buckner and Krienen (2013) posited, as we have discussed, that humans had evolved in their frontal cortexes new brain hardware ideally suited for such activities.

Apprehending death

Prior to our awakening, sometime in the Upper Paleolithic, death does not seem to have been the kind of problem that it later became for *H. sapiens sapiens*. Porges (2011) indirectly addressed this changing attitude towards death through his research into the evolving functions of the Vagus nerve. The Vagus, or wanderer, is the longest of the cranial nerves, appearing first in reptiles, then mammals, and, ultimately, in primates, and us. It bundles multiple connections between brain and body, conveying information bidirectionally to and about the state of the body as opposed to perceptual information about the world in which the Self resides. In the best interests of evolutionary utility, it serves as an excellent example of old structures acquiring new functions. "It contains efferent fibers of the parasympathetic nervous system that enervate the heart and the smooth muscle of much of the gastrointestinal tract and afferent sensory fibers that communicate the state of these organs to the brain" (Leffert, 2013, p. 119). It is a part of what is called the Brain-Heart-Vagus Circuit (BHVC) that includes, in primates, the expressive muscles of the face, wired through the V, VI, and VII cranial nerves. The Vagus mediates a response to the apprehension of death at least beginning with mammals and birds that grows out of a "freeze response" to danger in which the heart slows, cognition quiets, and fear seems to be suppressed (Panksepp & Biven, 2012). In extremis, it provides a path to death with dignity. This response exists in humans and can appear in the last stages of terminal illness. It can, however, be cognitively overshadowed by emotions ranging from anxiety to terror.

For as long as we have been human, that is, autonoetically Conscious, we have seen our loved ones die around us, and mental time travel tells us both that they will continue to do so and that we too will die. As we have evolved into individual reflective beings, our anxieties over personal death, the cessation of the Self, have increased. Consciousness and the attendant death anxiety originally had great adaptive value (Humphrey, N., 2011) (it made Humans struggle harder to stay alive in a dangerous World) and was evolutionarily conserved across generations. But as we shifted from encountering World to reflecting on it and ourselves, death morphed into a psychological problem of major proportions. We have struggled to understand it and to mitigate its finality. The name for systems that first formed to accomplish this mitigation is, of course, religion, and they function through the operation of belief, not logic. These systems undoubtedly had prehistoric origins (we find evidence of them in our ancestors' mortuary practices, perhaps going back as far as 200,000 years). Existing into the present they have, comparatively recently, encountered a postmodern response to death: Existentialism and Phenomenology. In our contemporary world, the latter exists as a higher level of cognitive practice with people mostly having recourse to the older, more primitive solutions to the problem.

Denial of death is common at least at some points in the life cycle. A recent survey (Humphrey, N., 2011) revealed that 90% of Americans believe in the immortality of a soul that transcends death. Humphrey describes three ways of accomplishing this, a sort of three "Ds" of denial. The first is to *"discount the future,"* to live *only* in the moment, *never* looking up to a future. The second is to *"disindividuate,"* to think of oneself as part of a social, cultural, or religious group that lives on after us.[16] Finally, there is a common form of *"denial"* of death, that bodily death does not preclude the existence of a separate and immortal self (an immortal soul if you wish). To these, I would add a fourth, a denial of death contained in a *fantasy* of physical, bodily immortality. Although we don't often think of it this way, patients do consult us when one or more of these mechanisms break down, even if the problem is displaced onto something more mundane like failing to receive a promotion at work.

Apprehending the social

If one group involves our ability to grasp death, a second involves a form of social knowledge. We've just spoken about how Machiavellian intelligence and Theory of Mind offer ways by which Human Beings can navigate the social groups to which they belong. Some kind of supra-ordinate rules of behavior facilitates this process: In their most basic form, they involve socially derived information concerning right/wrong and good/bad. The kind of knowledge that enabled one to make a fire or, for that matter, to boot up a computer was of no help here. However, if there were socially agreed upon rules of conduct laid down along the lines of what was good/bad or right/wrong, groups functioned more effectively. These rules also fit rather smoothly into the death-religion epistemology. Problems occurred (and still do occur) for individual group members who didn't buy into the system or, on a larger scale, when different groups clash because of disagreements about the content of these rules (or the religious ones).

Problems dealing with the dangerous unpredictability of the *Umwelt* and the social unpredictability of the *Mitwelt* led to the development of two new kinds of knowing: belief and judgments made under uncertainty (Tversky & Kahneman, 1974/1982). Belief is to be found in the spaces between the bits and pieces of demonstrable knowledge of these worlds, with many of those spaces appearing as a result of the newfound capacity for future time travel (Schacter, Addis, & Buckner, 2008). And indeed, belief, in its various forms, offered common answers to problems arising out of dealing with life in these two worlds and death. Belief resides in the Conscious "hat" and the nearby parts of the sphere we talked about at the beginning of the chapter. It bridges Conscience[17] and reality testing. Judgments made under uncertainty employ Heuristics and Biases and are, despite appearances, made unconsciously in the rest of the sphere, outside of the conscious hat. Ultimately, we moved beyond these ways of apprehending the world to engage our inner world, the *Eigenwelt*,[18] and the attendant study of Being.

Being in World

Consciousness brought us the knowledge that we had to be careful about being-in-the-world and would be rewarded for doing so, but burdened us with the knowledge of physical death—that, inescapably, we (and those around us) are bound to die. This reality was so painful and frightening that we turned (sooner rather than later) to the religious sector of belief in an attempt to mitigate it. And it is at this point that we stepped upon a bridge between the paleoanthropology and philosophy that led, by a very circuitous path, to Phenomenology and Existentialism.

The distinction between the two, Phenomenology and Existentialism, has been at best obscurely rendered in the postmodern literature. Some tendency to identify the former with Heidegger and the latter with Sartre and Camus has not proven instructive. My own ideas about that distinction have evolved over the course of this volume and the two preceding ones (Leffert, 2016, 2017). I have come to view Phenomenology as the study of Being-in-the-World, the study, to employ Heidegger's very difficult term, of Dasein and its *Geography*. It is a general study of Ontology. Existentialism constitutes a much more specific, complementary study, that of the *Psychology* of Being. If Phenomenology strives to locate Dasein, Existentialism looks at what is going on in her mind. In keeping with this, literature and the performing arts occupy an important place within it. Camus makes this point most eloquently in his early Notebooks (1962/1963) when he asserts: If you want to do philosophy, write novels. In their different discussions of Being, both disciplines engage in the related discourses of Man's search for meaning (Frankl, 1959/2006) and how finding it enables her to creatively face death.

Going back even before our awakening, humans have tried to comprehend death and mitigate the terror that has accompanied it. Beliefs in some form of afterlife, life in a "heaven," reincarnation, or searches for ways of extending life beyond the possible all offer mitigations or denials of the finitude of life and the inevitability of death. These beliefs extend back into prehistory. A phenomenological critique of these posited "solutions" would describe these as *fallen* states, whereas Phenomenology and Existentialism, to the contrary, attempt to deal with the finitude of life and the inevitability of its ending in death. The remedy *they* offer is to fill life with meaning in the face of an apprehended inevitable death that renders it more precious and more beautiful. Permanence need not be a characteristic of such strivings or of what they accomplish. Failure to come to terms with these realities involves an existential collapse, which is also a kind of death. "Death contains the possibility of an impossibility of Dasein having any existence at all" (Leffert, 2016, p. 46).

Although what I have offered here is a short but by no means novel critique of religious doctrine as a "solution" to the ontological problem of death, it is *not* meant as a critique of a group of higher order ideas that are found within some religions but can also exist independently of them. What I am talking about is

Spirituality, the experience of humanness as having a transcendent meaning of its own and a sense of meaning and connectedness to be found in our inevitably being part of a group. Groups come in different sizes, ranging from Dunbar's number up to vast swathes of humanity. As Christakis and Fowler (2009) tell us, this connectedness, and the pleasure and meaning it brings us take place mostly outside of awareness. Much of it is unconscious, offering unconscious solutions to the problems of existence and death. Although this "groupness" has sometimes been portrayed as regressive (and certainly can be) in the service of the ego or otherwise, it is much more a positive capacity of the Self.

What our awakened reflection tells us is that we were gratuitously introduced into the world via a series of biological and social accidents and that we are left to make what we can of our situation. A narcissistic injury in its own right, many of us still resort to religion as a kind of narcotic to treat the pain of our acknowledged unimportance. Many others of us, however, do not, and here the therapeutic situation comes into play to help make meaning out of accident. It is not hard to see where *thrown* and *fallen* come down in the face of this dilemma. As Sartre (1997/2007) puts it, we are thrown into *existence* and left to create our *essence*.

Along very similar lines, N. Humphrey (2011) begins his arguments on "Cheating Death" with a quote from Milan Kundera's (1978/1999) *The Book of Laughter and Forgetting* to the effect that there is a border between what in life has meaning and the loss of all those things that are meaningful—the human values of love, intimacy, reciprocity, and historicity. And it is in these borderlands, with the decent into meaninglessness always a risk, that we live our lives. Perhaps paradoxically, it is the presence of that border that also makes our lives meaningful. It is in just these borderlands that we psychotherapists have set up shop. What do we do, really, other than help our patients move to the meaningful borderlands? Another way of describing the "wrong" side of the border in terms other than the antithesis of meaning is to say that it is characterized by the absurd, accompanied by despair, and that the analysis of the absurd is, in the end, what we are about.

If this last chapter has seemed incomplete, it's because it is. Adequate explorations of Existentialism, absurdity, and death proved beyond the limitations of space that they needed to conform to in this present volume. I hope to address them shortly in a subsequent one.

Notes

1 Informed speculation is the bread and butter of paleoanthropologists. Falk's work on Taung (Falk, 2011; Falk & Clarke, 2007) is a good example of this.
2 I have had more to say about Paleoanthropology because I recognize it to be a discipline less well-known to psychotherapists.
3 In an extreme form, this is probably what is going on for people with multiple personality disorder.
4 This is also a representation of the solution of the mind-body problem contained in our definition of Self.
5 The term *Superego* is so laden with baggage, including a subscription to ego psychology, and accounts for so few of the functions that are contained in this part of the Self that it

has lost meaning. Modern usage of the term seems to have become dissociated from its origins—always a bad sign.
6 The origin of our slower ancestor, *H. sapiens* is murkier. Current research finds him in several different parts of Africa about 200,000 ya, living side by side with other advanced hominins.
7 *Emerge* is not a word chosen because it reads well. It is chosen because it refers to the developmental process of *emergence*, in which higher order properties emerge from lower order properties and their interaction with the social and physical world.
8 There are *many* developmental studies that demonstrate the advent of Consciousness in young children; this one (Gopnik & Graf, 1988) was chosen for illustrative purposes because of its elegance.
9 In my experience, some majority of us is unfamiliar with the distinctions between anoetic, noetic, and autonoetic memories, and the corresponding states of consciousness that accompany them.
10 This would be particularly problematic for Kleinian therapists if they were aware of it.
11 I have elsewhere (Leffert, 2010) offered a contemporary discussion of memory theory.
12 Anoetic memory involves loosely defined procedural memories of World and Self whereas noetic memory involves semantic or factual memory: the contents of the drawer. They develop in that order with autonoetic memory appearing last; all three continue, unless damaged by trauma or illness, into the adult present and future.
13 An obvious example involves the way displayed family photographs of very young children are subsequently remembered by them episodically in terms of when they were taken.
14 In some respects, we still struggle with them.
15 Also still a problem, e.g., global warming.
16 Paradoxically, disindividuation allows people to risk death, or even certain death in war, or extreme environmental events.
17 In French the closeness of the two resides in the word *conscience*, which can mean either conscious or conscience depending on how it is used.
18 Psychoanalysis has, in the past, exclusively concerned itself with the *Eigenwelt* (new language for an old theoretical stance). We return to it now, however, not as a stand-alone feature, but as an integral part of the disparate apparatuses of being we have been talking about.

References

Baars, B. J. (2003). How does a serial, integrated, and very limited stream of consciousness emerge from a nervous system that is mostly unconscious, distributed, parallel and of enormous capacity? In B. J. Baars, W. P. Banks, & J. B. Newman (Eds.), *Essential sources in the scientific study of consciousness* (pp. 1123–1129). Cambridge: MIT Press. (Original work published in 1993.)

Baron-Cohen, S., Tager-Flusberg, H., & Cohen, D. J. (2000). *Understanding other minds: Perspectives from developmental cognitive science* (2nd ed.). Oxford: Oxford University Press.

Buckner, R. L., & Krienen, F. M. (2013). The evolution of distributed association networks in the human brain. *Trends in Cognitive Sciences, 17*, 648–665.

Camus, A. (1963). *Notebooks 1935–1942* (P. Thody, Trans.). Chicago: Ivan R. Dee. (Original work published in 1962.)

Christakis, N. A., & Fowler, J. H. (2009). *Connected: The surprising power of our social networks and how they shape our lives*. New York: Little, Brown and Company.

Crick, F. C., & Koch, C. (2005). What is the function of the claustrum? *Philosophical Transactions of the Royal Society Biological Sciences, 360*, 1271–1279.

Doidge, N. (2007). *The brain that changes itself*. New York: Viking.

Doidge, N. (2015). *Remarkable discoveries and recoveries from the frontiers of neuroplasticity*. New York: Viking.
Dunbar, R. (2016). *Human evolution: Our brains and behavior*. Oxford: Oxford University Press.
Falk, D. (2011). *The fossil chronicles: How two controversial discoveries changed our view of human evolution*. Berkeley: University of California Press.
Falk, D., & Clarke, R. (2007). Brief communication: New reconstruction of the Taung endocast. *American Journal of Physical Anthropology, 134*, 529–534.
Fonagy, P. (1999). Memory and therapeutic action. *The International Journal of Psychoanalysis, 80*, 215–224.
Frankl, V. E. (2006). *Man's search for meaning* (I. Lasch, Trans.). Boston: Beacon Press. (Original work published in 1959.)
Freud, S. (1953). Totem and taboo. In J. Strachey (Ed.), *Standard edition* (Vol. XIII, pp. 1–161). (Original work published in 1913.)
Freud, S. (1961). Civilization and its discontents. In J. Strachey (Ed.), *Standard edition* (Vol. XXI, pp. 64–145). London: Hogarth Press. (Original work published in 1930.)
Gopnik, A., & Graf, P. (1988). Knowing how you know: Young children's ability to identify and remember the sources of their beliefs. *Child Development, 59*, 98–110.
Humphrey, N. (1999). *A history of the mind: Evolution and the birth of consciousness*. New York: Springer. (Original work published in 1992.)
Humphrey, N. (2011). *Soul dust: The magic of consciousness*. Princeton: Princeton University Press.
Humphrey, N. K. (1988). The social function of intellect. In R. Byrne & A. Whiten (Eds.), *Machiavellian intelligence: Social expertise and the evolution of intellect in monkeys, apes, and humans* (pp. 13–26). Oxford: Oxford University Press. (Original work published in 1976.)
Husserl, E. (1983). *Ideas pertaining to a pure phenomenology and to a phenomenological philosophy: Book one: General introduction to a pure phenomenology* (F. Kersten, Trans.). New York: Springer (Original work published in 1913.)
Husserl, E. (1999). *Cartesian meditations* (D. Cairns, Trans.). Dordrecht: Springer. (Original work published in 1931.)
Kahneman, D. (2011). *Thinking, fast and slow*. New York: Farrar, Strauss and Giroux.
Kandel, E. R. (2006). *In search of memory*. New York: W. W. Norton & Co.
Kundera, M. (1999). *The book of laughter and forgetting*. New York: Penguin Books. (Original work published in 1978.)
Leffert, M. (2010). *Contemporary psychoanalytic foundations*. London: Routledge.
Leffert, M. (2016). *Phenomenology, uncertainty, and care in the therapeutic encounter*. New York: Routledge.
Leffert, M. (2017). *Positive psychoanalysis: Aesthetics, desire, and subjective well-being*. New York: Routledge.
May, R. (1958). Contributions of existential psychotherapy. In R. May, E. Angel, & H. F. Ellenberger (Eds.), *Existence* (pp. 37–91). New York: Simon & Schuster.
Nelson, K., & Fivush, R. (2004). The emergence of autobiographical memory: A social cultural developmental theory. *Psychological Review, 111*, 486–511.
Panksepp, J., & Biven, L. (2012). *The archaeology of mind: Neuroevolutionary origins of human emotions*. New York: W. W. Norton & Co.
Porges, S. W. (2011). *The polyvagal theory: Neurophysiological foundations of emotions, attachment, communication, self-regulation*. New York: W. W. Norton & Co.
Premack, D. (1988). "Does the Chimpanzee have a theory of mind?" revisited. In R. Byrne & A. Whiten (Eds.), *Machiavellian intelligence: Social expertise, and the evolution of intellect in monkeys, apes, and humans* (pp. 160–179). Oxford: Clarendon Press.

Sandler, J., & Fonagy, P. (Eds.). (1997). *Rediscovered memories of abuse: True or false?* Madison: International Universities Press.

Sartre, J.-P. (2007). *Existentialism is a humanism.* New Haven: Yale University Press. (Original work published in 1997.)

Schacter, D. L. (1996). *Searching for memory.* New York: Basic Books.

Schacter, D. L. (2001). *The seven sins of memory.* Boston: Houghton Mifflin Company.

Schacter, D. L., Addis, D. R., & Buckner, R. L. (2008). Episodic simulation of future events concepts, data, and applications. *Annals of the New York Academy of Science, 1124,* 39–60.

Schore, A. N. (2009). Right-brain affect regulation: An essential mechanism of development, trauma, dissociation, and psychotherapy. In D. Fosha, D. J. Siegal, & M. F. Solomon (Eds.), *The healing power of emotion: Affective neuroscience, development, and clinical practice* (pp. 112–144). New York: W. W. Norton & Co.

Tulving, E. (2003). Memory and consciousness. In B. J. Baars, W. P. Banks, & J. B. Newman (Eds.), *Essential sources in the scientific study of consciousness* (pp. 575–591). Cambridge: MIT Press. (Original work published in 1985.)

Tulving, E. (2005). Episodic memory and autonoesis: Uniquely human? In H. S. Terrace & J. Metcalfe (Eds.), *The missing link in cognition: Origins of self-reflective consciousness* (pp. 3–56). Oxford: Oxford University Press.

Tversky, A., & Kahneman, D. (1982). Judgment under uncertainty: Heuristics and biases. In D. Kahneman, P. Slovic, & A. Tversky (Eds.), *Judgment under uncertainty: Heuristics and biases* (pp. 3–20). Cambridge: Cambridge University Press. (Original work published in 1974.)

INDEX

2011 Psychoanalytic Professional Activities Benchmark Study 23, 26

Abbott, I.F. 52, 53
abstract notation systems 107
absurdity 77, 132–133, 136, 138, 139, 146–147
adolescent pruning 69, 99–100
affective states 64, 74, 99
affect-trauma frame of reference 12
African Grey Parrot 45, 101
allostasis 144
American Board of Psychoanalysis 16
American Psychoanalytic Association (APsaA) 15, 23, 26
amnesia 45
amygdala 75, 76
anatomical localization of consciousness 39–40, 56–57
anatomically modern humans (AMH) 5, 95, 104, 107, 112, 113, 119, 155
anchorite, therapist as 78
Anglin, J.M. 121–122
animal studies 64; mother-child relationship 69, 70, 80–81; play 74–75; transgenerational epigenesis 80–81, 83; vocalizations 118
anoetic consciousness 3, 45–46, 106, 108, 155
anoetic memory 43, 44, 45, 46, 47, 158
antianxiety medication 23
antidepressants 21–22, 23
archaic humans 5, 95, 104, 107, 112, 113, 119, 155

Artificial Intelligence (AI) systems 155
attachment 69, 74, 116, 144
attachment behavioral system 98–99
attachment deactivation strategies 6, 144, 145–146
attachment hyperactivation strategies 6, 144
attention 40
attention deficit hyperactivity disorder 75
Aurignacian period 104
Australopithecus 94–98
autonoetic consciousness 3, 45, 46–47, 51, 55, 56, 100–101, 152; development of 115–117, 156–158; evolution of 106–115, 154–156, 158–159; language and 106
autonoetic memory 44–45, 46–47, 54, 63, 105, 108, 117; development of 156–158

Baars, B.J. 42, 106, 155
Bachelard, G. 78
Bainbridge, Kate 38–39
belief 160
Bell, J.A. 101
Benjamin, J. 17
biases 43, 76, 108, 113, 160
Bill (patient) 140–141
Bio-Psycho-Social Self 43–44, 47, 54, 153, 154
bipedal locomotion 95, 96–97
bipolar disorder 22
Biven, L. 74, 75
Blitzsten, Lionel 15
Board on Professional Standards (BoPS) 16, 26

Bogen, J.E. 39, 41
Boss, Medard 4, 71, 131, 147
boundary violations: analyst-patient sex 17–18; loving feelings in therapeutic practice and 72–74; touch in therapeutic practice and 4, 71, 72
Bowlby, John 69, 74, 93, 98–99
brain: adolescent pruning 69, 99–100; anatomical localization of consciousness 39–40, 56–57; Broca's area 118, 120; caloric needs of 97, 112, 155; changes in maternal brain during pregnancy 69; claustrum 39, 49, 57, 106, 155; corpus callosum 40–41, 114–115; cortical midline structures 100; cortical thickening 73, 75; development 5, 42, 99–100; functional neuroanatomy 20–21, 39–40, 49, 56–57; global neuronal workspace 49–50; in hominin evolution 95–96, 98, 101–104, 106, 107, 108, 112, 113, 155; infants and early childhood 5, 115, 116, 120–121; language and 117–120; laterality 42–43, 98, 118; left-sided dominance 41, 42; longevity of neurons 67; Mirror Neuron System (MNS) 20–21, 55, 64, 100, 119; myelination of left cerebral cortex 99, 101, 115, 120, 156; neural basis of mind 48–49, 54; neural correlates of consciousness 52; neuroplasticity 73, 78, 84, 99, 145; parallel distributed processing networks 40, 50; play and 74–76; reticular formation 39, 56; size 5, 66, 96, 98, 99–100, 102, 112, 113, 115, 116, 155–156; social group size and 112, 113, 155–156; split-brain studies 40–41, 46, 109; synapses 69, 96, 99–100, 116; vegetative states 38–39
Brain-Heart-Vagus Circuit (BHVC) 159
Bråten, S. 116
Breckenridge, K. 4
British School 139–140
Broca's area 118, 120
bullying 76
Burghardt, G.M. 74, 76, 97

caloric needs of hominins 97, 112, 155
Cambrian Period 65
Camus, Albert 5, 132, 133–135, 136–137, 138–139, 147, 161
Carbamazine 22
cardiovascular disease 83
Carey, N. 82
Carlson, D.A. 26
Carol (patient) 78–79

Carroll, S.B. 65, 66
Cartesian separation of mind and body 48, 54
Casement, P.J. 4, 71
cell phones 55–56
Champagne, F.A. 80, 81
chaos theory 48
chimpanzees 102, 116, 118, 119–120
Chiron, C. 42
Christakis, N.A. 55, 113, 155, 162
chromatin 66–67
chromosomes 66–67
Churchland, A.K. 52, 53
Churchland, P.M. 48, 52, 68
Churchland, P.S. 48
Clactonian industry 103
claustrum 39, 49, 57, 106, 155
clinging behavior 144
clinical listening 135
Clowry, G.J. 118
cognitive archaeology 101–104
cognitive development 101, 116
Collins, T.F.T. 50
commissurotomy 40–41, 109
complexity 47–48
conscious social behavior 113
consciousness 1–2, 3, 6, 37–58, 104–117, 154–161; anatomical localization of 39–40, 56–57; anoetic 3, 45–46, 106, 108, 155; attention and 40; belief 160; brain development and laterality 42–43; complexity and 47–48; content of 40; cultural definitions of 55; current understanding of 51–53; of death 54, 132, 153, 158, 159–160, 161; decision-making and 43, 113; denial of death 160, 161; development of 115–117, 156–158; different kinds of 43, 44–47, 54; as emergent property 47, 56–57; evolution of 105–115, 154–156, 158–159; Existentialism and 133, 152–153; *Iliad* and 109–110; individual differences 50–51; intentionality 113, 116, 117; as interpersonal 54–56; judgments made under uncertainty 160; language and 42, 55; level of 40; mental time travel 44–45, 105, 108, 110, 116, 159; modular or general-purpose system 106–108, 109; neural correlates of 52; noetic 3, 45, 46–47, 106, 108, 109, 116, 155; parallel distributed processing model of 40, 50; phenomenology of 53–54; physicalism 48–49, 68; religion and 161; simultagnosia 40; social group size and 112, 113, 155–156; social intelligence

consciousness *continued*
and 110–111, 156, 160; Social Media and 55–56; split-brain studies 40–41, 46, 109; Theory of Mind 108, 115, 116, 156, 160; unconsciousnesses 43–44; vegetative states 38–39; as workspace 49–50; *see also* autonoetic consciousness
contagion 55, 113
conversational styles 122
corpus callosum 40–41, 114–115
cortical midline structures 100
cortico-thalamic complex 39
countertransference 13, 16, 73
Craighero, L. 119
Crick, F.C. 39, 49
cultural definitions of consciousness 55

Damasio, Antonio 48
Dart, Raymond 95
death 54, 132, 153, 158, 159–160, 161; denial of 160, 161
decision-making 43, 113
degrees of separation 113
Dehaene, S. 47, 49
denial of death 160, 161
Dennett, D.C. 116
Depakote 22
Depersonalization/Derealization Disorder 139
Derrida, J. 9
Descartes, René 48
despair 146–147
Deuteronomy 154
development 63, 65–66; brain 5, 42, 99–100; cognitive 101, 116; consciousness 115–117, 156–158; episodic memory 156–158; first year of life 5, 98–99, 115, 117, 120–121; internal working models (IWMs) 99, 101; language 117, 120–122; mirror self-recognition test 101, 115; *see also* Evo-Devo
developmental psychology 63
diabetes mellitus 83
Diagnostic and Statistical Manual of Mental Disorders 5th Edition (DSM-5) 139
Diener, E. 81–82, 135–136
Dissociative Disorders 139
DNA 65, 66; methylation 66–67, 82; mitochondrial 107–108
Doidge, N. 153
domain-specific intelligence 108
Donald, Merlin 111–112, 113
Dunbar, Robin 111–113, 117, 119, 155
Dunbar's Number 112, 113

Dutch Hunger Winter 4, 82–83
dyadic meaning making 42, 43–44

Ecclesiastes 138
education *see* psychoanalytic education
efficacy research 24–26
Ehrenberg, D.B. 78
Eichler, E.E. 96
Elavil 21
emergent properties 47, 56–57
emotions, absurdity and 146–147
epigenetics 3–4, 57–58, 66–68, 79–85; autonoetic consciousness and 114; DNA methylation 66–67, 82; Dutch Hunger Winter 4, 82–83; histone modifications 66–67, 82; inheritance 4, 68, 80–85; marking 67–68, 80, 82, 84; monozygotic twin studies 67–68; Överkalix study, Sweden 4, 82, 83; play and 76; regulatory genes 65, 66; transgenerational 4, 68, 80–85
episodic memory 44–45, 46–47, 54, 63, 105, 108, 117; development of 156–158
Erikson, Erik 66, 77, 139
everydayness 97, 101, 103, 108, 110, 132
Evo-Devo 3–5, 57–58, 63–66, 93–123, 152; brain 5, 95–96, 98, 99–100, 101–104, 106, 107, 108, 112, 113, 155; cognitive archaeology 101–104; first year of life 5, 98–99, 115, 117, 120–121; hominin evolution 94–98, 101–104, 105–115, 158–159; mirror self-recognition test 101, 115; mother-child relationship 4, 64, 69–70, 79, 80–81, 99, 121; neoteny 96, 97; ontogeny of consciousness 115–117, 156–158; ontogeny of language 117, 120–122; phylogeny of consciousness 105–115, 154–156, 158–159; phylogeny of language 117–120; play 4, 74–79; signaling by infants and parents 97–98; *see also* epigenetics
evolution 63, 64, 65–66; brain 95–96, 98, 101–104, 106, 107, 108, 112, 113, 155; consciousness 105–115, 154–156, 158–159; language 117–120; *see also* Evo-Devo; hominin evolution
Existentialism 5–6, 12, 64, 131–147, 152–153, 161; absurdity 132–133, 136, 138, 139, 146–147; Camus 5, 132, 133–135, 136–137, 138–139, 147, 161; consciousness and 133, 152–153; death 132, 153; despair 146–147; Existential failures 133–141; Existentialist approach 5–6, 141–146; Hemingway 5, 133–135,

137–138, 139, 147; unconscious and 152–153

Fadiga, L. 119
Fairbairn, W.R.D. 139
Falk, D. 95, 96, 97, 117–118, 120
Faulkner, William 133–134
Feig, L.A. 81
Fenichel, Otto 16
Field, T. 70, 72
First World War 136
Fivush, R. 156
Fonagy, P. 157
Fosshage, J.L. 4
Fowler, J.H. 55, 113, 155, 162
FOXP2 gene 118–119
Fraga, M.F. 67–68
France 135, 136
Frank, J.B. 25
Frank, J.D. 25
freeze response 159
Freud, Sigmund 4, 11–12, 13–14, 15, 20, 70, 158
functional neuroanatomy 20–21, 39–40, 49, 56–57
functional somatic disorder (FSD) 6, 142–146
future of psychoanalysis 23–29; biological treatments and 29; psychoanalytic education 26–27; psychoanalytic politics and 28; psychoanalytic practice 28–29; psychoanalytic research 24–26; public perception of psychoanalysis 24, 29

Gamble, C. 107
games 76
Gay, P. 13–14
Gazzaniga, M.S. 41
Gerber, A.J. 27
Germany 136
gestural communications 119–120
global neuronal workspace 49–50
Gluck, A.L. 48
Gogtay, N. 100
Goldner, V. 17
Gopnik, A. 156–157
Graf, P. 156–157
Greenfield, S.A. 50
grooming, in primates 112
Groos, K. 76
group process 17–20, 27, 28
Guntrip, H. 139

hand ax 103–104
handshakes, in therapeutic practice 72

Harlow, H. 70
Hartmann, Heinz 66
Heidegger, Martin 55, 97, 108, 110, 132, 137, 141, 161
Hemingway, Ernest 5, 133–135, 137–138, 139, 147
heuristics 43, 76, 108, 113, 160
histone modifications 66–67, 82
history of psychoanalysis 8–23; birth of relational psychoanalysis 16–17; care in clinical psychoanalysis 13–14; medicalization of psychoanalysis in America 14–16; neuroscience and 20–21; phenomenological inquiry into 11–13; psychopharmacology and 10, 21–23; regressive group process in psychoanalytic organizations 17–20
Hoekzema, E. 69
Hofer, M.A. 64, 65, 66, 69, 70, 72, 80–81
Hoffman, I.Z. 16–17
Holmes, D.S. 43
Homer 109–110
hominin evolution 5, 94–98, 101–104, 105–115, 158–159; anatomically modern humans (AMH) 5, 95, 104, 107, 112, 113, 119, 155; *Australopithecus* 94–98; bipedal locomotion 95, 96–97; brain 95–96, 98, 101–104, 106, 107, 108, 112, 113, 155; cognitive archaeology 101–104; consciousness 105–115, 154–156, 158–159; consciousness of death 153, 158, 159–160; language 117–120; Neanderthals 106, 107, 108, 112, 116, 117, 119, 155; Out of Africa Event 107–108, 119; social group size 112, 113, 119, 155–156; Upper Paleolithic package 106–108, 114, 119, 153, 155
Homo erectus 103
Homo habilis 102–103
Homo heidelbergensis 103
Homo sapiens (archaic) 5, 95, 104, 107, 112, 113, 119, 155
Homo sapiens sapiens 5, 45, 97, 101, 104; autonoetic consciousness 113–114, 155, 158–159; consciousness of death 153, 158, 159–160; language 119, 120; Out of Africa Event 107–108, 119; social group size 112, 113, 119, 155–156; Upper Paleolithic package 106–108, 114, 119, 153, 155
Horton, J.A. 4, 71–72
humor, in therapeutic practice 77
Humphrey, N. 156, 160, 162
Humphrey, N.K. 110–111, 116, 156

Husserl, E. 9, 11, 37, 53, 54

Iceberg Theory 134–135, 139, 153
Iliad (Homer) 109–110
immortality 160
Inaba, M. 80
infants and early childhood: autonoetic consciousness 115–117, 156–158; brain 5, 115, 116, 120–121; cognitive development 101, 116; first year of life 5, 98–99, 115, 117, 120–121; intentionality 116, 117; intersubjectivity 99, 115, 116; language 117, 120–121; mental time travel 116; mirror self-recognition test 101, 115; neoteny 96, 97; signaling by 97–98; story telling 117; Theory of Mind 115, 116
inheritance of epigenetic changes 4, 68, 80–85
insecure attachment 144
intelligence: brain size and 96; domain-specific 108; social 110–111, 156, 160
intentionality 113, 116, 117
Interdisciplinary Studies 28–29, 153
internal working models (IWMs) 99, 101
Interpersonal Psychoanalysis 12
Intersubjective Psychoanalysis 12–13, 16–17, 132, 153

Jacobson, Edith 16, 93
Jacoby, R. 15
Jake (fictional character) 134, 135, 137–138, 139, 147
Jaynes, Julian 109–110, 114
Jennifer (patient) 84–85
judgments made under uncertainty 160

Kaati, G. 83
Kahn, M.M.R. 139
Kahneman, D. 113; heuristics 43, 76, 108, 113, 160; judgments made under uncertainty 160
Kandel, E.R. 84, 153
KE family 118–119
Kernberg, O.F. 27
Kinsbourne, M. 108
Klein, R.G. 107
Knopf, L.E. 27
Koch, C. 39, 40, 49
Kohut, H. 12
Krauss, J. 119
Kuhl, P.K. 120, 121
Kundera, Milan 162

Lamictal 22

Lampl-de Groot, Jeanne 13–14
language 42, 55, 93–94, 112, 117–122; autonoetic consciousness and 106; conversational styles 122; development of 117, 120–122; evolution of 117–120; FOXP2 gene 118–119; Motherese 121; vocabulary 121–122; word usage 121–122
Latour, B. 53
laughter 112
Lear, J. 73
Lewy, Ernst 15–16
Lithium Carbonate 22
Little, M.I. 71
Loewald, H.W. 73
long-term memory 84
loving feelings, in therapeutic practice 72–74
Lucas, R.E. 81–82
Luyten, P. 143–144, 145

Machiavellian intelligence 110–111, 156, 160
Mahler, M.S. 93
Marinsek, N.L. 40
massage therapy 4, 70, 72
maternal deprivation 70
May, Rollo 131, 141–142, 154
Mayo Clinic 145, 146
meaninglessness 5, 135
Meares, R. 77–78
medical school curricula 15
medication *see* psychotropic medications
meditation 73
Mellars, P. 107
memory: anoetic memory 43, 44, 45, 46, 47, 158; development of 156–158; different kinds of 44–47; episodic 44–45, 46–47, 54, 63, 105, 108, 117, 156–158; long-term 84; narrative memory 44–45, 46–47, 54, 63, 105, 108, 117; noetic memory 44, 45, 46–47, 54, 116, 157–158; procedural 43, 44, 45, 46, 47, 158; semantic 44, 45, 46–47, 54, 116, 157–158; short-term 84
mental time travel 44–45, 105, 108, 110, 116, 159
mentalization 6, 143, 144, 145, 146
messenger-RNA (mRNA) 67, 76
Metaphysics 49
metapsychologies 10–11, 12, 25–26, 141; in psychoanalytic education 27
methylation of DNA 66–67, 82
Meursault (fictional character) 134, 135, 136–137, 138–139, 147

Michels, R. 27
mind-body separation 48, 54
Mirror Neuron System (MNS) 20–21, 55, 64, 100, 119
mirror self-recognition test 101, 115
Mithen, S. 101, 106–107, 111, 115, 116
mitochondrial DNA 107–108
mode-epigenesis 66
modern critical stance 53
monozygotic twin studies 67–68
mood stabilizers 22, 23
mother-child relationship 4, 64, 69–70, 79, 80–81, 99, 121
Motherese 121
Murray, E.A. 114
music 112
Myth of Sisyphus, The (Camus) 136, 137

Naccache, L. 39, 47, 49
narcissism 12
narrative memory 44–45, 46–47, 54, 63, 105, 108, 117; development of 156–158
natural selection 95
Nazi state 136
Neanderthals 106, 107, 108, 112, 116, 117, 119, 155
Nelson, K. 156
neocortex 39, 57, 76, 95–96
neoteny 96, 97
Netherlands 4, 82–83
neural correlates of consciousness 52
Neurophenomenology 51, 53–54, 57
Neurophilosophy of consciousness 3, 37–58; anatomical localization of consciousness 39–40, 56–57; brain development and laterality 42–43; complexity 47–48; consciousness as interpersonal 54–56; consciousness as workspace 49–50; current understanding 51–53; different kinds of consciousness 43, 44–47, 54; different kinds of memory 44–47; individual consciousness as unique 50–51; phenomenology of consciousness 53–54; physicalism 48–49, 68; Social Media 55–56; split-brain studies 40–41, 46; unconsciousnesses 43–44; vegetative states 38–39
neuroplasticity 73, 78, 84, 99, 145
neuroscience 20–21, 37–38, 53, 152, 153; in psychoanalytic education 27; *see also* brain
Nisbett, R.E. 42–43, 113
noetic consciousness 3, 45, 46–47, 106, 108, 109, 116, 155

noetic memory 44, 45, 46–47, 54, 116, 157–158
non-interpretive mechanisms 13
Novick, J. 73
Novick, K.K. 73

object relations 13
obstetrical dilemma 96
Olduvian technology 102
orbitofrontal cortex 75, 112
origins of the self 4–5, 93–123; cognitive archaeology 101–104; first year of life 5, 98–99, 115, 117, 120–121; hominin evolution 94–98, 101–104, 105–115, 158–159; mirror self-recognition test 101, 115; ontogeny of consciousness 115–117, 156–158; ontogeny of language 117, 120–122; phylogeny of consciousness 105–115, 154–156, 158–159; phylogeny of language 117–120
Orr, Douglass 15
Out of Africa Event 107–108, 119
Överkalix study, Sweden 4, 82, 83
Owen, Adrian 38–39
oxytocin 144

Pain Rehabilitation Center, Mayo Clinic 145, 146
Paleoanthropology 5, 6, 152, 153, 158–159; *see also* hominin evolution
Panksepp, Jaak 20, 44, 45, 64, 74, 75, 93, 99
panpsychism 49
parallel distributed processing networks 40, 50
parenting 64; *see also* mother-child relationship
Parsons, C.E. 99
pathological narcissism 12
patient experiences 13–14
Pellegrini, A.D. 76
Pellis, S. 74
Pellis, V. 74
personal analysis of students 19, 26, 27
personality 81–82
phenomenological time 54
Phenomenology 5, 12, 64, 131–132, 161; of consciousness 53–54; unconscious and 152, 153
phenotype transmission 4, 68, 80–85
physicalism 48–49, 68
Piaget, J. 70
play 4, 74–79
play therapy 74

politics, psychoanalytic 28
Polleux, F. 96
Porges, S.W. 159
post-traumatic stress disorder (PTSD) 5–6, 78–79, 139, 140, 142–143
prefrontal cortex 49, 75, 113
pregnancy: changes in maternal brain during 69; malnourishment during 82–83
primary intersubjectivity 99
primates 64; Brain-Heart-Vagus Circuit (BHVC) 159; consciousness 45, 109; gestural communications 119–120; grooming 112; intentionality 116; mirror self-recognition test 101; social group size 112; toolmaking 102; vocalizations 118
problem-solving, play and 76
procedural learning 100
procedural memory 43, 44, 45, 46, 47, 158
Prozac 21–22
psychoanalytic education 15; future of 26–27; group process experiences in 19, 27; metapsychologies in 27; neuroscience in 27; psychopharmacology in 26; psychotherapy cases in 26; training analysis 19, 26, 27; tripartite model of 18–19, 26
psychoanalytic organizations 17–20; politics of 28
psychoanalytic politics 28
psychoanalytic practice: future of 28–29; see also therapeutic practice
psychoanalytic research 24–26
psychoanalytic theories see metapsychologies
psychological depth 132
psychopharmacology 10, 21–23, 29, 57; in psychoanalytic education 26
psychotropic medications 10, 21–23, 29, 57; antianxiety medication 23; antidepressants 21–22, 23; mood stabilizers 22, 23; in psychoanalytic education 26
public perception of psychoanalysis 24, 29
Pulver, S.E. 20

Reardon, S. 39, 95
regard médicale 12, 14
regressive group process 17–20, 27, 28
regulatory genes 65, 66
Relational Psychoanalysis 12–13, 16–17, 152–153
religion 161
Renfrew, C. 101

repression 38, 43, 132, 152, 153
reticular formation 39, 56
ribonucleic acid (RNA) 66; messenger-RNA (mRNA) 67, 76
Risse, G.L. 41
Roazen, P. 14
rodent studies 64; mother-child relationship 69, 70, 80–81; play 74–75; transgenerational epigenesis 80–81, 83
Rosenberg, K.R. 97, 98
rough-and-tumble play 74–76

Saavedra-Rodriguez, L. 81
Sachs, J. 78
Sacks, Oliver 2, 57
Sam (patient) 142–143, 144, 145–146
Sartre, Jean-Paul 133–134, 161, 162
Schechter, K. 26
Schore, A.N. 20, 42, 79, 93, 99
Second World War 136
secondary attachment strategies 6, 144, 145–146
secondary autonomy 66
secondary intersubjectivity 99, 115
secure attachment 116, 144
Segal, E.M. 101–102
selective serotonin reuptake inhibitors (SSRIs) 21–22
self, origins of *see* origins of the self
self-awareness 45, 101
self-experience 45
Self-Psychology 131–132
self-reflection 51, 100–101, 108
semantic memory 44, 45, 46–47, 54, 116, 157–158
sentience 52
sex, analyst-patient 17–18
sexual abuse, childhood 78–79, 157
short-term memory 84
silence 14
simultagnosia 40
single-celled organisms 65
skull, delayed fusion of 96
social anxiety 140
social bonding 112
social contagion 55, 113
social group size 112, 113, 119, 155–156
social intelligence 110–111, 156, 160
Social Media 55–56
social networks 113, 155
Solms, Mark 20
somatic conditions 6, 142–146
speech 42, 93–94, 117; *see also* language
Sperry, R.W. 41, 109
Spinoza, Baruch 48

spirituality 161–162
Spitz, R. 70
split-brain studies 40–41, 46, 109
SRGAP2 gene 5, 95–96
Stein, Gertrude 138
Stem Cell transplants 29
Stern, D.N. 13
Stolorow, Robert 132
story telling 117
Stranger, The (Camus) 5, 134–135, 136–137, 138–139, 147
Strawson, G. 49
stress regulation 144
Stringer, C. 107
Subjective Well-Being (SWB) studies 70, 81–82, 135–136
Sullivan, R.M. 64
Sun Also Rises, The (Hemingway) 5, 134–135, 137–138, 139, 147
Surplus Resource Theory (SRT) 76, 97
Sweden 4, 82, 83
symbolic systems 107, 108
synapses 69, 96, 99–100, 116

Taung fossil 95
Terrace, H.S. 120
tertiary intersubjectivity 99, 116
thalamus 39
theoretical orientations *see* metapsychologies
Theory of Mind 108, 115, 116, 156, 160
theory of omission *see* Iceberg Theory
therapeutic practice: clinical listening 135; Existentialist approach 5–6, 141–146; humor in 77; loving feelings in 72–74; play in 77–78; touch and massage in 4, 70–72
third order intentionality 116, 117
thrownness 101, 103, 108, 110
Tofranil 21
toolmaking 102, 103–104
Toronto, E.L.K. 72
touch in therapeutic practice 4, 70–72

Touch Research Institute 70
training analysis 19, 26, 27
transcription 67
transcription factors 118
transference 13, 16, 73, 77–78
transgenerational epigenesis 4, 68, 80–85
trauma 139, 140; childhood memories of 157
Trevarthen, C. 99, 116
Trevathan, W.R. 97, 98
tricyclic antidepressants 21
tripartite model of psychoanalytic education 18–19, 26
Tronick, E.Z. 43–44
Tsuchiya, N. 40
Tulving, Endel 3, 44, 45, 46, 54, 100, 105, 109, 114
Tversky, A. 113
twin studies 67–68
two-person psychology 16–17

unconscious 38, 41, 43–44, 111, 113, 132, 152–153, 154, 162
universal grammar 118
Upper Paleolithic package 106–108, 114, 119, 153, 155

Vagus nerve 159
Vanderkerckhove, M. 44, 45
Vargha-Khadem, F. 118–119
vegetative states 38–39
Vietnam War 140, 142–143, 145
vocabulary, size of 121–122
Vogel, P.J. 41

Whitelaw, Emma 83
Wilson, T. 42–43, 113
Winnicott, D.W. 4, 71, 78, 139
word usage 121–122

Yalom, Irwin 132

Zebra Finches 118

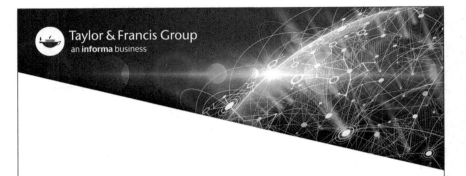

PGMO 06/05/2018